100 WEEKEND PROJECTS ANYONE CAN DO

100 WEEKEND PROJECTS ANYONE CAN DO

Easy, practical projects using basic tools and standard materials

THE FAMILY
Handyman | The Family Handyman
Eagan, Minnesota

Editorial and Production Team
Vern Johnson, Peggy McDermott, Rick Muscoplat,
Marcia Roepke, Mary Schwender

Photography and Illustrations
Ron Chamberlain, Tom Fenenga, Bruce Kieffer, Mike Krivit,
Don Mannes, Ramon Moreno, Shawn Nielsen, Doug
Oudekerk, Frank Rohrbach III, Eugene Thompson,
Bill Zuehlke

Text, photography and illustrations for *100 Weekend Projects
Anyone Can Do* are based on articles previously published
in *The Family Handyman* magazine (2915 Commers Dr.,
Suite 700, Eagan, MN 55121, familyhandyman.com).
For information on advertising in *The Family Handyman*
magazine, call (646) 293-6150.

ISBN: 978-1-62145-329-1

The Family Handyman
Editor in Chief   Gary Wentz
Project Editor   Eric Smith
Design & Layout   Diana Boger, Teresa Marrone
Project Manager   Mary Flanagan
Senior Editor   Travis Larson
Associate Editors   Jeff Gorton, Mark Petersen, Jason White
Office Administrative Manager   Alice Garrett
Set Builder   Josh Risberg
Senior Copy Editor   Donna Bierbach
VP, Group Publisher   Russell S. Ellis

Published by Home Service Publications, Inc.,
a subsidiary of Trusted Media Brands, Inc.

PRINTED IN CHINA

10 9 8 7 6 5 4 3 2 1

A Note to Our Readers
All do-it-yourself activities involve a degree of risk.
Skills, materials, tools and site conditions vary widely.
Although the editors have made every effort to ensure
accuracy, the reader remains responsible for the selection
and use of tools, materials and methods. Always obey
local codes and laws, follow manufacturer instructions
and observe safety precautions.

CONTENTS

1 CLOSET & ENTRYWAY STORAGE | 6

2 KITCHEN & BATHROOM STORAGE | 18

3 SHELVES | 36

SS SPECIAL SECTION
MAKE YOUR PROJECTS LOOK GREAT WITH THESE PRO TIPS | 52

4 FURNITURE & DECORATING | 60

5 GARAGE & UTILITY SHELVES & ORGANIZERS | 78

6 SHOP ORGANIZERS | 96

7 SAWHORSES & STANDS | 112

8 WORKBENCHES & WOODWORKING EQUIPMENT | 120

9 ORGANIZATION AROUND THE HOUSE | 140

10 OUTDOOR STORAGE | 148

11 GARDEN PLANTERS | 162

12 DECK & WINDOW PLANTERS | 176

13 BENCHES | 188

14 GARDEN & DECK CHAIRS | 204

15 YARD PROJECTS | 226

16 GARDEN FEATURES | 240

17 GARDEN TOOLS & EQUIPMENT | 254

18 OUTDOOR TABLES | 268

19 QUICK PROJECTS | 282

Twin closet shelves 7
Throw & go bins.. 8
Stud-space cabinet... 12
Quick projects for beginners............................. 13
Hide-the-mess lockers 14

1 CLOSET & ENTRYWAY STORAGE

Twin closet shelves

There's a whole lot of unused real estate above most closet shelves. It seems logical that if one shelf is good, two would be better. And that upper shelf could be 15 in. deep instead of 12 in. because there's no closet rod hanging out below. The deep baskets help with the organization; cabinet knobs make for easier access. We show a two-tier shelf; you can install three if your closets (and you) are tall enough.

WHAT IT TAKES

TIME: 1 hour
SKILL LEVEL: Beginner

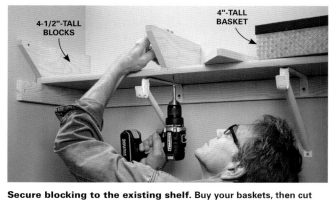

Secure blocking to the existing shelf. Buy your baskets, then cut spacer blocks 1/2 in. wider than the baskets are tall. Cut the ends of the blocks at an angle to accommodate the wider top shelf. Screw blocks to the bottom shelf, spacing them 1/2 in. farther apart than the baskets are wide. Then install and secure the top shelf.

Figure A
Closet shelf

1-5/8" SCREW

15" SHELF

3/4" x 4-1/2" BLOCK

BASKET

CLOSET ROD

1-5/8" SCREW

BRACKET OR WOODEN SUPPORT, AS SHOWN IN PHOTO

Throw & go bins

Storage for a family on the move

Shelves and cabinets are great places to store kid stuff, but when you're in a hurry (and kids always are), it's nice to just throw and go. That's why we built these bins. They're great for sports gear but handle all kinds of miscellaneous garage clutter.

We wanted something with a little character, so we loosely based the design on a row of bins at an old-fashioned country store. It was worth the little bit of extra effort to build something that brings back good memories yet serves a practical purpose in the present.

Cut the parts

Cut the sides, top and bottom from 3/4-in. plywood using a table saw or circular saw. We used "BC" plywood, which is good enough for paint, but you may want to buy birch veneer plywood if you plan to use stain.

This project requires a full sheet of plywood plus a 2 x 4-ft. section. Many home centers carry 4 x 4-ft., and some even stock 2 x 4-ft., so you don't have to buy two full sheets. However, they charge a premium for smaller sheets, and you won't save more than a few bucks. We bought two full sheets and used the leftover on other projects. The same goes for the 1/4-in. plywood—you

WHAT IT TAKES

TIME: One day to build, plus painting

SKILL LEVEL: Beginner to intermediate

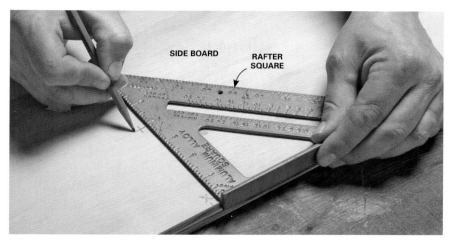

1 **Lay out the side profiles.** After measuring and marking the location of the bin fronts, use a square to mark the recessed portion of the front.

SIDE BOARD RAFTER SQUARE

3 **Cut two at a time.** Clamp two sides down and cut them both at the same time. That way, if you make any small cutting errors, the pair of sides will still match up. Make most of the cut with a circular saw, and then finish it off with a jigsaw.

2 **Connect the dots.** Use a straightedge to connect the dots. You only need to lay out one side board. Once it's cut, that board will act as a pattern for the rest.

only need a 4 x 4-ft. sheet, but a 4 x 8-ft. is a better value.

The fronts of the bins get the most abuse, so we built them from a solid 1x6 pine board. Solid wood holds up better than a plywood edge. You can rip down the two center boards when you're cutting up the other parts, but hold off on cutting them to length until the top and bottom boards are in place. That way you can cut them exactly to size.

Mark the side profile

This part of the process seems a little tricky, but it's really quite simple if you follow these directions. Hook a tape measure on the bottom front of one of the side boards. Measure up and mark the edge of the board at: 0, 4 in., 15-1/2 in., 19-1/2 in., 31 in. and 35 in. Now go back and measure over 4 in. at the following locations: the bottom, 15-1/2 in., 31 in. and the top (Photo 1). These marks represent the indented portion of the side. Start at the end of the board, and connect the dots (Photo 2). It's just that easy.

Cut and sand the sides

Clamp two side boards down to your work surface. Arrange them so the best sides of the plywood will be on the outside of the bins. Use a circular saw to make most of each cut. (Sometimes it's necessary to hold the blade guard up when you start a cut at an angle.) Finish the cuts with a jigsaw (Photo 3). A handsaw will work fine if you don't own a jigsaw.

Sand the edges with 80-grit sandpaper while the sides are still clamped together (Photo 4). Use one of the two cut side boards to mark one of the other uncut side boards, and repeat the process.

If you've already chosen a color for your project, now would be a good time to sand and finish all the parts. That way, you'll only have to touch up the fastener holes after assembly. Some of the plywood edges may have voids, which can be filled with wood putty or patching compound.

Figure A
Bin overview

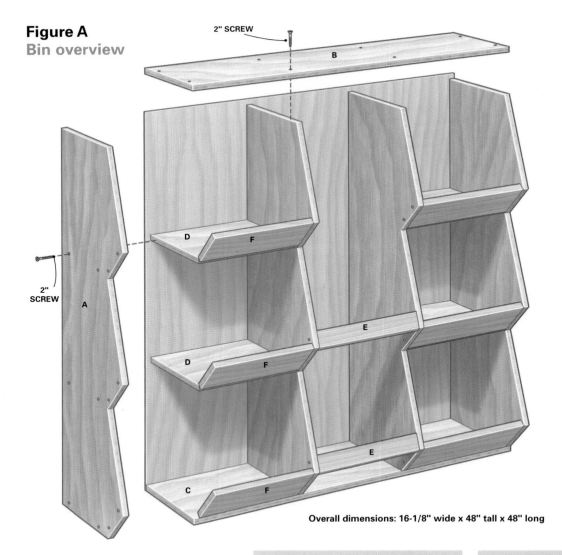

2" SCREW

B

2"
SCREW

A

D   F

D   F

E

E

C   F

Overall dimensions: 16-1/8" wide x 48" tall x 48" long

Assemble the bins

Lay out two of the sides back to back with the good side of the plywood facing down. Using a straightedge, mark lines between the notches to serve as a reference line for the bottoms of the bins. The bottom of the whole unit will serve as the bottom of the lowest bins, so fasten the bottom on the second lowest bin first. Align the board above the reference line.

Fasten the bottoms and the fronts with three 1-1/2-in. brads. Once it's all put together, go back and reinforce it all with two 2-in. trim head screws in each side of every board.

Once the bottoms are in place, come back and install the 1x6 fronts (Photo 5). Align them flush with the outside edge of the plywood. You'll notice a small gap between the bin bottom and the front.

Materials List

ITEM	QTY.
4' x 8' x 3/4" BC sanded plywood	2
1x6 x 8' pine	1
4' x 8' x 1/4" underlayment plywood	1
2" trim head screws	
1-1/2" 18-gauge brads	
Gallon of paint/primer	

This makes assembly easier, especially if your side cuts weren't perfect. It won't be noticeable when it's up against the wall. Once the first bank of bins is done, assemble the second one.

Finish it up

Fasten the top and bottom flush with the outside edges of the bins. Again, drive three brads into each side board and then

Cutting List

KEY	QTY.	SIZE & DESCRIPTION
A	4	15-7/8" x 46-1/2" x 3/4" BC sanded plywood (sides)
B	1	12-1/2" x 48" x 3/4" BC sanded plywood (top)
C	1	12-1/2" x 48" x 3/4" BC sanded plywood (bottom)
D	4	15" x 11-1/4" x 3/4" BC sanded plywood (bin bottom)
E	2	2" x approx. 15" BC sanded plywood (center board)
F	6	15" x 5-1/2" pine 1x6 (bin front)

go back and secure them with a couple of trim head screws.

Use the 1/4-in. plywood back to square up the project. Start with the two factory-cut sides of the plywood, and start fastening it to either the top

Figure B
Side layout

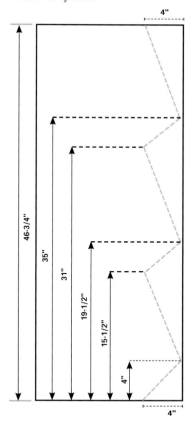

Figure C
Cutting diagram for 3/4" plywood

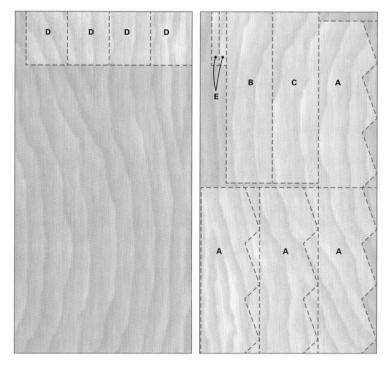

4 **Sand two at a time.** Smooth out the cuts before you unclamp the sides. Make sure to keep each pair together when you assemble the bins.

or bottom, making sure it's perfectly flush with the edge. Then fasten one side, working away from the previously fastened top or bottom, straightening and nailing as you go. Install one screw through the back into each bin bottom for a little extra support. Before you finish the other two sides, set up the project and check that things are square.

18-GAUGE BRAD NAILER

5 **Assemble the bins.** Build the bin sections before you install the top and bottom. If you have a brad nailer, make assembly easier by tacking all the parts together before you drive in the screws.

Measure between the two banks of bins, and cut your center boards to that size. Pin them in with brads and secure them with a screw. The center boards can be located anywhere you want depending on the type of items you're going to store.

If your project is going to be sitting on concrete, you may want to install a couple of strips of treated lumber on the bottom. Rip 5/8-in. strips of treated lumber and tack them onto the perimeter of the bottom.

You can screw the project to the wall if you know your kids will be using it as a ladder, but it's pretty stable as it is. All that's left is to go tell the family that there are no more excuses for throwing stuff on the floor.

Stud-space cabinet

Bonus storage space! Take a few hours and remove the drywall from between two studs, then construct a shallow cabinet to fit the space.

When you can't find a convenient nook for a set of shelves, you can often create one by recessing the shelves into the wall itself. Choose the location before you build the project to make sure it will fit. Start by looking for a space with no obvious obstructions. Locate the studs with a stud finder. Some stud finders can also locate electrical wires and plumbing pipes inside walls. When you've found a promising spot, cut a 6-in.-square inspection hole between the studs. Use a flashlight and a small mirror to inspect the stud cavity for obstructions. You often can modify the size of the cabinet to avoid obstructions.

When you find a good space, mark the perimeter of the opening and use a drywall keyhole saw to cut it out. Measure the opening and subtract 1/4 in. from the height and width to determine the outer dimensions of your cabinet.

For standard 2x4 stud walls with 1/2-in.-thick drywall, build the cabinet frame from 1x4s that measure 3-1/2 in. wide (see illustration). If your walls are different, adjust the depth of the frame accordingly. Then add a 1/4-in. back. Screw 1/4-in. pegboard to the back so you can hang stuff from pegboard hooks.

Add casing that matches the trim in your house. Drill holes into the sides to accept shelf supports. Shelf supports fit in 3mm, 5mm or 1/4-in. holes depending on the style.

Install the cabinet by slipping it into the opening, leveling it and nailing through the trim into the studs on each side. Use 6d finish nails placed every 12 in. along both sides.

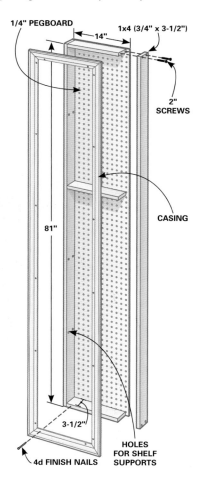

1/4" PEGBOARD
14"
1x4 (3/4" x 3-1/2")
2" SCREWS
CASING
81"
3-1/2"
4d FINISH NAILS
HOLES FOR SHELF SUPPORTS

WHAT IT TAKES

TIME: Half-day

SKILL LEVEL: Beginner to intermediate

Quick projects for beginners

Build this double-duty step stool from six pieces of 3/4-in. plywood.

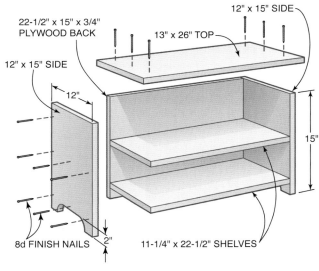

22-1/2" x 15" x 3/4" PLYWOOD BACK

12" x 15" SIDE

12" x 15" SIDE

13" x 26" TOP

12"

15"

2"

8d FINISH NAILS

11-1/4" x 22-1/2" SHELVES

Shoe-storage booster stool

Build this handy stool in one hour and park it in your closet. You can also use it as a step to reach the high shelf. All you need is a 4 x 4-ft. sheet of 3/4-in. plywood, wood glue and a handful of 8d finish nails. Cut the plywood pieces according to the illustration. Spread wood glue on the joints, then nail them together with 8d finish nails. First nail through the sides into the back. Then nail through the top into the sides and back. Finally, mark the location of the two shelves and nail through the sides into the shelves.

No more wet boots!

What do you get when you mix boots and winter weather? A dirty, slippery floor (and wet socks). Make life neater and safer for everyone in your house by building this simple boot tray. All you need is a plastic tray or a large metal baking sheet with a lip. Put a layer of medium-size stones in the tray so the boots can drain. To keep the stones in place and give the tray a handsome finished look, build a 1x2 frame around the tray and paint it the same color as the trim in your entryway.

Hide-the-mess lockers

Build simple boxes and add store-bought doors

Most houses have a nice big coat closet by the front door. The problem is, since the garage is in the back, everyone, including the dog, uses the back door.

We designed and built these hide-the-mess lockers with those houses in mind. Each locker is big enough to stash a coat, backpack, boots, hats, and odds and ends that normally wind up on the floor. Since they're modular and space efficient, you can build one for each member of the family—including the dog (leashes, toys, food, you name it). Now everyone has a personal place for stashing stuff—and the responsibility for keeping it organized.

The louvered door is made from one of a pair of closet bifold doors, which you can buy at almost any home center. Since the doors come in pairs and you can get two locker "boxes" from each sheet of plywood, you'll make the best use of materials by building them in twos. Here's how to do it.

WHAT IT TAKES

TIME: 2 days
SKILL LEVEL: Intermediate

Money, materials and tools

Our total materials cost was around $100 per locker. Since we were planning to paint the lockers, we used inexpensive "AC" plywood. If you plan to stain your lockers, and use hardwood plywood such as oak or birch and hardwood doors, you'll spend more for each locker. On a row of lockers, only the outer sides of the end lockers show, so you can use inexpensive plywood for the inner parts and more expensive material for the outer parts. Expect to spend at least a day buying materials, rounding up tools and building a pair of lockers. Set aside another day for finishing.

A table saw is handy for cutting up plywood, but a circular saw with a guide will provide the same results. You'll also need a miter saw to cut the screen molding. A finish nailer will help you work faster, but hand-nailing will work too as long as you drill holes to prevent splitting.

Buy the doors first

There are a variety of bifold doors available. If you need more ventilation, use full louvered doors; if ventilation isn't an issue, use solid doors. The doors you buy may not be exactly the same size as ours, so you may have to alter the dimensions of the boxes you build. Here are two key points to keep in mind as you plan your project:

■ You want a 1/8-in. gap surrounding the door. So to determine the size of the box opening, add 1/4 in. to the height and width of the door. Since our bifold doors measured 14-3/4 x 78-3/4 in., we made the opening 15 x 79 in.

■ To determine the depth of the shelves, subtract the door thickness from the width of the sides (including the 1/4-in. screen molding). Our doors were 1-1/8 in. thick, so we made

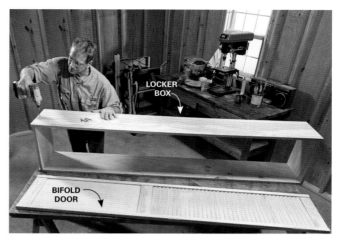

1 **Build a simple box.** Cut the plywood parts and assemble them with trim-head screws. Make sure the box opening is 1/4 in. taller and wider than the door itself.

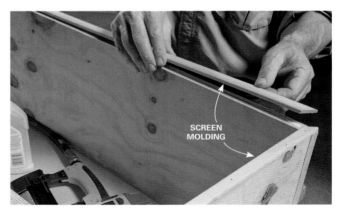

2 **Square it up.** Take diagonal corner-to-corner measurements, then adjust the box until the measurements are equal and the box is square. Install the back, using one edge of the back to straighten the box side as you fasten it. Check once again for squareness, then secure the other edges of the back.

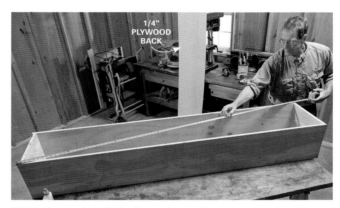

3 **Cover the plywood edges.** Install screen molding over the front edges of the box. Apply wood glue lightly and use just enough nails to "clamp" the molding in place while the glue dries.

the shelves 10-7/8 in. deep (12 minus 1-1/8 equals 10-7/8 in.). When the doors are closed, they'll rest against the shelves inside and flush with the screen molding outside.

4 **Build slatted shelves.** Plywood shelves would work fine, but slatted shelves allow better ventilation so wet clothes and shoes can dry. Space the slats with a pair of wood scraps.

5/16" SPACER

THICKNESS OF DOOR

5 **Install the shelves.** Stand your locker up and position the shelves to suit the stuff that will go in it. Mark the shelf locations, lay the locker on its back and screw the shelves into place. Make sure the shelves are inset far enough to allow for the door.

"NO-MORTISE" HINGE

6 **Mount the hinges.** Remove the hinges from the doors (they'll be pointed the wrong way) and reinstall them on the door based on the direction you want it to swing. Prop up the door alongside the box and align the door so there will be a 1/8-in. gap at the top and bottom of the box. Then screw the hinges to the box.

Get building!

Use a table saw or straight-cutting guide to cut the plywood sides (A) and top and bottom (B). The Cutting List on p. 15 gives the parts dimensions for the lockers. If you plan to paint or stain the lockers, it's a good idea to prefinish the insides of parts. Once the lockers are assembled, brushing a finish onto the insides is slow and difficult.

Assemble the boxes with 2-in. trim-head screws (Photo 1). Trim-head screws have smaller heads than standard screws and are easier to hide with filler. Cut the 1/4-in. plywood back (C) to size. Make certain the box is square by taking diagonal measurements (they should be equal; see Photo 2), and then secure the back using 1-in. nails. Use the edges of the back as a guide to straighten the edges of the box as you nail the back into place.

Cut 1/4 x 3/4-in. screen molding and use glue and 1-in. finish nails or brads to secure it to the exposed front edges of the plywood (Photo 3). Cut the shelf front and back (D), sides (E) and slats (F) to length, then assemble the three slatted shelf units (Photo 4). With the locker box standing upright, position the shelves and hold them temporarily in place with clamps or a couple of screws. Adjust the shelf spacing based on the height of the locker's user and the stuff that will go inside. Once you have a suitable arrangement, lay the locker on its back and screw the shelves into place (Photo 5). The shelves are easy to reposition in the future as needs change.

Add the hardware and finish, then install

Remove the hinges that hold the bifold doors to each other. Determine which way you want the door to swing, then mount the hinges onto the door accordingly. (Note: You'll need to buy another set of hinges if you're building two lockers.) Remember, you want the louvers to point downward on the outside! With the locker on its back, position the door and secure the hinges to the plywood side (Photo 6). Install door handles and magnetic catches to hold them closed.

Remove the doors (but don't finish them yet!) and install the locker boxes. Your lockers can stand against baseboard, leaving a small gap between the backs of the lockers and the wall. Or—if you remove the baseboard—they can stand tight against the wall. Either way, installing them is a lot like installing cabinets: Fasten all the boxes together by driving 1-1/4-in. screws through the side of one locker into the next. Then screw the entire assembly to wall studs.

Install the unfinished doors to make sure they all fit properly, then remove them again. This may seem like a waste of time, but there's a good reason for it: Your locker boxes may have shifted a little during installation, and the doors may not fit properly. If a door or two need some edge sanding, you want to do that before finishing.

When you've checked the fit of all the doors, remove them one last time for finishing. Whether you're using paint or a natural finish, louvered doors are a real pain. If your plans include a clear coat, consider polyurethane or lacquer in spray cans: You'll get better results in far less time, though you'll spend a little extra. After finishing, install the doors and load up those lockers!

Figure A
Locker construction

Overall Dimensions:
16-1/2" wide x 81" tall x 12-1/4" deep

Materials List
(for one locker)
Because bifold doors are sold in pairs, and one sheet of 3/4-in. plywood yields two lockers, you can make the best use of materials by building an even number of lockers.

ITEM	QTY.
30" bifold door pack (2 doors)	1
3/4" x 4' x 8' plywood	1
1/4" x 4' x 8' plywood	1
1/4" x 3/4" x 8' screen molding	5
3/4" x 1-1/2" x 8' solid wood	9

2" trim-head screws, 1-1/4" screws, 1" nails, 1-1/2" nails, wood glue, no-mortise hinges, door handles and magnetic catches.

Cutting List
(for one locker)
These locker parts suit a door measuring 14-3/4 x 78-3/4 in. Verify the exact size of your doors before building.

KEY	QTY.	SIZE & DESCRIPTION
A	2	11-3/4" x 80-7/8" sides (3/4" plywood)
B	2	11-3/4" x 15" top/bottom (3/4" plywood)
C	1	16-1/2" x 80-1/2" back (1/4" plywood)
D	2	3/4" x 1-1/2" x 15" shelf front/back (solid wood)
E	2	3/4" x 1-1/2" x 9-3/8" shelf sides (solid wood)
F	6	3/4" x 1-1/2" x 15" shelf slats (solid wood)

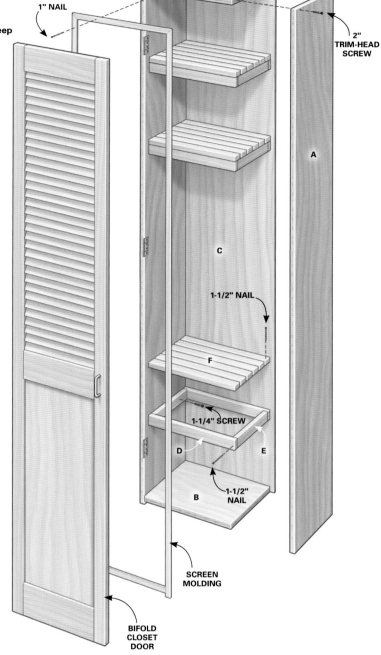

Figure B
Cutting diagrams

3/4" PLYWOOD

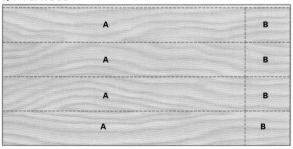

1/4" PLYWOOD

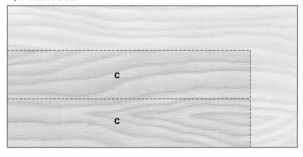

Quick projects for beginners 19

Cabinet door rack 20

Simple kitchen shelf 22

Two-tier spice drawer 28

Space-saving wall niche 30

Bathroom shelving unit 33

Bigger medicine cabinet 34

Customize your cabinets 35

2 KITCHEN & BATHROOM STORAGE

Quick projects for beginners

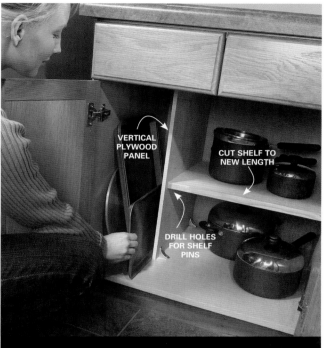

Under-sink organizer

To tame the clutter under your bathroom sink, make this organizer from scraps of 3-in. PVC. Cut the pipe into short lengths and then glue them to 1/2-in. plywood with polyurethane construction adhesive. Space the pipe pieces to accommodate liquid soaps, shampoos and other bottles and leave spaces between the pipe sections for odd-shaped spray bottles. Now things will be organized and won't topple over every time you reach for something.

VERTICAL PLYWOOD PANEL

CUT SHELF TO NEW LENGTH

DRILL HOLES FOR SHELF PINS

Cookware organizer

Most kitchen base cabinets lack vertical storage space for big, flat cookware like cookie sheets and pizza pans. To provide it, just remove the lower shelf, cut a vertical panel of plywood and fasten it at the cabinet bottom with furniture braces and at the top with a strip of wood. Drill holes for the adjusting pins to match the original locations and trim the shelf to length.

Toilet paper shelf

Here's an easy way to make a little extra space. Buy or make a deep "shadow box" picture frame, then apply a couple of coats of white enamel paint on the frame and hang it around your toilet paper holder. It gives you two convenient shelves for small items.

Cabinet door rack

A super-simple solution for cabinet chaos

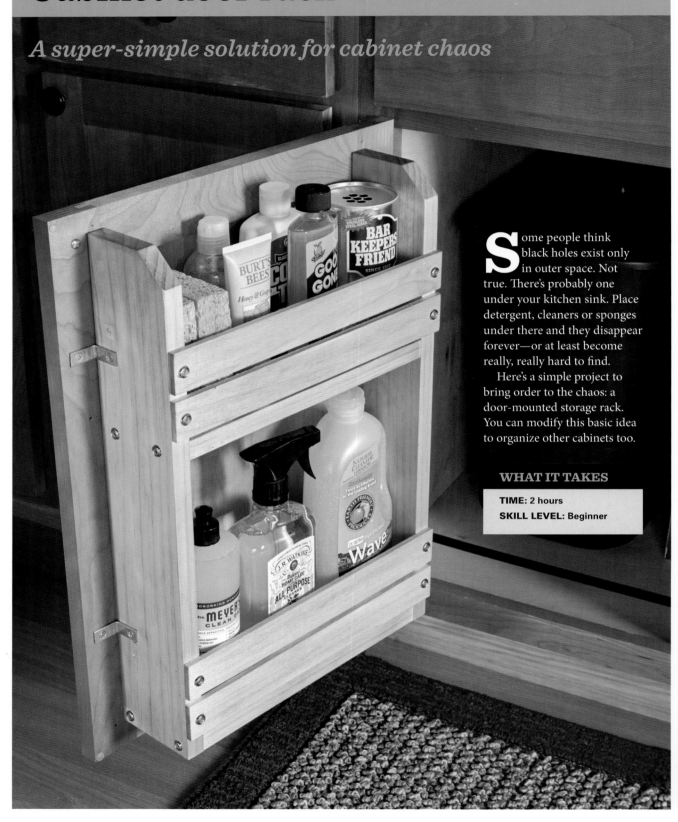

Some people think black holes exist only in outer space. Not true. There's probably one under your kitchen sink. Place detergent, cleaners or sponges under there and they disappear forever—or at least become really, really hard to find.

Here's a simple project to bring order to the chaos: a door-mounted storage rack. You can modify this basic idea to organize other cabinets too.

WHAT IT TAKES

TIME: 2 hours
SKILL LEVEL: Beginner

Planning and materials

As you plan your rack, consider building multiple racks. Building two or three doesn't take much more time than building one. Also think about (and measure!) the items you want your rack to hold. You may want to mount the upper shelf a little higher or lower than we did.

Most home centers carry everything you'll need, including 1/4-in.-thick wood strips in species like pine, oak and poplar. If you don't find thin material alongside the other lumber, look for "mull strip" or "mullion" in the millwork aisle. The wood quantities on our Materials List will yield a rack sized for most cabinet doors, but you may need a little more or a little less.

How to do it

Begin by looking inside your cabinet. With the door closed, this rack will project 3-3/4 in. into the interior. Make sure the installed rack won't bump into your sink, pipes, garbage disposal or other fixed object.

Measure the cabinet door and opening to determine the measurements of the sides and shelves (Photo 1). Mark the position of the upper shelf on the sides: We positioned ours 12 in. from the bottom, but you can adjust the location based on your needs. Secure the shelves to the sides using 2-in. screws and finish washers (Photo 2). Drill holes in the four cross slats 3/8 in. from the ends and fasten them to the sides with 3/4-in. screws.

With the rack assembled, we gave it two coats of lacquer. Lacquer is a durable finish, dries in minutes and comes in spray cans for quick, no-mess application.

After the finish dries, screw the four L-brackets to the

Materials List

QTY	DESCRIPTION
6'	1x4
6'	1/4" x 1-1/2" strip
4	1" L-brackets
	3/4" screws
	2" screws
	finish washers
	spray lacquer

Figure A
Cabinet door rack

1/2" MINIMUM

45-DEGREE MITER

1-1/2"

SLAT

1/4" x 1-1/2"

1x4

SIDE

L-BRACKET

1x4

SHELF

2" SCREW AND FINISH WASHER

1/4" x 1-1/2"

sides of the racks, making sure to position them so they won't interfere with the door hinges. Clamp the rack to the door, predrill mounting holes using the L-brackets as guides, and secure the rack to the door (Photo 3). Put a strip of tape 4 in. back from the front of the cabinet to indicate a "No Parking" zone for items stored inside.

1 **Measure to size the rack.** Measure the width of the door and cut the rack shelves 4-1/2 in. shorter than that measurement. Measure the height of the cabinet opening and cut the rack sides 1 in. shorter.

2 **Build the rack.** Mark the location of the top shelf on the sides. Drill screw holes and fasten the sides to the shelves using 2-in. screws and finish washers. Add the slats, apply a finish and screw brackets to the rack.

3 **Mount the rack.** Center the rack on the door and drill screw holes. Wrap tape around the drill bit to act as a depth guide so you don't drill through the door. Clamps aren't absolutely necessary for this step, but they're a big help.

Simple kitchen shelf

Easy for anyone to build— and fun to customize!

L ots of kitchens have a little wall space that would be perfect for a storage or display shelf. Plenty of bathrooms do too. This shelf is a great project for a beginning woodworker, and since it's so easy to adapt to different uses, a more advanced DIYer can have a lot of fun customizing it.

WHAT IT TAKES

TIME: 1/2 day
SKILL LEVEL: Beginner

Tools and wood

You'll need a jigsaw, a drill and two accessories for the drill. The first is a No. 8 combination drill bit and countersink (shown on p. 21), which you can find anywhere drill bits are sold. The second accessory is a small sanding drum (shown on p. 21 and in Photo 3), which you can find at home centers or online. The only other tool you might need is a nail set, for setting the heads of finish nails below the surface. Obviously, if you have a band saw and a miter saw, they will make this project a piece of cake.

You can build this shelf from just about any type of wood. Resist the urge to use the least expensive knotty pine, unless that's the look you're after. Knotty pine will be harder to work with and to paint well. Instead, get clear pine, poplar or any other knot-free board. If you're planning to paint the shelf, avoid oak. We used clear alder.

Cut out the shelf and brackets

Begin by cutting the shelf to length with a jigsaw (Photo 1). Then cut a piece 6 in. long from which you can cut the two brackets (Photo 2). Jigsaws often make a rougher cut on the top surface, so label that "top." The roughness will be hidden by the edging, even if the top of the shelf is visible after hanging it. But use a fine-tooth blade and set your oscillating feature (if your saw has it) to zero.

You can trace the curve for the brackets from the full-size pattern on p. 22, or even easier, use the bottom of a coffee can or a small plate. The exact curve isn't important. After the brackets are cut, smooth the sawn edges with a file, sanding block and the sanding drum in your drill (Photo 3) until the wood is smooth. You can stop sanding at about 150 or 180 grit.

Install edging strips on the shelf

Start edging the shelf by cutting the end strips to length. Instead of measuring, just hold the molding to the end of the shelf and mark it for cutting. It won't hurt if it's a hair too long. Mark one edge of the shelf as the front edge, then nail on the side strips (Photo 4), keeping the front edge flush. Make sure the rounded edge faces out. Put a thin bead of glue on the shelf edge before nailing, and keep the bottom edge as flush as you can. If the strips are a little long in back, you can easily sand or file off the excess, and if they stick out a little on the bottom edge, that can be sanded off too. Finally, nail on the edging strip in front.

Now set the nails and put a little painter's putty on them. When the putty is dry, sand the edging so the corners are smooth and the bottom edge is flush with the shelf. The bottom of the shelf will have a seam between the shelf and the edging. It's pretty much impossible to eliminate that seam permanently. Expansion and contraction of the wood will open it up even if you caulk or putty it, so don't be too much of a perfectionist. However, if your cut on

Low-tech woodworking

This is a low-tech project. A jigsaw and a cordless drill are the only power tools you need, though there are more accurate and faster options. You'll also need some basic hand tools and two specialized accessories for the drill: a sanding drum and a combination drill/countersink bit. (See the text for more info.)

COMBO DRILL/ COUNTER-SINK

SANDING DRUM

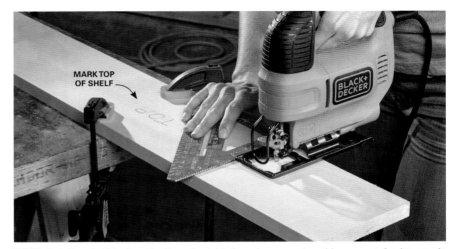

MARK TOP OF SHELF

1 Cut the shelf to length. Use a fresh blade and a square to guide your cut. A miter saw is the best tool for the job, but if you don't have access to one, you can substitute almost any other saw.

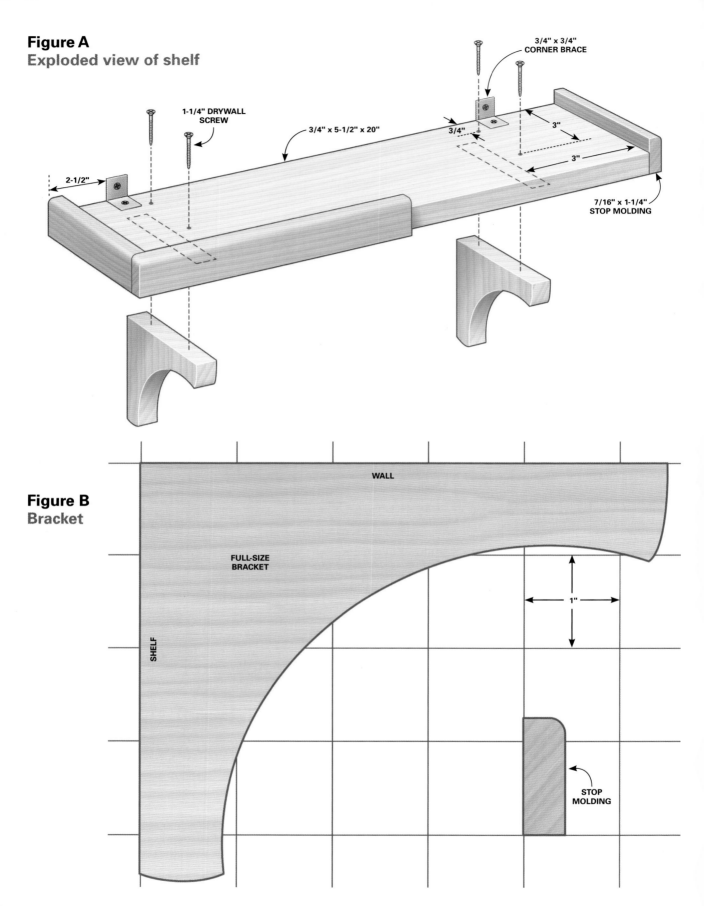

Figure A
Exploded view of shelf

1-1/4" DRYWALL
SCREW

3/4" x 3/4"
CORNER BRACE

3/4" x 5-1/2" x 20"

3/4"

3"

3"

2-1/2"

7/16" x 1-1/4"
STOP MOLDING

Figure B
Bracket

WALL

FULL-SIZE
BRACKET

SHELF

1"

STOP
MOLDING

Materials List

ITEM	QTY.
1x6 clear paint-grade softwood or hardwood	3'
7/16" x 1-1/4" pine stop molding	3'
1-1/4" drywall or utility screws	4
3/4" x 3/4" corner braces or brackets	2
Plastic or metal screw-in drywall anchors	2
Aerosol paint	1 can
Sandpaper	
Wood glue	

the 1x6 is particularly rough, some putty there will help clean things up.

Screw the brackets to the shelf

The next step is to drill some screw holes in the shelf for attaching the brackets. The idea is simple: two screw holes on each side of the shelf so you can screw down into the brackets. Here's what to do. First, hold a bracket where you want it to be, but on the top of the shelf. Trace around the bracket, then do the same thing for the other bracket. Mark the screw locations and drill screw holes in the shelf from the top, using your combination drill/countersink bit.

Now hold a bracket in position on the bottom of the shelf, make sure the back edge is flush with the back edge of the shelf and that the screw holes are centered on the bracket. You can do it by eye, but if that's hard, put the two screws in their holes and use the points of the screws to guide you. Drive the screws by hand into the bracket (Photo 5), then repeat with the other bracket. Now is a good time to step back and admire your work, because you're almost done. But if for some reason you messed this part up, just drill new holes and fill the old ones with putty. You can shift the position of the brackets if you want.

Paint your shelf

Begin this part of the project by unscrewing the brackets. It's always easier to paint a project well if you can do the parts separately. Sand the pieces

2 **Cut the curved brackets.** For a curve like this, a smooth continuous cut is more important than following the line exactly. Any bumps or blips will be hard to sand out.

3 **Sand the curves with a sanding drum.** The trick is to go against the direction of rotation of the drill, with the drill going fast. If you make a gouge, angle the drum slightly to remove it.

4 **Nail on the edging.** The edging is a stock molding from home centers. It keeps stuff from falling off the shelf and covers the rough ends of the shelf.

thoroughly to about 150 to 180 grit, removing sharp edges and corners, but not rounding them over too much. Wipe the sanding dust off with a rag and vacuum the parts thoroughly. Now set up your painting area. We highly recommend using spray paint for this project because it'll get you the smoothest finish.

Cover your work surface with paper or plastic, and set your shelf on strips or blocks to get it up off the surface. The shelf is pretty easy to paint, but go light on the edges to avoid drips. After the first coat of paint is thoroughly dry, sand it lightly with fine sandpaper, just enough to take off any roughness. Wipe and vacuum, then apply two final coats.

There's a trick to painting the brackets: Drive a long screw in one of the holes and use it as a little handle. That way you can spray the whole piece evenly in one shot (Photo 6). Then carefully set it down on a couple strips of wood to dry. When the paint is dry on all the parts, reassemble your shelf.

Hang your shelf

We recommend using small angle brackets to hang your shelf (Photo 7). Normally the top of a shelf is above eye level and the brackets are hidden, especially with items on the shelf. If your brackets are more exposed, give them a little spray paint to match the shelf, and paint the part that goes on your wall to match your wall. They'll be barely noticeable. Generally, though, this step isn't necessary.

To hang the shelf, use drywall anchors. Don't worry about hitting studs; there shouldn't be enough weight on this shelf to require it. Just put the shelf where you want it to go, make sure it's level, mark through the brackets where the anchors will go, and install the anchors. If it seems like you need a third hand to manage everything, you could draw a level line on the wall where the shelf will go. With the anchors in place, use the screws that came with the anchors to attach the shelf. Your shelf is complete! When you're ready to build more, check out the variations on p. 25.

5 **Screw the brackets to the shelf.** Notice that we've traced the shape of the bracket on the top of the shelf to help position the screw holes. We used a combination countersink/drill bit for the holes.

6 **Spray-paint the shelf parts.** You'll get better results by unscrewing the brackets and painting everything separately. A screw in the top of the bracket is a handy handle.

7 **Hang your shelf with small angle brackets.** For a light-duty shelf like this, you don't need to screw it to the studs. Just make sure the shelf is level and use drywall anchors in the wall.

Customize your shelf

Go ahead—play with this project! It's easy to make your shelf as long as you want it to be. Just put more brackets underneath it, maybe one every 2 ft. or so. You could also scale it up by using 1x8 lumber, or even wider stock, as long as you also scale up the brackets. Some other variations are shown below. However, we have one strong recommendation: If you're doing anything more than changing the size or color, first make a prototype out of inexpensive pine. Your plates, pot lids, cooking tools or whatever will be different from ours, so make sure they fit.

Pothooks and lids

This shelf has hooks screwed underneath to hold frying pans. We gave the hooks a dark finish by heating them with a torch as shown below. On our shelf, we cut off some of the threaded part of each hook with a bolt cutter because they were too long. The pot lids are held in place with two rows of 5/16-in. dowels. For heavier lids, use 3/8-in. dowels.

Blacken screw hooks with oil. Working outside, burn off the plating with a torch. Dip the hook into cooking oil and heat it until the oil burns off. You may need to repeat a couple times. This makes a hard, baked-on coating that resists wear. It's like seasoning a cast iron pan.

Plates and spoons

This shelf has a strip of molding (any kind will work) nailed on the top a couple inches from the back edge. This will keep plates from sliding off. The rod is 5/16-in.-diameter steel available at hardware stores. Cut it with a hacksaw and file the ends smooth. The trick is to drill the brackets before assembly, both at the same time, so the rod is perfectly aligned. The hooks are simple S-hooks, also a hardware item, opened up with a pair of pliers.

A wood strip makes it a plate rack. Tack a piece of molding to the top of the shelf to keep plates from sliding. Experiment to find the best location for the molding.

Two-tier spice drawer

WHAT IT TAKES

TIME: 3 hours
SKILL LEVEL: Seasoned beginner

Recently we remodeled our kitchen: new cabinets, countertops, appliances, the works. Yet the first thing we show off when people visit isn't the fancy new stove, but the ingenious two-tier spice tray. When we open the drawer, we can slide the top tray all the way back into the cabinet to access the entire bottom layer; no need to lift out a separate tray or sort through layers of stuff. It's not only a space-saver but also a smart organizer since all the spices are in one place, face up. We used the same basic design to make a two-tier utensil drawer too.

Do a little measuring before diving into this project. You can install the 1-3/4-in.-thick tray (like ours) if your drawer is at least 4 in. deep on the inside. Also, these trays are most useful if your existing drawers have (or you install) full-extension slides on the main drawer.

DRAWER BACK

1 **Cut the drawer back.** Use a jigsaw to cut away a little more than half of the drawer back.

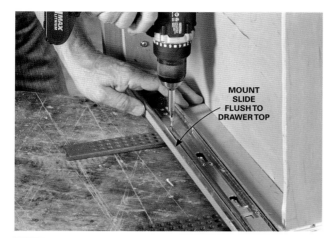

2 **Install the tray slides.** Secure full-extension drawer slides to the top inside edges of the drawer. Install them "backward" so they extend toward the back of the drawer. It's OK if they run an inch or so beyond the back of the drawer; most cabinets have extra space in back.

MOUNT SLIDE FLUSH TO DRAWER TOP

3 **Build the upper tray.** Since most standard drawer glides are 1/2 in. wide, build your tray 1 in. narrower (or a hair less) than the inside width of the drawer. Build your tray the same length as the inside drawer length. Install partitions according to your needs.

1/4" PLYWOOD BOTTOM

4 **Install the tray.** Attach the plywood bottom to the tray with nails or brads. Screw the tray to the drawer slides so the top of the tray is flush with the top of the drawer. Then reinstall the drawer.

Figure A
Spice drawer

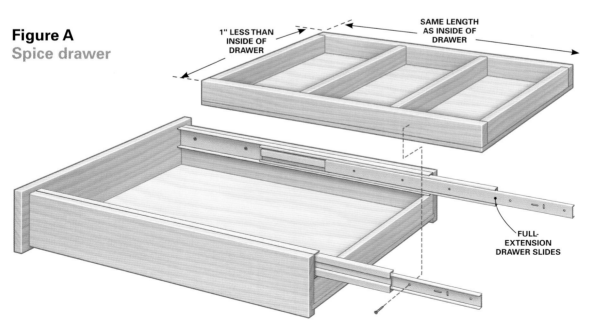

1" LESS THAN INSIDE OF DRAWER

SAME LENGTH AS INSIDE OF DRAWER

FULL-EXTENSION DRAWER SLIDES

Space-saving wall niche

The cabinet fits between studs inside the wall, so it'll work in even the tiniest bathroom. Unlike a wall-hung shelf, the cabinet lets you gain storage space without sacrificing elbow room.

I f you need to carve out more storage space in your bathroom, this is the project for you. Bathrooms are notoriously cramped, so this cabinet is designed to fit inside a wall where it won't take up valuable space. The width is slightly narrower than the 14-1/2-in. stud space, so the cabinet will fit even if the studs are a little off center or bowed.

The following pages show you how to build and install the cabinet. You can complete the project in just one weekend: Build and stain (or paint) it on Saturday, then stick it in the wall on Sunday.

Tools and materials

Everything you need for this project is available at home centers.

To complete the project, you'll need a miter saw, a circular saw or table saw, and a drywall saw. A brad nailer will make nailing fast and easy, but it's not absolutely necessary (you can hand-nail instead). You'll also need a router with a 1/4-in. round-over bit and a 1/4-in. Roman ogee bit to rout the shelves and sill nose.

Where to put the cabinet

This cabinet is installed next to the shower, but it'll also fit nicely behind the bathroom door if there's no other available space. In most cases, it won't work over the toilet because there's a vent pipe in the wall. Also avoid exterior walls because they're filled with insulation.

When choosing a location, check both sides of the wall for obstructions. A light switch or showerhead on the other side of the wall means the wall contains electrical cable or plumbing pipes.

You could also choose a different room. The cabinet can store—or display—anything you like in the hallway, bedrooms or family room.

Cut, rout and drill the pieces

Get started by cutting all the pieces to size (refer to Figure A). Then run a router with a Roman ogee bit along the bottom front and both bottom sides of the sill nose. Use a round-over bit to rout the top and bottom front of the shelves.

Apply wood glue along the front edge of the sill, center the sill nose over it, then clamp the pieces together until the glue dries. Use a damp cloth to wipe away any glue that oozes out. If the sill and sill nose surfaces aren't flush, sand the pieces flat with 80-grit sandpaper.

Lay out the sides for the shelf bracket holes, following Figure A. Drill the holes 3/4 in. from the edges and spaced 1 in. apart. Use a 1/4-in. drill bit (or whatever bit size is required for your brackets). You only need to drill the holes 3/8 in. deep (wrap tape 3/8 in. from the end of the drill bit to mark the depth), although it's OK to drill all the way through the sides since the other side will be hidden inside the wall.

After drilling the holes, sand off the pencil lines remaining on the sides with 120-grit sandpaper.

Assemble the cabinet

Use wood glue and 1-1/4-in. brad nails to assemble the cabinet frame (Photo 1), following Figure A. Then drill two 1/8-in. pilot holes in each corner and drive 1-1/2-in. screws to hold the corners together.

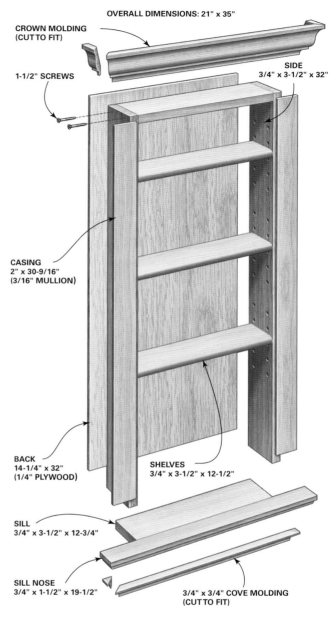

Figure A:
Wall niche

OVERALL DIMENSIONS: 21" x 35"

CROWN MOLDING (CUT TO FIT)

1-1/2" SCREWS

SIDE 3/4" x 3-1/2" x 32"

CASING 2" x 30-9/16" (3/16" MULLION)

BACK 14-1/4" x 32" (1/4" PLYWOOD)

SHELVES 3/4" x 3-1/2" x 12-1/2"

SILL 3/4" x 3-1/2" x 12-3/4"

SILL NOSE 3/4" x 1-1/2" x 19-1/2"

3/4" x 3/4" COVE MOLDING (CUT TO FIT)

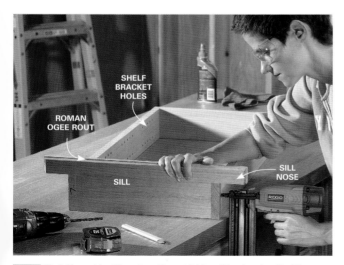

1 Tack the cabinet box together quickly with a brad nailer. Then add screws for rock-solid corners. Glue the sill nose to the sill before assembling the cabinet.

SHELF BRACKET HOLES

ROMAN OGEE ROUT

SILL

SILL NOSE

Materials List

ITEM	QTY.
1x4 x 96" oak	2
1x2 x 24" oak	1
1/4" x 24" x 48" oak plywood	1
3/16" x 2" x 72" mullion	1
11/16" x 3-1/4" x 36" crown molding	1
3/4" x 3/4" x 36" cove molding	1
Shelf brackets	12

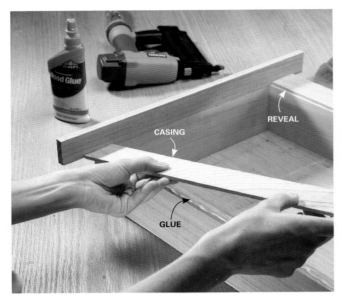

CASING

REVEAL

GLUE

2 Add casing to the box using as few nails as possible. Three nails will hold the casing tight while the glue dries.

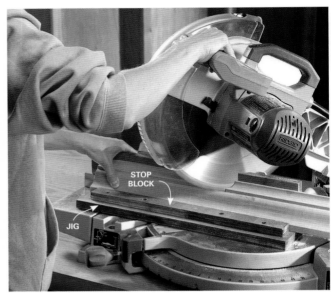

STOP BLOCK

JIG

3 Cut the crown molding using a simple homemade jig. The jig holds the crown upside down as you make the cuts.

4 Glue the crown corners together without nails or clamps. Just hold each return tightly in place for about 60 seconds. Set the completed crown aside for 20 minutes, then attach it to the cabinet.

Run a thin bead of glue along the back of the entire frame, then set the back panel over it. Use the back panel to square the frame, then tack the panel into place with 5/8-in. brad nails.

Lay the cabinet on its back and fasten the casing (Photo 2). Three 5/8-in. nails will hold the casing until the glue dries.

Precision cuts are required for the molding corners to fit tightly. Measure along the bottom edge of the molding when you make the cuts (the top measurements will vary depending on the type of molding).

To get accurate cuts, build a simple jig to hold the molding in place during cuts. Screw or nail wood scraps together at a 90-degree angle. Set the crown molding upside down in the jig so the flat part on the back (the part that sits against the cabinet after installation) is flush against the vertical part of the jig.

Fasten a stop block to the horizontal part of the jig along the top of the molding. Screw or hot-glue the jig to the fence on your miter saw so it won't move.

Set the crown molding upside down in the jig and cut it (Photo 3). If the molding moves in the jig even a tiny bit during the cut, recut the molding or the corners won't fit tightly together. To cut the molding returns (sides), use the jig to make the angle cuts, then cut the 90-degree angles.

Nailing the mitered corners together won't work—the molding will crack or move as you nail it. Instead, simply glue the corners (Photo 4). Cut the cove molding for the bottom of the cabinet in the miter saw (without using the jig). Glue the cove molding pieces together.

Glue and tack the assembled crown and cove moldings to the cabinet with 5/8-in. brad nails.

Apply a finish and stick the cabinet in the wall

Sand the entire cabinet with 120-grit sandpaper and wipe away the dust with a clean cloth. Then brush on a finish. This cabinet has a golden oak stain followed by two coats of polyurethane.

Then get the wall ready. Using a drywall saw, cut a small inspection hole in the wall where the cabinet will go. Shine a light in the opening and use a small mirror to look for obstructions in the wall. If you find electrical cable or plumbing pipe, patch the hole and move over a stud space.

Make an outline on the wall (between two studs) 1/4 in. larger than the cabinet back (so it'll fit easily) and cut out the drywall with a drywall saw. Be careful not to cut into the drywall on the other side of the wall.

Finally, put the cabinet into the wall, level it, then nail through the stiles into the studs with 2-1/2-in. finish nails.

Bathroom shelving unit

In a small bathroom, every single square inch counts. These shelves make the most of wall space by going vertical. The version shown here, made of cherry, cost about $100. But you can build one for less if you choose a more economical wood like oak or pine. All you need is a 6-ft. 1x4, a 6-ft. 1x6 and a 6-ft. 1x8.

Cut the middle spacers and the shelves 12 in. long. Cut the bottom spacer 11 in. long to allow for a decorative 1-in. reveal. Cut the top spacer to fit (the one shown was 7-1/4 in.). Measure 1 in. from one edge of the backboard and draw a guideline for the shelves and spacers along its length. Nail the bottom spacer in place, leaving a 1-in. reveal at the bottom edge. Center the first shelf by measuring 3-1/4 in. in from the edge of the backboard and nail it in place. Work your way up the backboard, alternating between spacers and shelves (Photo 1).

On the back side, use a 1/8-in. countersink bit to drill two holes, one at the top and one at the bottom of each spacer. Drill two holes spaced 1 in. from each side of the backboard into each shelf ledge. Drive 1-1/4-in. drywall screws into each hole (Photo 2). Paint or stain the assembled unit. If you'd like to clearcoat it, use a wipe-on poly or spray lacquer—using a brush would be really tough. Mount the unit on the wall with two 2-1/2-in. screws and screw-in drywall anchors. Drive the screws where they won't be seen: right below the bottom shelf and right above the top shelf.

WHAT IT TAKES

TIME: 1 day
SKILL LEVEL: Beginner

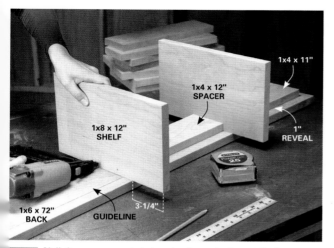

1 Nail the spacers and shelves in place, starting at the bottom and working your way up. Place the bottom spacer 1 in. from the lower edge of the backboard.

1x4 x 11"
1x4 x 12" SPACER
1x8 x 12" SHELF
1" REVEAL
1x6 x 72" BACK
GUIDELINE
3-1/4"

2 Strengthen the shelves by driving screws through the backboard into the shelves and spacers. Drill screw holes with a countersink bit.

Bigger medicine cabinet

Surface-mounting a large medicine cabinet is simply a matter of centering it, leveling it and screwing it to the wall studs.

An old cabinet may be surface-mounted or recessed into the wall cavity between the framing. Remove a recessed unit simply by opening the door, backing out the screws in the side of the cabinet and pulling it out of the recess. Cut around it with a utility knife if it's caulked or painted in around the edges. Have a helper support surface-mounted cabinets, then back out the screws; or if working alone, hold the cabinet by screwing a temporary 1x2 support ledger under the cabinet as shown in Photo 1. Move or replace the lighting beside or above the old cabinet, if needed.

Hold the new medicine cabinet against the wall and adjust it up and down to find the perfect height, then mark the bottom and set the cabinet aside. Use the mark to draw a level line for positioning the 1x2 ledger (Photo 1). Then follow Photos 2 and 3 for installation details.

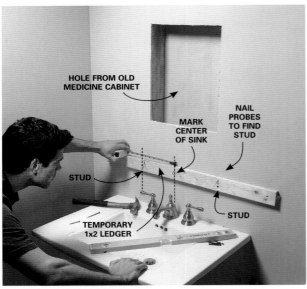

1 Mark the height of the bottom of the cabinet and draw a line with a 2-ft. level. Find the studs by probing with a nail and mark the stud positions above the level line. Screw a temporary 1x2 ledger board through the drywall into the studs. Mark the center of the sink on the ledger, and then measure over from the center mark to the left and right studs.

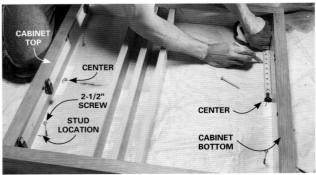

2 Mark the center of the cabinet at the top and bottom and transfer the center-to-stud locations inside the cabinet. Start 2-1/2-in. screws at those marks.

3 Set the cabinet on the ledger and line up the center of the cabinet with the center mark on the ledger. Drive the screws into the studs, then remove the ledger. Fill the screw holes with surfacing compound and touch up the paint.

WHAT IT TAKES
TIME: 1/2 day
SKILL LEVEL: Beginner

Customize your cabinets

If you have a short cabinet flanked by two taller cabinets, you can add this combination shelf/wine glass rack/plate rack.

Cut the shelf to length, then add mounting strips on each end. Cut four 9-in. sections of wine glass molding from a 3-ft. length, then glue and nail them to the bottom of the pine shelf. Wine glass molding is available from woodworking stores and online. Cut curved brackets from each end of a 1x6 board that matches your cabinets and cut the center 1 in. wide to serve as shelf edging (Photo 1). Finally, install the unit by driving screws through the mounting strips and into the cabinets on each side.

To display your plates and keep them accessible and chip-free, build and install this plate rack (Photo 2).

To create the two plate rack "ladders," measure the cabinet, then build each ladder so the finished height equals the height of the inside of the cabinet. The finished width should be equal to the width of the face frame opening. Drill 3/8-in. holes, 3/8 in. deep in 3/4-in. x 3/4-in. square dowels and space them every 1-1/2 in. Cut the dowels to length, add a drop of glue in each hole, insert the dowels, then use elastic cords or clamps to hold things together until the glue dries.

A drill press comes in handy, but you can also get good results using a cordless drill, a steady hand and a 3/8-in. drill bit with masking tape wrapped around it as a depth guide for the holes in the rails.

WHAT IT TAKES

TIME: 1 day
SKILL LEVEL: Intermediate

WINE GLASS BRACKET

1 Build a shelf to fit snugly between adjacent cabinets. Use a jigsaw to create curved brackets, nail wine glass brackets to the bottom of the shelf, then install the entire unit as one piece.

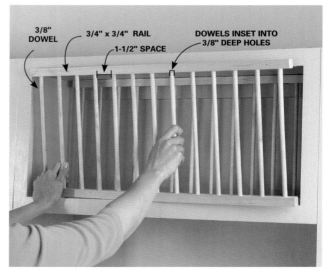

3/8" DOWEL **3/4" x 3/4" RAIL** **DOWELS INSET INTO 3/8" DEEP HOLES** **1-1/2" SPACE**

2 Cut, assemble and install the two plate rack "ladders." Use short screws to secure the ladders in the cabinet opening. Set the rear ladder 4 in. away from the back of the cabinet and the front ladder snug against the back of the face frame.

Above-door display shelf 37
Stackable shelving 38
Quick projects for beginners 45
Floating shelves 46
Hanging tips 49
Sturdy multipurpose storage shelves 50

3 SHELVES

Above-door display shelf

Your house has a couple dozen windows and doors. Which means you have a couple dozen places for installing display shelves.

As a bonus, if you increase the height and depth of the "box" that forms the core of each shelf, these shelves can double as valances for window curtains or blinds.

Your materials will vary based on the size of your window or door. There are a few key measurements to keep in mind as you customize this design to fit:

■ Make the inside of the box 1/8 in. longer than the door or window trim. That way, the box will easily fit over the trim.

■ The height of the box should be about the same as the width of the window or door trim (or you risk having the door hit the shelf when it opens). If this is doubling as a valance, the box can hang below the trim.

■ The top shelf should overhang the three edges (the front and the two sides) of the box equally so the crown molding fits symmetrically.

Crown molding comes in a variety of styles and widths (from 2-1/4 in. to 6 in. and larger.) Mock up a small section of shelf to determine the best size and proportion of molding for your project.

Mount the completed shelf to the wall above the window or door. In most cases you'll be able to secure the shelf to the trim and framing along the sides and top of the opening. If not, use L-brackets mounted to the top of the shelf. Note: Use extra care if you mount this over an entry door (or one that your teenager slams a lot). Be sure all the displayed items are arranged securely behind the "lip" created by the cove molding.

1 **Build the core of the shelf.** Build the three-sided 1x3 box so it fits over your door trim. The 1x6 shelf should overhang the ends the same amount as it does the front.

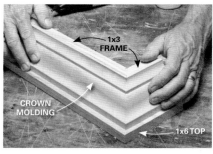

2 **Install the crown molding.** Cut and install the crown molding. Install the 3/4-in. cove molding along the edge of the top shelf, letting it protrude 1/4 in. upward to create a lip.

WHAT IT TAKES

TIME: 3 hours
SKILL LEVEL: Intermediate

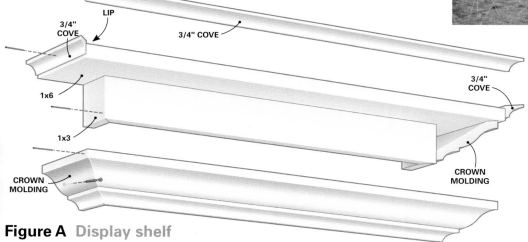

Figure A Display shelf

Stackable shelving

A simple board-and-channel design allows you to easily adapt this shelving to any wall space

WHAT IT TAKES

TIME: 2 weekends
SKILL LEVEL:
Intermediate

If you're looking for a way to maximize the storage on a wall, look no further. These shelves are easy to build, stylish enough to display your collection of favorite things, yet strong enough to hold plenty of books. In addition, you can easily customize the versatile system to fit around windows, doors, desks and other features and make every inch of wall space count.

Here, we'll show you how to make these handsome shelves with plywood and iron-on edge veneer. Then we'll show you how to mount them in simple grooved 1x2 uprights that you fasten to the walls.

Cutting the groove in the uprights (Figure B) and making square, splinter-free crosscuts on the plywood are the only tricky parts of the project, and we'll show you foolproof methods for both. Even though the shelves are simple, you'll be cutting out a lot of parts, so plan to spend a weekend on this project. Allow a few more days for staining and finishing.

You'll need a circular saw with a sharp 40-tooth carbide blade for cutting the plywood. To cut the groove in the 1x2, you'll need a table saw and standard blade. You'll also need a drill and countersink bit, a level and a clothes iron to melt the glue on the iron-on edging. The edge-trimming tool we show isn't mandatory (a sharp utility knife and patience give good results), but it simplifies the job.

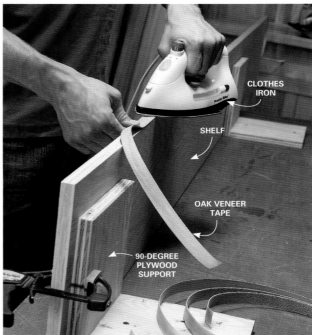

CLOTHES IRON

SHELF

OAK VENEER TAPE

90-DEGREE PLYWOOD SUPPORT

1 Rip the plywood to width and iron on the veneer tape. Align one edge with the plywood edge, set the iron to "cotton" and move it slowly along the veneer to melt the glue.

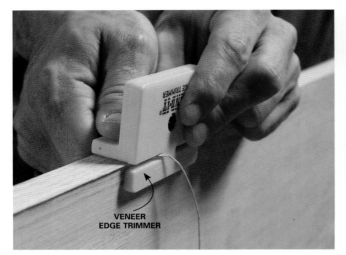

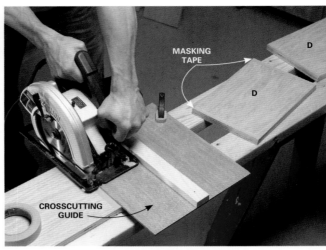

2 Trim the ends flush with a utility knife. Then trim the long edges flush with a special trimming tool. Finish by lightly sanding the edges flush with 220-grit paper.

3 Crosscut the 8-in.-wide strips of plywood. Use a crosscutting jig with a circular saw to get perfectly square cuts. Masking tape minimizes splintering.

You'll need 1-1/2 sheets of 3/4-in. plywood. to build the 8-ft.-long section shown. We purchased 3/4-in. veneer-core oak plywood with two good faces. Less-expensive plywood may just have one good side, but since only the uprights require two good sides, you may be able to work around any defects on the less desirable side. For a contemporary look, we stained these oak shelves black and applied two coats of sealer, but you can choose any paint or stain color to match your decor.

Cut the plywood and iron on the edge veneer

Start by cutting the 4 x 8-ft. sheet of plywood into four 10-in.-wide strips (Figure C). Cut the 4 x 4-ft. sheet into five 8-in.-wide strips. We used a table saw, but clamping an 8-ft. straightedge to the plywood as an edge guide for your circular saw will also work. Sand any saw marks from the edge of the plywood strips, being careful not to round over the corners. Then vacuum the edges to remove the sawdust.

The next step is to cover one long edge of each plywood strip with veneer tape (Photo 1). You'll find iron-on veneer tape at woodworking stores and home centers. Start by cutting strips of veneer tape a few inches longer than the plywood. Then align one edge of the tape with the face of the plywood and press the tape into place with a hot iron. Move the iron slowly enough to melt the glue, but fast enough to avoid scorching the veneer. An 8-ft. strip should take about 10 seconds. While the glue is still hot, rub a small chunk of wood along the tape to press and seal it to the plywood. Inspect the seam between the tape and the plywood for gaps, and reheat and press any loose areas. Use a sharp utility knife to trim the ends of the tape flush. Then use a special trimmer (Photo 2), a utility knife or a block plane to trim the long edges flush. Finish by sanding the edges of the tape flush to the plywood. Wrap 220-grit sandpaper around a small block of wood and angle it slightly when sanding to avoid scuffing through the thin veneer on the plywood face. Cover the ends of the shelves with veneer tape later, after you cut the short shelves (E) to length.

Figure A
Crosscutting jig

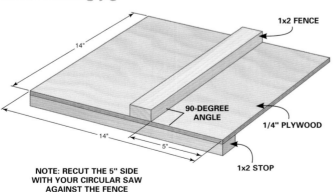

14"

1x2 FENCE

14"

5"

90-DEGREE ANGLE

1/4" PLYWOOD

1x2 STOP

NOTE: RECUT THE 5" SIDE WITH YOUR CIRCULAR SAW AGAINST THE FENCE

Materials List

ITEM	QTY.
3/4" x 4' x 8' A1 grade plywood	1
3/4" x 4' x 4' A1 grade plywood	1
1x2 x 6' oak	3
1x2 x 4' oak	1
3/4" or 7/8" iron-on veneer tape	60 ft.
1-5/8" flathead screws	32
2-1/2" flathead screws	20
1-1/4" trim head screws	4
3/4" x 3" mending plates	12
3/4" x 1-1/2" angle braces	4
3/4" x No. 6 flathead screws	52

Figure B
Shelf details

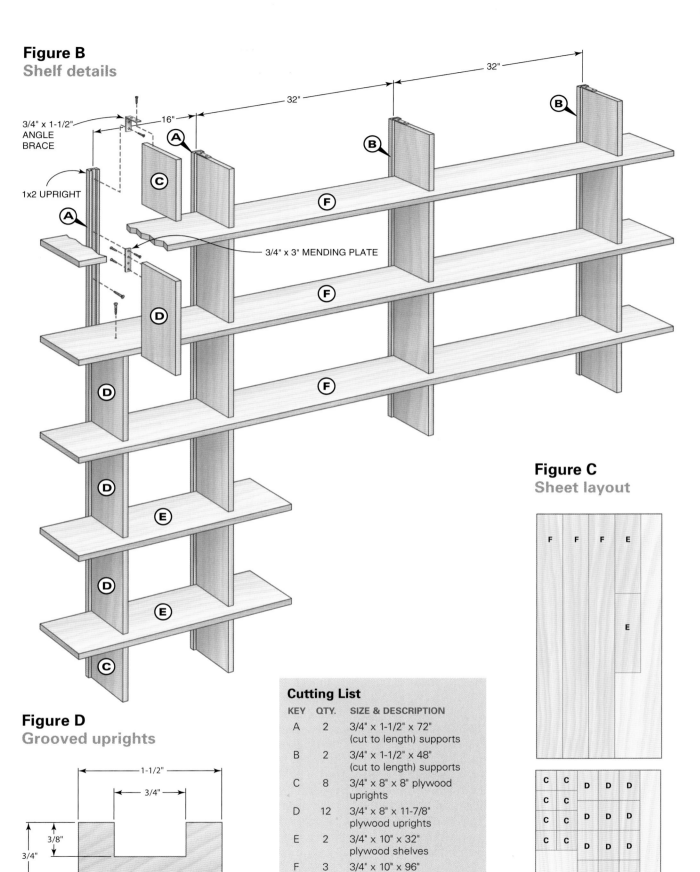

3/4" x 1-1/2"
ANGLE
BRACE

16"

32"

32"

Ⓑ

Ⓑ

Ⓐ

Ⓒ

Ⓑ

Ⓕ

1x2 UPRIGHT

Ⓐ

3/4" x 3" MENDING PLATE

Ⓕ

Ⓓ

Ⓕ

Ⓓ

Ⓓ

Ⓔ

Ⓓ

Ⓔ

Ⓒ

Figure C
Sheet layout

F   F   F   E

E

C   C   D   D   D
C   C
C   C   D   D   D
C   C
        D   D   D
        D   D   D

Cutting List

KEY	QTY.	SIZE & DESCRIPTION
A	2	3/4" x 1-1/2" x 72" (cut to length) supports
B	2	3/4" x 1-1/2" x 48" (cut to length) supports
C	8	3/4" x 8" x 8" plywood uprights
D	12	3/4" x 8" x 11-7/8" plywood uprights
E	2	3/4" x 10" x 32" plywood shelves
F	3	3/4" x 10" x 96" plywood shelves

Figure D
Grooved uprights

1-1/2"

3/4"

3/8"

3/4"

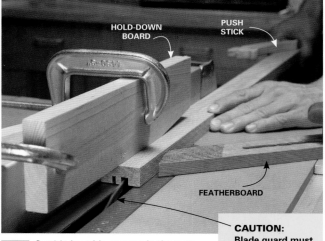

HOLD-DOWN BOARD

PUSH STICK

FEATHERBOARD

4 Cut 3/4-in.-wide grooves in the 1x2s by making a series of passes on the table saw. Practice on a scrap to set the exact width and depth of the cut.

CAUTION: Blade guard must be removed for this operation.

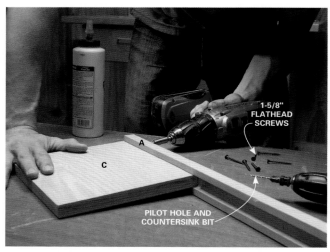

1-5/8" FLATHEAD SCREWS

A

C

PILOT HOLE AND COUNTERSINK BIT

5 Predrill and glue and screw one 8-in.-square upright piece to each 1x2, making sure to keep the bottom of the upright aligned with the bottom of the 1x2.

A

STUD LOCATION

4' LEVEL

C

B

2-1/2" FLATHEAD SCREWS

6 Cut the 1x2s to length. Then locate the studs, plumb the first 1x2 support and screw it to a stud. Predrill and space your screws every 16 in.

Build a jig for accurate crosscutting

It may take a half hour to build, but an accurate crosscutting jig is essential for perfectly square, splinter-free cuts (Figure A). Start by cutting a 14-in. square of 1/4-in. plywood on your table saw. Align a 1x2 stop with the edge of the plywood and attach it with 3/4-in. screws. Keep the screws 3 in. from the ends to avoid sawing through them. Countersink the screw heads.

On the opposite side, attach another 1x2 perpendicular to the first one and about 5 in. from the edge of the plywood. Use a Speed square or combination square to align this 1x2 90 degrees to the first one. Clamp the jig to a scrap of plywood. With the saw's base tight to the fence, saw through the jig and plywood (check for screws in the path of the blade before

cutting). Check the test cut on the plywood with a framing square. If it's not perfectly square, adjust the position of the stop slightly. You'll have to make new screw holes for each adjustment. You can also use the jig as a measuring guide for the longer uprights by cutting the jig to 11-7/8 in. wide on the table saw. For repetitive cuts without measuring, line up one end of the jig with the end of the plywood and cut along the opposite end.

To avoid splintering the plywood, press high-adhesive masking tape over the cutting path (Photo 3) and cut slowly with a sharp, thin-kerf 40-tooth carbide blade.

A

14-1/2"

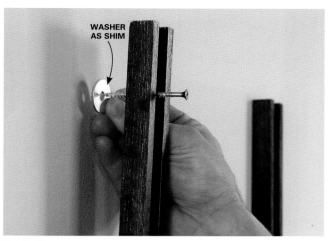

WASHER AS SHIM

8 Check the 1x2 supports for dips and bows with a straightedge. Remove screws and shim behind the 1x2s with 1-in.-diameter washers to straighten them if necessary.

A

1-5/8" FLATHEAD SCREW

SPEED SQUARE

E

C

7 Level the top of the next 1x2 support to the first 1x2 and fasten it near the top. Then use the level to plumb the sides and screw it to the stud every 16 in.

9 Center the first shelf with an equal overhang at each end. Square the upright (C) to the front of the shelf and predrill and drive a 1-5/8-in. screw through the shelf into the upright.

Use your table saw to cut a groove for the uprights

There are many ways to cut the grooves in the 1x2s. We'll show you how to do it with your table saw and a standard blade. Of course, if you own a set of dado blades for your table saw, cutting the groove will take less time. You could also use a router mounted in a router table to cut the groove, but we won't show this technique here.

The first step is to use a scrap of wood to set the exact width of the groove. Cut a 16-in. length from one of the 6-ft. 1x2s as a practice piece. Adjust the height of the blade to 3/8 in. above the saw's table and set the fence 11/16 in. from the blade. Set up a featherboard and clamp a hold-down board to the fence (Photo 4). Run the 1x2 through the saw. Use a push stick when the board gets within 6 in. of the blade. Rotate it end-for-end and run it through again. You should have a groove that's about

1/8 in. wide. Move the fence about 1/8 in. closer to the blade and make two more cuts on the 1x2. Repeat this process to make the groove progressively wider. When the groove gets close to 3/4 in. wide, make finer adjustments with the fence. Test after each pair of passes until the 1x2 fits snugly over the edge of the plywood. Make sure the mending plates also fit in the groove (Photo 10). With the width of the cut perfectly set, cut the grooves on the 1x2 uprights in reverse, starting from the outer edges and moving in (Photo 4). Run each 1x2 through the saw twice, once in each direction. Then move the fence about 1/8 in. farther from the blade and repeat the process until the groove is complete. Remove slivers of wood from the grooves with a sharp chisel.

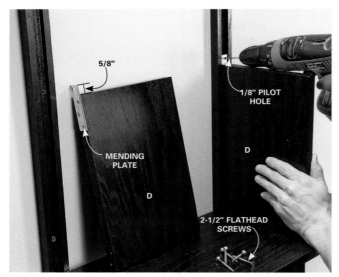

10 Screw a mending plate to the back of each upright. Set the uprights into the groove, predrill and drive a screw through the mending plate and 1x2 into the stud.

11 Rest a long shelf across two uprights. Align the bottom short 1x2 supports with the shelf, plumb them and screw the supports to studs.

Prepare the 1x2s and mount them on the wall

First attach the 8-in.-tall plywood uprights to the low end of the 1x2s (Photo 5). Determine the length of each 1x2 by literally stacking uprights and scraps of plywood in the groove to simulate the shelving system you want. Then cut the 1x2s to length.

Photos 6 – 8 show the process for mounting the 1x2s to the wall. Start by locating the studs with a stud finder. Mark the studs with a strip of masking tape centered about 80 in. from the floor. Then screw the long 1x2s to the studs (Photos 6 and 7). If the wall has a stud that's bowed, the 1x2 will be crooked and the shelves won't fit well. To avoid this problem, hold a straightedge against the face of the 1x2 after you've screwed it to the wall. If it's crooked, back out the screw near the low spot and add washers to shim the 1x2 straight (Photo 8).

With the long 1x2s in place, add shelves and uprights until you get to the level of the first long shelf. Photo 11 shows how to make sure the long shelf will be straight when you mount the short 1x2s. The rest is simple. Stack the parts and screw them together until you reach the top. Photo 12 shows how to anchor the top shelf with an angle brace. If you also want to anchor the bottom of the final upright, drive a trim screw at an angle through the shelf from underneath.

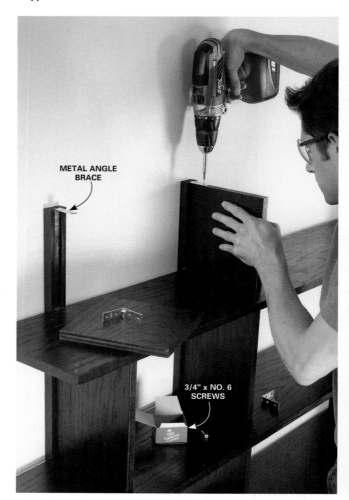

12 Stack the remaining shelves and uprights following the procedure in Photos 9 and 10. Secure the top upright to the 1x2 with a metal angle brace.

Quick projects for beginners

Portable bookshelf

Here's a cool knock-down shelf for a dorm room or den. You just slide the shelves between the dowels, and they pinch the shelves to stiffen the bookshelf. It works great if you're careful about two things:

- Make the space between the dowel holes exactly 1/16 in. wider than the thickness of the shelf board.
- Be sure the shelf thickness is the same from end to end and side to side.

After test-fitting a dowel in a trial hole (you want a tight fit), drill holes in a jig board so the space between the holes is your shelf thickness plus 1/16 in. Clamp the jig board on the ends of the risers and drill the holes. Cut the dowels 1-3/4 in. longer than the shelf width, then dry assemble (no glue). Mark the angled ends of the risers parallel to the shelves and cut off the tips to make the risers sit flat. Disassemble and glue the dowels in the riser holes. When the glue dries, slide the shelves in and load them up.

Cutting List

Perfectly flat 1x12 lumber or plywood
2 shelves: 11-1/4" wide x 3' long
4 risers: 2-1/4" wide x 24" long
8 dowels: 3/4" dia. x 13" long

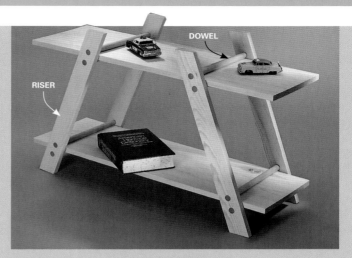

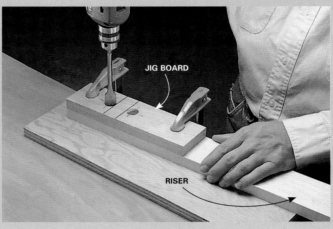

Above-the-door bookshelf

The space above a doorway is an over-looked storage bonanza! It's the perfect spot for a cookbook cubby in the kitchen. Consider adding a cubby over the doorways in your home office, laundry room and bedrooms too. You'll be surprised how many books, knickknacks and other items you can find room for in these valuable unused spaces.

Floating shelves

WHAT IT TAKES

TIME: 1 day
SKILL LEVEL:
Beginner

These "floating" shelves are perfect for displaying your collectibles, photos, travel mementos or just about anything. Without the brackets and clunky hardware you'd find with store-bought shelves or kits, they seem to be suspended in midair.

These shelves are strong, too. While they're not designed to hold your collection of kettlebells, they're certainly capable of it. No one would believe that they're made from plain old lightweight and inexpensive hollow-core doors.

Here, you'll learn how to install these shelves (and shorter ones) securely with basic tools. Even if you think you have no DIY skills you can tackle this project.

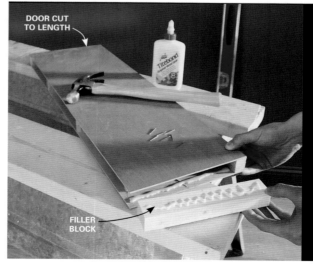

DOOR CUT
TO LENGTH

FILLER
BLOCK

Making it fit your space

Build shorter shelves by cutting the shelf to length. Glue a filler block flush with the end and nail each side with small brad nails.

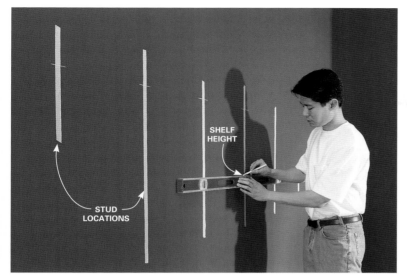

1 Trace the horizontal location for each shelf using a 4-ft. level as your guide. Use a stud finder to mark the locations of the studs and lightly press masking tape over each one. If you don't have a string line, use a long straightedge and mark the wall with a pencil. Check your marks with the 4-ft. level.

Surprise—a low-cost project that requires only basic tools

Each shelf is made from half of an 18-in. hollow-core door. You can buy new hollow-core interior doors at a home center or lumberyard (just be sure the door doesn't have predrilled holes for locksets). You may find only 24-in.-wide doors, but the door can be any width; just try to minimize the waste. And you might be able to get doors free from yard sales or other sources.

As far as tools go, you can get by with just a circular saw and edge guide (Photo 2) to cut the door. However, it's recommended that you use a table saw to cut the cleat because a clean, straight cut is important for a good-looking shelf. (If you don't own a table saw, use a friend's or have the cleat cut at a full-service lumberyard.) You'll also need a stud finder, a chisel, a hammer, a wrench, 1-in. brads, 3-1/2-in. lag screws, carpenter's glue and a level.

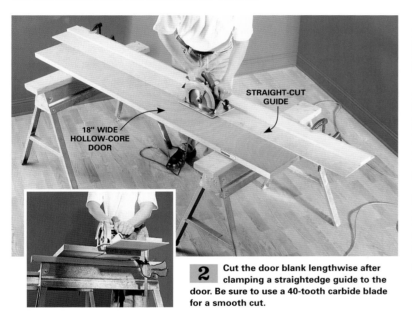

2 Cut the door blank lengthwise after clamping a straightedge guide to the door. Be sure to use a 40-tooth carbide blade for a smooth cut.

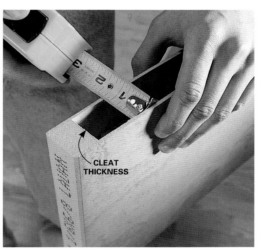

3 Measure the space between the outer veneers of the door and cut cleats from a 2x4 to this thickness. Our measurement was 1-3/32 inch. Use straight, dry lumber for cleats.

4 Predrill 1/4-in.-dia. holes at the stud locations after you cut the cleats to length (the measurement between the end blocks of the door half). Hold the cleat to your line on the wall and drill into the stud with a 1/8-in. bit. Using a wrench, install one lag screw into each stud until it's tight. Use 1/4-in. x 3-1/2-in. lag screws. Each cleat must be straight as an arrow.

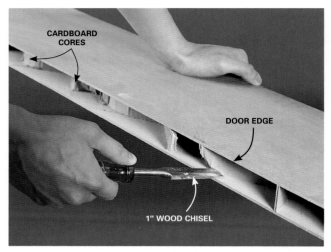

5 Cut away the corrugated cardboard cores at least 1-1/2 in. from the cut edge. Scrape away the glue carefully without gouging the wood surface.

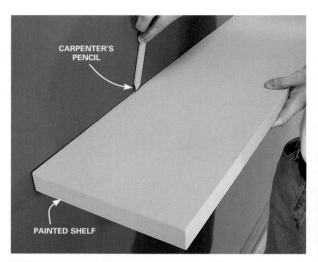

6 Dry-fit the shelf to make sure the blank fits over the cleat. Check the back side of the shelf and scribe it to the wall if necessary. Use a block plane or sander to remove material from the back edge for a tight fit.

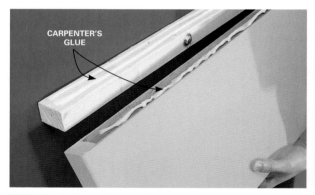

7 Apply glue to the top of the cleat and the inside bottom edge of the door blank. Slide the shelf over the wood cleat.

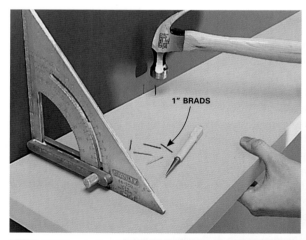

8 Nail the shelf to the cleat using a square as your guide. Start at the middle and work your way to each end. Use 1-in. brad nails spaced 8 in. apart.

If you want a different look . . .

We chose to paint our shelves, but if you want the beauty of real wood, you can buy the door in wood veneers like oak or maple (ours was lauan). If you decide on a natural wood finish, you'll need to cover the exposed edges with a matching wood trim. If you go this route, first shave off 1/8 in. from the front and side edges with a table saw to eliminate the slight bevel on each edge, then apply the matching trim. You can also cover the entire shelf with plastic laminate if you want a tough, hard-surfaced shelf.

You may want to change the depth of your shelves as well. Don't exceed 9 in. or you'll start to weaken the cantilever strength of the shelf. Feel free to make narrower or shorter shelves.

Create a rock-hard finish with a low-gloss enamel paint

The whole job will go a lot smoother if you paint the shelves before you install them. If you intend to paint the room, also do that before you install the shelves because it's a drag to cut around each shelf with a paint brush. Just be sure to sand your wood door with 150-grit sandpaper before you paint. If the surface is still rough and porous after sanding, fill the pores by applying a paste wood filler with a 3-in. drywall knife. Let it dry and sand the surface again.

These shelves are permanent— they're tough to remove!

The glue not only makes the shelves strong but also impossible to remove without ruining them. You'll have to cut them in place 2 in. away from the wall with a circular saw to expose the lag screws and then remove the cleats with a wrench. That's unfortunate, but you can always make another set cheaply and easily.

Handy hint

Use needle-nose pliers or a Popsicle stick with a split end to hold the 1-in. brads while nailing.

Hanging tips

Figure-eights simplify the job

These nifty little fasteners are actually designed to attach table and desktops to aprons (the vertical skirt around the perimeter), but they're also a handy solution for hanging shelves. You can buy a pack of eight at woodworking stores or online.

The only caveat is that the top of the figure-eight shows above the surface of the shelf, so it may be visible if you hang the shelf low. Try to position the figure-eights where there are studs, if possible. You can use good-quality hollow-wall anchors if the studs don't line up with the figure-eights.

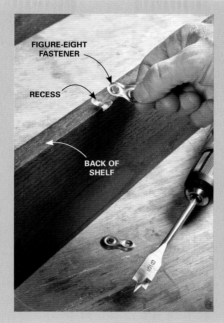

FIGURE-EIGHT FASTENER

RECESS

BACK OF SHELF

Drill a recess for the figure-eight. Use a spade bit or Forstner bit to drill a slight recess in the back of the shelf to accommodate the thickness of the figure-eight. Then chisel out the remaining wood until the figure-eight sits flush to the shelf. Attach the figure-eight with a screw.

Attach to the wall. Mount the shelf by driving screws through the figure-eights either into hollow-wall anchors or into studs.

French cleats for fast, solid hanging

Pairs of beveled strips that interlock to support shelves, cabinets or pictures are called French cleats. They're great for hanging any shelf or cabinet and have a few advantages in certain situations.

First, the cleats work well for heavy cabinets because you can easily mount the wall cleat and then simply lift the cabinet and "hook" it on. There's no need to support a heavy cabinet temporarily while you drive screws to anchor it.

Another common use for French cleats is to create a flexible system of shelves or cabinets. You can screw one or more lengths of wall cleats across the entire wall, and then easily relocate shelves, or add more shelves at a later date. Make cleats by ripping strips of 3/4-in. plywood with a 45-degree bevel on one edge. Screw one strip to the wall and the other to the back of the shelf or cabinet.

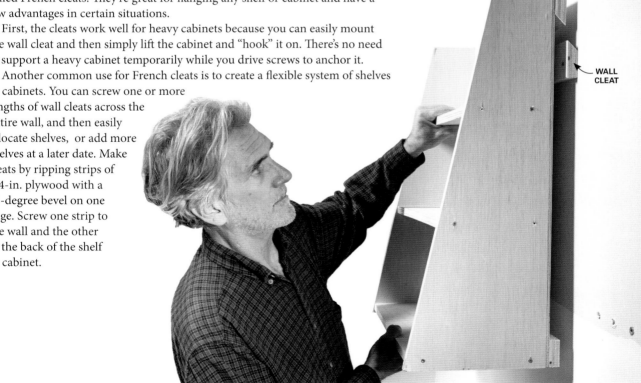

SHELF CLEAT

WALL CLEAT

Sturdy multipurpose storage shelves

Build sturdy, simple shelves, custom sized to hold boxes or other storage containers.

You can modify the sturdy storage shelves above and create a great-looking storage center. Simply add one shelf and change the 22-1/2-in. measurement to 14 in. and the 4-in. measurement to 6 in. Apply the finish of your choice.

Store-bought shelving units are either hard to assemble, flimsy or awfully expensive. Here's a better solution. These shelves are strong, easy to build and inexpensive. The sturdy shelf unit is sized to hold standard records and storage boxes. If you want deeper storage, build the shelves 24 in. deep and buy 24-in.-deep boxes. If you prefer to use plastic storage bins, measure the size of the containers and modify the shelf and upright spacing to fit.

Refer to the dimensions in Figure A to mark the location of the horizontal 2x2 on the back of four 2x4s. Also mark the position of the 2x4 uprights on the 2x2s. Then simply line up the marks and screw the 2x2s to the 2x4s with pairs of 2-1/2-in. wood screws. Be sure to keep the 2x2s and 2x4s at right angles. Rip a 4 x 8-ft. sheet of 1/2-in. MDF, plywood or OSB into 16-in.-wide strips and screw it to the 2x2s to connect the two frames and form the shelving unit.

Figure A Shelf unit

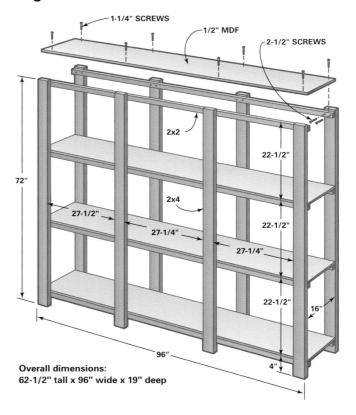

1-1/4" SCREWS
1/2" MDF
2-1/2" SCREWS
2x2
72"
22-1/2"
27-1/2"
2x4
27-1/4"
22-1/2"
27-1/4"
22-1/2"
16"
96"
4"

Overall dimensions:
62-1/2" tall x 96" wide x 19" deep

SPECIAL SECTION

MAKE YOUR PROJECTS LOOK GREAT WITH THESE PRO TIPS

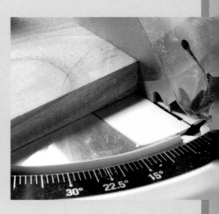

Cut narrow strips with a sliding jig 53
Prevent clamp stains with wax paper 53
Hold it square 53
Sanding tips 54
Ease sharp edges with a round-over bit 56
Bump and shave 56
Hide the nail heads 57
Circular saw jigs for table saw-quality cuts 58
Make sure your blade is sharp 59
Seal oil-based stain 59
Slow down your glue 59

Cut narrow strips with a sliding jig

To make a series of identical narrow strips for shelf edging, you don't need to remove the blade guard or move the fence for every cut. Just attach a short strip of wood slightly thinner than the width of the rip cut to the end of a 1x6 or straight piece of 3/4-in. plywood. Then hold the board against it and push the jig through. The jig keeps your hands well away from the blade, and you can rip as many pieces as you need without ever moving the fence.

To make the jig, attach a 6-in.-long strip of wood, 1/16 in. narrower than the width of the desired rip, to the end of a 1x6 as shown. Add a handle near the end of the jig to give yourself better control as you run the jig through the saw.

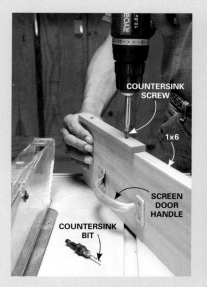

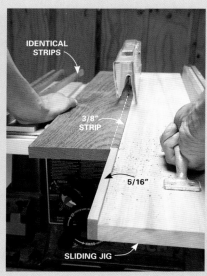

Prevent clamp stains with wax paper

Moisture in glue triggers a reaction between iron and chemicals in wood called "tannins." The result is black stains on the wood, especially with tannin-rich woods like oak or walnut. A strip of wax paper acts as a barrier between the clamp and the wood. You can also use wax paper to keep glue off your cauls (pieces of wood used to spread clamping pressure evenly).

Hold it square

When you're clamping bookshelves or cabinets together, getting a square assembly is half the battle. These simple blocks, made from three layers of 1/2-in. plywood, pull the cabinet into square and keep it there. After the squaring blocks are in place, you can use pipe clamps to squeeze the joints tightly together.

Sanding tips

Sand faster with suction

Connecting to a vacuum doesn't just cut down on dust. It actually allows your random orbit sander to work faster. Even with the sander's built-in dust collection system, the sander rides on a thin cushion of dust that prevents full contact between the grit and the wood. So by increasing dust removal, a vacuum improves sander efficiency. On some sanders, hooking up to a vacuum doubles the sanding speed.

Know when to stop

How smooth is smooth enough? We put that question to professional woodworkers—and couldn't get a straight answer. (Woodworkers are notoriously noncommittal.) "It depends ..." was the typical response. Here's what that means:

"Open-grain" woods like oak and walnut have coarse grain lines and a rough texture, so sanding to very fine grits is a waste of time. "Closed-grain" woods like maple and cherry have a smoother, more uniform texture, so they need to be sanded with higher grits before the sanding scratches will disappear.

The finish matters, too. For thick coatings like polyurethane, varnish or lacquer, most of the people we talked to stop at 150 grit on open-grain woods, 180 on closed. For oil finishes, which don't create much buildup, higher is better; 220 on open grain, 240 on closed.

Pre-sand your stock

Before cutting up boards for your next project, sand them all with 80 or 100 grit. You might waste a little time sanding areas that will end up as scraps, but you'll come out ahead in the long run. The initial sanding—removing scratches, dents and milling marks—is the heaviest sanding. And if you sand boards before cutting or assembly, you can use the tool that does deep sanding fastest: a belt sander. Sanding whole boards also eliminates the repetition of stopping, starting and setup for individual parts.

Stop the swirls

For faster hand sanding, you just press harder and move faster. But with a random orbit sander, that strategy will actually slow you down. Too much pressure or speed creates tiny swirling scratches that you'll have to sand out sooner or later (often later, after stain makes them visible). A light touch and patience are the key to avoiding those swirls. Just rest your hand on the sander; don't press. The weight of your arm provides enough pressure. Move at a snail's pace—no more than 1 in. per second. Going that slow feels unnatural and takes some self-discipline. So try this: Stretch out a tape measure along your project and watch the second hand on a clock while you sand. After about 30 seconds (or 30 in.), you'll get used to the right speed.

Skip a grit

You don't have to use every single grit as you sand your way from coarse to fine. Instead, use every other grit; 80-120-180 or 100-150-220, for example.

Sand across the grain

The first commandment of sanding: Sand with the grain. But when you have a lot of wood to grind off, break that rule and run your belt sander diagonally across the grain (at about 45 degrees). Instead of scratching away at the wood fibers, the belt will rip them out. It's incredibly fast—and dangerous. Be careful not to gouge too deep, and expect to follow up with some heavy sanding to smooth the "plow marks" left behind.

Premium paper works faster

Better sandpaper has sharper particles of grit, which bite into wood faster. And not just a little faster—a lot faster. Premium paper removes wood at two or three times the rate of standard paper. It costs a bit more, but the grit stays sharp much longer, so you actually save money, whether you're using sheets, discs or belts.

Prevent glue spots

Glue spots are cruel. When you think all the tedious sanding is done and you apply stain or even varnish, they'll appear like bleached smudges. Getting rid of them means more sanding. On a flat surface, glue drips aren't a big deal. You'll remove them automatically as you run through the normal sanding process. But in hard-to-sand spots like inside corners, prevention is the best strategy, and a little masking tape will save you a lot of hassle.

Stack 'em and sand 'em

"Gang sanding" with a random orbit or belt sander lets you smooth a bunch of edges in one pass. As a bonus, the wider surface prevents the sander from grinding too deep in one spot or tilting and rounding over the edges. This trick also makes sanding a self-correcting process; all the parts will end up exactly the same.

Ease sharp edges with a round-over bit

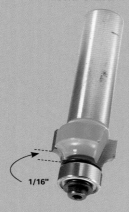

1/16"
ROUND-OVER BIT

1/16"

Whether you're building shelving or furniture, avoid leaving sharp edges on wood. They're more likely to chip, splinter or dent with everyday use. Sharp edges also create weak spots in paint and other finishes, leading to cracking and peeling, especially outdoors. Fussy carpenters often ease sharp edges with sandpaper or a file. But a router with a 1/16- or 1/8-in. round-over bit does the job more consistently and neatly. These small-profile bits are difficult to set at the correct cutting depth, so always test the cut on scrap wood first.

Bump ...

... then shave

Bump and shave

When you need to trim just a smidgen off a board or molding, try this: Lower the blade of your miter saw and press the end of the workpiece against it. Then raise the blade, pull the trigger and cut. Depending on how hard you pushed against the blade, you'll shave off from 1/16 to 1/32 in. Once you get the feel of it, you'll be able to adjust the pressure and the width of the shave.

Hide the nail heads

Bad

Good

GRAIN LINE

1 Predrill and drive nails in the darker grain lines when possible. Holes there are much easier to hide.

2 Touch up bad matches with a colored felt-tip pen. Or drill out the old putty and refill.

If you want your trim work to have a rustic, distressed look, go ahead and make the nail holes stand out. But if you're seeking a smooth, furniture-like finish, you have to make those nail holes disappear. Hiding nail holes takes a little more time and patience, but you'll get the fine, flawless appearance you want.

Begin by staining and sealing the trim before you put it up. Then buy colored putties to closely match the stain colors on the wood (Photo 3). (The other option, filling the holes with stainable filler before staining, is tricky unless you have a lot of experience.) Prestaining also makes the darker grain lines of the wood stand out. Position your nails there for the least visibility.

Buy several putty colors and mix them to match the wood color. Wood tone is rarely uniform, even when the wood is stained, so you can't rely on only one color to fill every hole (Photo 3). Fine-tune your blends and set your test piece alongside the trim to check the visibility of the nail holes under real light conditions. Lighting can significantly affect whether the filler blends or stands out.

Keep in mind that you can correct old mistakes or fix a situation where the wood has darkened after a year or two (with cherry, for example). Simply buy wood-tone felt-tip pens and touch up the filler (Photo 2). Or lightly drill out the most unsightly old filler holes with a small drill bit and refill them. Colored putties and touch-up pens are available at most hardware stores, paint stores and home centers.

COLORED PUTTY

TEST PIECE

3 Blend putty colors to more closely match the finished wood colors. One color won't do it all.

Circular saw jigs for table saw-quality cuts

If you have a full-size table saw, you're all set for making plywood cuts. And if you have a portable table saw, you can use it for smaller ripping jobs like making shelving and drawer parts. But you can also do a fine job with only a circular saw fitted with a cabinet-grade, smooth-cutting blade and a couple of simple screw-together jigs made from cheap melamine closet shelving stock.

Ripping jig

Use an 8-ft. length of 16-in.-wide shelving to build the ripping jig. Draw a line 3 in. from the edge and cut along it with the circular saw. Screw this piece to the larger piece about 3 in. away from one edge, with the factory edge facing the widest section of shelving as shown. Then use that edge as a guide to cut off the melamine. Now it's just a matter of lining up that edge with marks on plywood stock and clamping it to make perfect cuts up to 8 ft. long on any piece of plywood.

FACTORY EDGE
3"
3"
6"

STOP
4"
FACTORY EDGE

FENCE
6"
FACTORY EDGE

Crosscutting jig

You can use the ripping jig for crosscutting, too, but this crosscutting jig has the advantage of a stop on the bottom. Push the stop against the plywood, align it with the cutting mark and clamp for quick, accurate crosscuts. Make it from a 4-ft. length of 24-in.-wide melamine shelving (or plywood if wide shelving isn't available). Cut a 4-in.-wide strip for the stop from one end and another 4-in.-wide strip from one edge

for the fence. Align the factory edge of the short piece with the factory edge at the other end of the shelving to make the stop. Then clamp and screw the two pieces together while checking alignment with a carpenter's square. Flip the jig over and measure from the long factory edge 6 in. to position and screw the long saw guide as shown. The key with both jigs is to use the straight factory edges for guiding the saw.

Make sure your blade is sharp

Choosing the right blade for your miter saw, and making sure it's sharp, are crucial for cutting tight-fitting joints. You can't make perfect cuts with a dull blade, one with too few teeth or one that's designed for ripping. Check your blade for sharpness by cutting a 45-degree miter on a 1x3 or larger piece of oak or other hardwood (photo at right). If the blade cuts smoothly with very little pressure and leaves a clean, almost shiny cut with no burn marks, it's sharp enough. When you check your blade or shop for a new one, here's what to look for.

If the cut end of the miter looks scorched, rough or chipped, have the blade sharpened or buy a new one.

TEAR-OUT

DULL BLADE CUT

SHARP BLADE CUT

SHARP BLADE

DULL BLADE

First, it should be labeled as a "trim" or "fine crosscutting" blade. A 10-in. blade should have at least 40 teeth, a 12-in. blade at least 60. If the blade is for a sliding miter saw, be sure the teeth have a hook angle of zero to negative five degrees. Teeth with a neutral or negative hook angle are less aggressive and safer for sliding miter saws. Expect to spend a little more money for a carbide-tipped blade that'll perform well and last.

Slow down your glue

It's hard enough to align and clamp joints without rushing to get it done before the glue begins to set (in five to 10 minutes, and even faster in warm, dry conditions). That's why there are slow-setting wood glues, which give you an extra 10 minutes or so.

If you can't find a slow version at your favorite home center, make your own. If you add one part water to 20 parts wood glue, you'll gain about five minutes of working time. The water will also weaken the bond very slightly. So if strength is critical, order slow-setting glue online.

Seal oil-based stain

Oil and water don't mix. Water-based poly can have adhesion problems when applied over an oil-based stain that's not thoroughly cured. Always apply a barrier coat of dewaxed shellac to seal oil-based stain. After the shellac dries, a light scuff-sand will leave an excellent surface for the poly to grip.

The instructions on the can will indicate that you can apply a water-based clear coat right over an oil-based stain if the stain has thoroughly cured. However, the curing time can be several days, especially with an open-grain wood such as oak where the stain can sit uncured deep in the pores. Play it safe and seal the stain with a dewaxed shellac.

Flip-flop step stool 61
Hacked! 63
    1. Modern console 64
    2. Craft center 66
    3. Built-in bench 68
Jigsaw stool 70
Fast furniture fixes 72
Knock-apart table 76
Photo sculptures 77
Quick table legs 77

4 FURNITURE & DECORATING

Flip-flop step stool

You'll find plenty of uses for a flip-flop stool. With the back swung up, it's the perfect chair for little kids to plunk down on. With the back swung down, it's the perfect step stool for reaching slightly-out-of-reach faucets, shelves and cabinets—for kids of all ages.

Begin by cutting the two sides to length and laying out the boards (Photo 1 and Figure A). Note that the sides will be mirror images. To mark the curved sides, hook your tape over the lower corners then swing 15-in.-radius curves

1 **Mark the two side pieces.** Use a tape measure to swing arcs for the edges as shown in Figure A, then mark the holes for the pivot screws and the back dowel stop.

2 Assemble the stool with 2-in. screws. First screw the back brace to the bottom shelf, then secure this L-shape assembly to the sides. Drill the holes for the pivot screw and the back dowel stop.

TEMPORARY 2x4 PROP BLOCKS

1x6 BACK

BACK STOP DOWEL

1x4 BACK BRACE

2" BOLTS WITH LOCKNUTS

WASHERS

3 Install the back. Screw the back to the pivot arms to create a U-shape. Drill the holes in the pivot arms, then secure the back using 2-in. bolts, washers and nuts. Don't permanently fasten the top until you've "test swiveled" the back to make sure you have enough clearance.

on each side. Use a pint can to create the rounded inner edges of the legs. The positions of the pivot and dowel holes are critical, so measure carefully. The pivot hole goes all the way through the board, but the dowel holes are only 1/2 in. deep. Drill the holes, then use a jigsaw to cut out the parts. Use a 1/4-in. round-over bit or sandpaper to soften all the edges.

Connect the 1x10 bottom shelf and 1x4 back brace to create an "L." Secure this assembly to the sides so the top edge of the 1x4 is flush with the upper back corner of the sides. Use 2x4 blocks to ensure the right spacing (Photo 2).

Cut the three parts for the back assembly (Figure A). To create the curved back, drive a pair of finish nails 3-1/2 in. from the edge of a 1x6, and flex a thin piece of wood upward between the nails to create an arc. Mark the arc with a pencil, then cut it out with a jigsaw. Secure the back to the two 1x4 sides to create a U-shape. Use 2-in. bolts (Photo 3) to secure the back assembly to the sides of the stool. (Tip: To install the washer between the back assembly and the stool, tape it over the hole in the side before installing the assembly.) Finally, position the top far back enough—about 1/2 in. from the front of the sides—so the back doesn't hit the front lip as it pivots.

Figure A
Flip-flop step stool

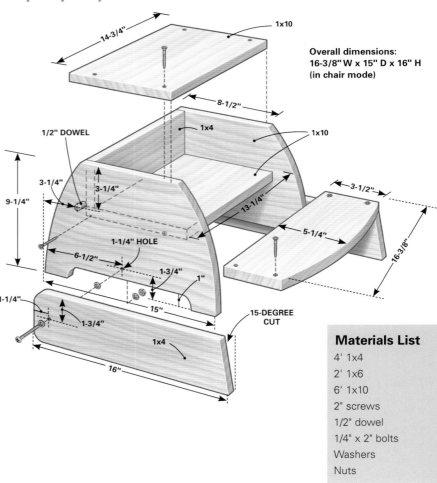

14-3/4"

1x10

Overall dimensions: 16-3/8" W x 15" D x 16" H (in chair mode)

8-1/2"

1/2" DOWEL

1x4

1x10

3-1/4"

3-1/4"

3-1/2"

9-1/4"

13-1/4"

5-1/4"

16-3/8"

1-1/4" HOLE

1-1/4"

6-1/2"

1-3/4"

1"

15"

1x4

15-DEGREE CUT

1-3/4"

1x4

16"

Materials List

4' 1x4
2' 1x6
6' 1x10
2" screws
1/2" dowel
1/4" x 2" bolts
Washers
Nuts

Hacked!

Customize store-bought "RTA" furniture to suit your needs

1. MODERN CONSOLE

Spend a little, get a lot. That's the idea behind ready-to-assemble (RTA) furniture. But RTA furniture isn't just inexpensive. It's also super adaptable. Because you assemble it yourself, RTA furniture invites tinkering. In fact, customizing RTA pieces is so common that it has its own name: "hacking."

We used furniture pieces from IKEA. You can also find RTA furniture at discount stores and home centers.

2. CRAFT CENTER

3. BUILT-IN BENCH

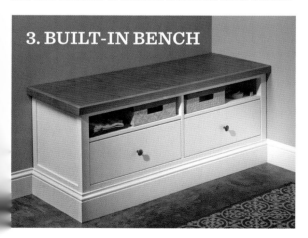

Hacked!

1. MODERN CONSOLE

Mimic a mid-century modern classic by turning a simple shelving unit on its side, wrapping it with plywood inside and out, and attaching legs.

WHAT IT TAKES

TIME: 1–2 days
SKILL LEVEL: Intermediate

Build it

Notice that the end panels of the original assembled Kallax shelving unit protrude beyond the sides. Remove both panels (Step 1) and trim off the protruding edges (Step 2). Then reattach both panels flush with the sides (Step 3). Cut hardwood plywood panels to wrap around the unit (Step 4). Make the top and bottom panels long enough to cover the side panels, and cut the side panels to fit tightly between the top and bottom pieces. Cut all the panels wide enough to create a 3/16-in. lip around the front of the shelving unit. Adhere iron-on edge banding to these pieces.

Fasten the panels with flat-head sheet metal screws after drilling countersink pilot holes through the unit. The unit's frames are hollow, so be careful not to punch through their thin faces when drilling the countersinks. Make sure the screw heads seat flush.

Cut plywood to cover the bottom and sides inside the unit (Step 5). Don't fasten these pieces with screws; instead, go for a friction fit. Apply iron-on edge banding to the exposed edges.

Remove all the plywood parts to apply finish. Finish the legs too. Reinstall the panels and inserts—tack the inserts with small nails or brads. Then attach the legs (Step 6).

Basic unit

Step 1
Remove end panels

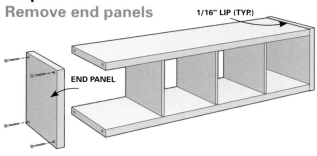

1/16" LIP (TYP.)

END PANEL

Step 2
Trim end panels

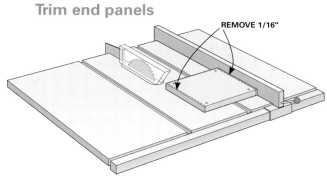

REMOVE 1/16"

Step 3
Attach end panels

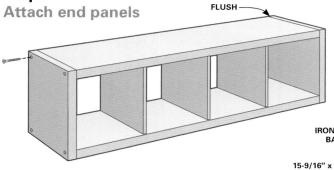

FLUSH

Step 4
Attach plywood panels

15-9/16" x 59-3/16" (TYP.)

IRON-ON EDGE BANDING

15-9/16" x 16-3/16" (TYP.)

2" NO. 12 SHEET METAL SCREW

COUNTERSINK PILOT HOLE

Step 5
Install plywood inserts

15-1/16" (TYP.)

Step 6
Attach legs

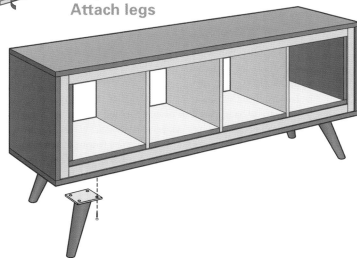

Materials List

ITEM	QTY.
IKEA Kallax Shelving Unit, Birch, No. 902.758.44	1
8" McCobb legs, soft maple (tablelegs.com)	4
Angle top plate for legs (tablelegs.com)	4
4' x 8' x 3/4" birch plywood	1
Birch iron-on edge banding	25'
No. 12 x 2" flat-head sheet metal screws	24
Wood stain and polyurethane	

Hacked!

2. CRAFT CENTER

Build a worktable with a huge surface, convenient storage and easy mobility by sandwiching three small storage units between a base with casters and a plywood top with hardwood edging.

WHAT IT TAKES

TIME: 1–2 days
SKILL LEVEL: Intermediate

Build it

Cut hardwood plywood for the top and base and install hardwood edging and iron-on edge banding as shown in Step 1. Position two Kallax shelving units back to back and fasten them to the base with flat-head sheet metal screws after drilling countersink pilot holes through the Kallax frames (Step 2). The frames are hollow panels, so be careful not to punch through their thin faces when drilling the countersinks. Make sure the screw heads seat flush.

Install the third Kallax unit across the front of the base, using the same method. Then tip the assembly over onto the top and fasten it as before (Step 3). Install locking swivel casters (Step 4). Then tip the assembly right-side up and round over all the top's sharp edges with a router and a round-over bit. Complete the job by installing Kallax drawer inserts and applying your favorite finish to the top (Step 5).

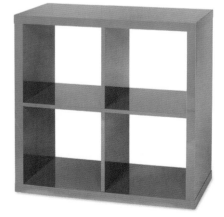

Basic unit

Step 1
Make the top and base

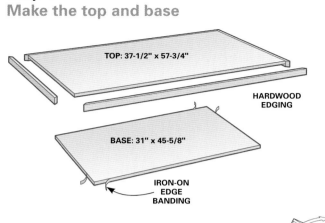

TOP: 37-1/2" x 57-3/4"

HARDWOOD EDGING

BASE: 31" x 45-5/8"

IRON-ON EDGE BANDING

Step 2
Fasten units to base

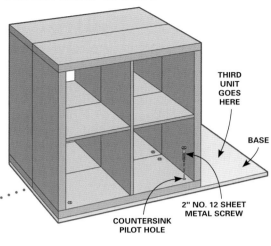

THIRD UNIT GOES HERE

BASE

2" NO. 12 SHEET METAL SCREW

COUNTERSINK PILOT HOLE

Step 3
Fasten top

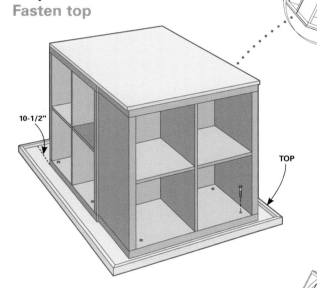

10-1/2"

TOP

Step 4
Attach casters

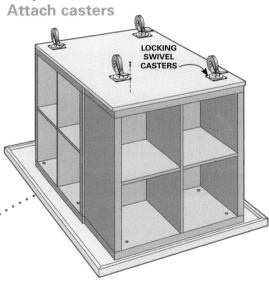

LOCKING SWIVEL CASTERS

Step 5
Round edges and install drawers

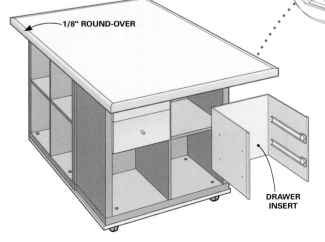

1/8" ROUND-OVER

DRAWER INSERT

Materials List

ITEM	QTY.
IKEA Kallax Shelving Unit No. 202.794.59	3
IKEA Kallax Insert with Two Drawers No. 702.866.50	2
4' x 8' x 3/4" birch plywood	2
Birch iron-on edge banding	25'
3/4" x 1-1/2" birch or maple solid wood	20'
3" locking swivel casters	4
No. 12 x 2" flat-head sheet metal screws	24
Polyurethane, wood glue	

Hacked!

3. BUILT-IN BENCH

Create a classic mudroom bench by fastening base molding and a new top to a cabinet designed to display a flat-screen TV.

WHAT IT TAKES

TIME: 1 day
SKILL LEVEL: Intermediate

Build it

Assemble the Hemnes TV unit through Step 27 of the manufacturer's instructions. Move it into position and shim the legs as necessary to level it. Then install a support block under the rails beneath the center divider (Step 1). This allows the unit to be used as a bench. Fasten the unit to the wall through its upper back rail (Step 2).

Build a new top by gluing hardwood edging to 3/4-in.-thick hardwood plywood and then rounding over all the sharp edges (Step 3). Sand the top, stain it and apply your favorite finish. Use corner brackets to fasten the top to the bench (Step 4). Then fasten base molding around the bench to build it in (Step 5). Install the drawers to complete the project.

Basic unit

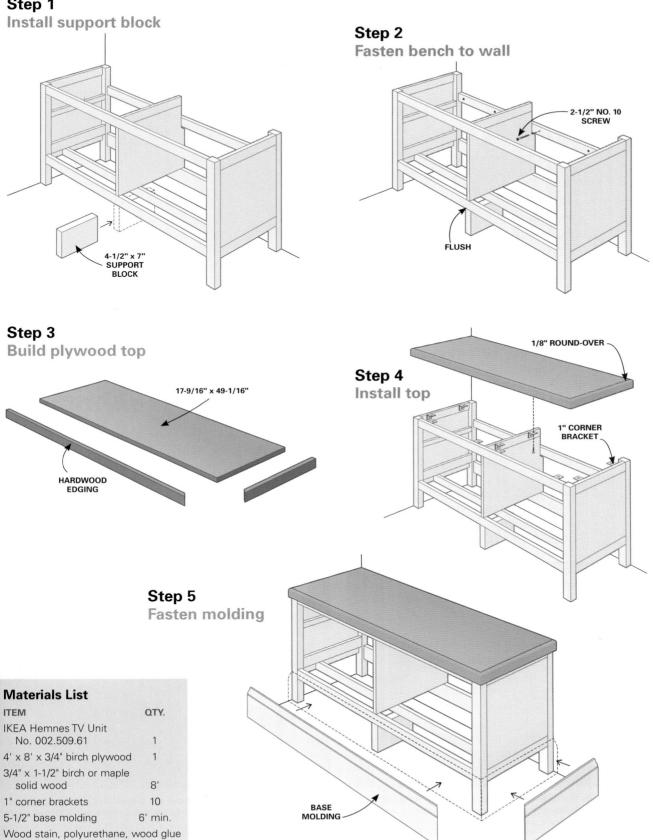

Step 1
Install support block

4-1/2" x 7"
SUPPORT
BLOCK

Step 2
Fasten bench to wall

2-1/2" NO. 10
SCREW

FLUSH

Step 3
Build plywood top

17-9/16" x 49-1/16"

HARDWOOD
EDGING

Step 4
Install top

1/8" ROUND-OVER

1" CORNER
BRACKET

Step 5
Fasten molding

BASE
MOLDING

Materials List

ITEM	QTY.
IKEA Hemnes TV Unit No. 002.509.61	1
4' x 8' x 3/4" birch plywood	1
3/4" x 1-1/2" birch or maple solid wood	8'
1" corner brackets	10
5-1/2" base molding	6' min.
Wood stain, polyurethane, wood glue	

Jigsaw stool

WHAT IT TAKES

TIME: 2 hours per stool
SKILL LEVEL: Beginner

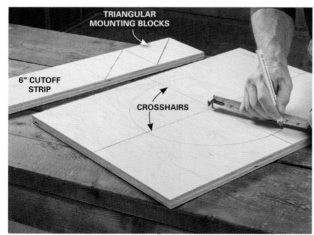

1 Lay out the legs and top. Rip the plywood into 18-in. and 6-in. strips. Draw "crosshairs" on the larger piece, drive a screw in the center, hook your tape over it, then with a pencil snugged against the 7-in. mark, draw the circle. Cut four support blocks from the narrow piece.

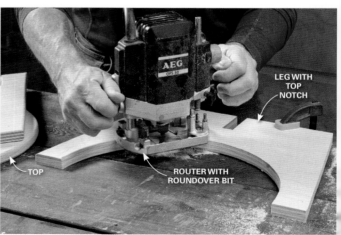

2 Cut out the parts and rout the edges. Use a jigsaw to cut out the parts (see Figure A), then use a router with a 1/4-in. round-over bit to ease the edges as shown.

You want simplicity and economy? These stools are designed so you can create eight of the short ones or four of the tall ones (or combinations thereof) from a single sheet of plywood. Here we'll show you how to build the short version; the taller stool is a couple inches wider, but employs the same concept to build.

Rip a 24 x 24-in. piece of plywood into 18-in. and 6-in. strips, then draw "crosshairs" (Photo 1) to locate the center of the larger board. Drive a drywall screw in the center and use that as a pivot point for swinging a 7-in.-radius circle. Draw lines 3/8 in. away from the crosshairs on each side (Figure A) to create 3/4-in.-thick layout marks for cutting the interlocking notches and installing the leg brace blocks later on.

Drill a 1/2-in. pilot hole in the lower notch as shown in Figure A, then insert a fine-tooth jigsaw blade and cut out the round top. Use your jigsaw to cut out the legs and the 3/4-in. x 2-1/2-in. notches for interlocking the legs. Use a router with a 1/4-in. round-over bit to soften both sides of the top and legs except for those edges along the tops of the two legs (Photo 2). If you don't have a router, ease the sharp edges with sandpaper. Cut the triangular blocks from the 6-in.-wide cutoff (Photo 1) and secure two of them to the underside of the top disc with glue and 1-1/4-in. all-purpose screws. Slip the legs into place as shown in Photo 3, then secure them to the blocks using 2-in. screws. Add the other two triangular blocks and apply a finish of your choice. We applied sanding sealer, a dark stain and then a coat of polyurethane.

Figure A
Jigsaw stool plywood layout (short version)

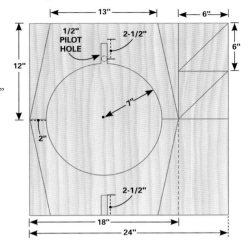

Overall dimensions

Short version:
18" W x 18" D x 12-3/4" H

Tall version:
20" W x 20" D x 21-3/4" H

Materials List

Short stool:
3/4" x 24" x 24" plywood

Tall stool:
3/4" x 24" x 48" plywood

1-1/4" screws, 2" screws, wood glue

Figure B
Jigsaw stool plywood layout (tall version)

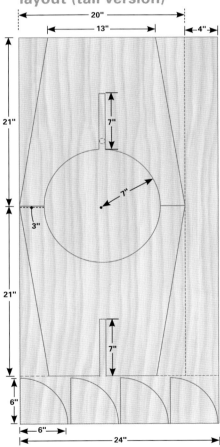

Figure C
Jigsaw stool assembly (tall version)

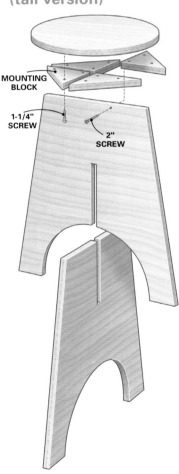

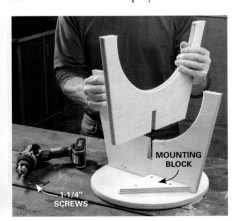

3 **Assemble the stool.** Screw two triangular blocks where the top layout marks intersect (kitty corner from each other), then secure the legs using 2-in. screws. Install the other two blocks, then apply a finish.

Fast furniture fixes

Easy repairs for everyday furniture

The creaking sound you hear each time you sit on that old kitchen chair is not a good sign. It has loose joints, and every time you sit on it, you're wearing down and further loosening them. Someday it's going to fall apart.

One of these tips will save that chair—and many other pieces of your favorite furniture, too! But keep in mind that these are fast, easy, practical fixes. They are not the best repairs for treasured heirlooms or valuable antiques.

WHAT IT TAKES

TIME: These repairs take from a few minutes to an hour
SKILL LEVEL: Beginner

You don't need a workshop to make these repairs—a few simple tools and a sturdy table will do. And you don't need any special skills. If you know the most basic stuff—how to cut plywood and drive screws—you can do it!

Add braces

Chair braces are an easy fix for a wobbly chair. They're better looking and much stiffer than L-brackets. Most hardware stores carry chair braces in finishes like chrome, brass or bronze. To avoid splitting the wood, be sure to drill 1/8-in. pilot holes before driving in the screws.

BACKER

3/4"
HOLE

Rescue a drawer

Drawer fronts that are just nailed or stapled to the drawer box often come loose or even fall off completely. You could simply pound the parts back together, but that kind of fix won't last long. For a repair that's stronger than the original construction, add a backer to the drawer front.

Make the backer from 3/4-in. plywood and cut it to fit tight inside the drawer. Using a spade bit, drill 3/4-in.-diameter holes in the plywood so you can access the screws that hold the drawer's handle. Fasten the backer to the inside front of the drawer, then screw the drawer sides to the ends of the backer.

Support sagging shelves

If your shelves sag, sometimes you can simply flip them over—but eventually they'll droop again. Here's a permanent solution: Add supports that fit tight between the shelves.

Pine stair tread, which has a rounded front edge, is perfect for this. It's available at all home centers. Many stores will cut it to length for you. You can paint or stain the supports to match the shelves, of course. But if the shelves hold books, consider staining them a color similar to your books. You'll be surprised at how well they blend in.

Fix a wobbly table

GLIDE

If you've got a table that rocks on an uneven floor, you've probably tried wedging something under the short leg. Doesn't last, does it? Here's a better way: Use washers and nail-on glides.

First, drill holes for the nails with a 1/16-in. bit and install the glides. Then set the table in place and slip washers under the low leg until the table is steady. When you've determined how many washers are needed, pull off the glide and reinstall it along with the washers.

Hide scratches with wax

To revive a finish, rub colored paste wax over the entire surface and buff. This isn't a perfect fix; heavy scratches or dents will still be visible. But light scratches and wear will almost disappear.

For the best camouflage, pick a color that's slightly darker than the finish. You can find colored paste wax at some paint stores or order it online.

DOWEL

Inject epoxy into loose joints

When one or two joints loosen on a chair but you can't get the rest of them apart, here's an advanced repair technique to try: Inject epoxy into the loose joints using a syringe.

Once mixed, most epoxy is too thick to push through a syringe. However, an epoxy used for fiberglass boat repair (like the one shown here) has just the right consistency. To inject the glue, drill 1/8-in. holes in an inconspicuous place in line with the dowels. Aim for the cavity behind each dowel. Insert the syringe into the hole, then inject the epoxy until it runs out of the joint. Push the joint together, then wipe off the excess epoxy.

This type of epoxy comes in small packets—you just tear off the top and squeeze. They're available online. This type of epoxy is more expensive than the hardware store variety. Plastic syringes are available at many pharmacies or online.

Save it with screws

When ready-to-assemble (RTA) particleboard furniture breaks—by being pushed across the floor, for example—the original knockdown fasteners often pull out of the wood and can't be replaced. The solution is to bypass them completely and screw the piece together from the outside.

Ordinary screws won't hold in particleboard, however. You need 2-1/2-in. to 3-in. screws with coarse threads and large, washer-style heads. (Large heads prevent the screws from being pulled through the particleboard.) Many home centers carry "cabinet installation screws" that are perfect for the job. Be sure to drill a pilot hole first, even if the screws have self-tapping points. You can also buy colored self-stick caps to cover the screw heads.

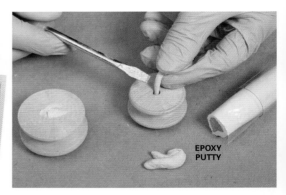

EPOXY PUTTY

Fill stripped-out screw holes

Wooden drawer knobs tend to strip out and then come loose or even pull off. Using a fatter screw or shoving matchsticks into the hole might work, but here's a sure fix: Fill the hole with epoxy putty, then drill a new hole. Epoxy putty is available at home centers and hardware stores.

Epoxy putty is easy to use. You just cut off the amount you want, knead the piece until the inner and outer layers blend together, then roll it between your fingers to form a thin string. Push the string of putty into the hole with a screwdriver. Then scrape off the excess before it hardens.

Strengthen ready-to-assemble furniture

New furniture that's put together with bolts and nuts often loosens up with use. If retightening the bolts every now and then seems like too much bother, you can take the piece apart and strengthen it with epoxy.

Most RTA furniture uses loose-fitting dowels to align each part. Spread epoxy inside the dowel holes and on the dowels themselves when you reassemble the piece. (If the dowels fit nice and tight, use yellow glue instead—it's more convenient.) Don't bother spreading glue on the ends of each part. They usually butt against a finished surface, and no glue will stick to a finish for very long.

Add metal braces

If appearance doesn't matter, screwing a brace or T-plate onto a piece of furniture is often the quickest way to fix it. Adding metal may not make the piece totally sound, but at least it won't come apart.

3 classic tricks

People who repair furniture for a living have all kinds of simple tricks up their sleeve. Here are a few that anybody can do at home:

■ Lubricate a sticking drawer with canning wax, which is made from paraffin. Paraffin works much better than candle wax.

■ When you're gluing a splinter or chip, use masking tape to hold it in place. A clamp isn't necessary.

■ Use steam to raise a dent. Place a wet towel on the dent, then press the pointed end of a hot iron onto the towel, right above the dent, for 10 seconds or so. Two or three applications may be necessary.

Shim a hinge

When a door won't close or won't align with a catch, placing a shim behind one of its hinges might solve the problem. The shim will kick out the upper or lower half of the door, depending on which hinge you choose.

Make the shim from one or more playing cards. Remove the hinge, then cut the cards to fit into the hinge's recess. Place each piece in the recess and punch screw holes in it using an awl or a small Phillips screwdriver. Remount the hinge with the original screws.

Epoxy a sloppy joint

When parts don't fit tightly, epoxy is the answer. Other woodworking glues—yellow, white or polyurethane—require a snug fit. The gap between parts can't exceed the thickness of a piece of paper. Epoxy, on the other hand, bonds across a gap of any size.

Epoxy won't stick well to old glue, so remove as much of the old glue as you can with a file or coarse sandpaper. Most epoxies must be used within five minutes of mixing, but you can buy a slower-setting epoxy if you need more time.

Knock-apart table

5/8" PLYWOOD

SLOT

15-1/2"

30"

4'

This table is made from a full sheet of 5/8-in. plywood for the interlocking base stand and a sheet of 3/4-in. plywood for the work surface and shelves. You'll also need four 10-ft. lengths of 1x3 pine for the edge banding and cleats.

Cut two 30-in.-high by 48-in.-long pieces from the 5/8-in. plywood for the base pieces. Then cut a slightly oversize 5/8-in.-wide slot in the bottom half of one base and in the top half of the other. Make both slots about 15-1/2 in. long. Assemble the base and position the top so the corners are aligned with the legs. Screw loose-fitting 12-in.-long 1x3s along each side of each leg to hold everything stable.

The table is much more stable if you use the 3/4-in. waste from the top to make triangular braces (which also act as shelves) with 20-in.-long sides. Using 1-1/4-in. drywall screws, attach 1x2s to the base about 12 in. up from the floor and screw the shelves down.

LOOSE FIT AGAINST LEG

4' x 4' 3/4" PLYWOOD

1" x 2" EDGE BANDING

19"

18-3/4"

20"

20"

SHELF/BRACE

Photo sculptures

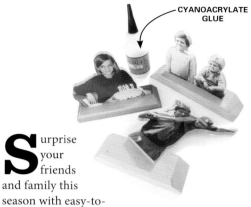

CYANOACRYLATE GLUE

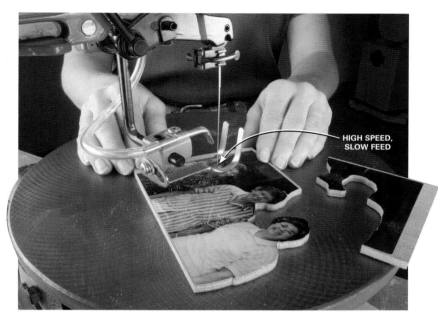

HIGH SPEED, SLOW FEED

Surprise your friends and family this season with easy-to-make photo sculptures. Your favorite folks will "pop" from your photos when you use this easy technique.

Here's how: Apply photo mount adhesive to pieces of 1/4-in. hardwood plywood, firmly press on the photos to be sculpted, then cut out the figures with a scroll saw. Make some wood bases from scrap wood and glue on the sculptured photos with cyanoacrylate glue. This glue will tightly bond the sculpture's bottom edge to the base, so you won't need to fiddle with notches or screws.

Hints for great-looking sculptures:

- Use a sharp No. 2 or No. 4 "skip tooth" blade.
- Change blades when the sawn "paper edge" appears slightly ragged.

- Select a medium or high speed and feed the work at a slow rate, pressing the wood firmly on the table as you saw.
- When choosing photos to sculpt, look for clearly outlined subjects so it's easy to follow the cutting line. Hair or clothing that blends into the background is difficult to cut.

WHAT IT TAKES

TIME: 1/2 day
SKILL LEVEL: Beginner

Quick table legs

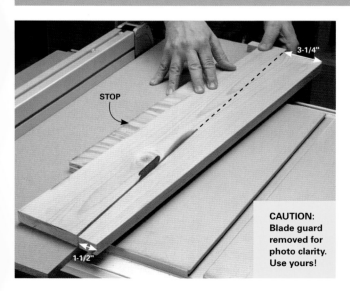

STOP

3-1/4"

1-1/2"

CAUTION: Blade guard removed for photo clarity. Use yours!

If you need to build a quick table, here's a great way to make the legs. Use this design to make tables for your house or utility tables for the shop and yard. Each leg is made from a 1x6, ripped to make two tapered pieces. Glue and nail (or screw) the two pieces together, sand as much as you feel is necessary, and you're done. The taper jig is quick to make, but it works only for this particular taper.

Laundry room ironing center..79
Double-decker garage shelf 80
Garage entry storage center 82
Yard tool slant rack...87
Quick projects for beginners 88
One-day garage storage system.....................................91

5 GARAGE & UTILITY SHELVES & ORGANIZERS

Laundry room ironing center

To keep your ironing gear handy but out from under foot, make this simple ironing center in a couple of hours. All you need is a 10-ft. 1x8, a 2-ft. piece of 1x6 for the shelves and a pair of hooks to hang your ironing board.

Cut the back, sides, shelves and top. Align the sides and measure from the bottom 2 in., 14-3/4 in. and 27-1/2 in. to mark the bottom of the shelves (Photo 1). Before assembling the unit, cut a 1 x 1-in. dog ear at the bottom of the sides for a decorative touch.

Working on one side at a time, glue and nail the side to the back. Apply glue and drive three 1-5/8-in. nails into each shelf, attach the other side and nail those shelves into place to secure them. Clamps are helpful to hold the unit together while you're driving nails. Center the top piece, leaving a 2-in. overhang on both sides, and glue and nail it into place (Photo 2). Paint or stain the unit and then drill pilot holes into the top face of each side of the unit and screw in the hooks to hold your ironing board. Mount the shelf on drywall using screw-in wall anchors.

WHAT IT TAKES

TIME: 1/2 day
SKILL LEVEL: Beginner

1 Place the sides next to each other and mark the shelf positions. For easier finishing, sand all the parts before marking and assembly.

1x8 x 34" BACK

1x8 x 12-3/4" TOP

1x8 x 36" SIDES

1x6 x 7-1/4" SHELVES

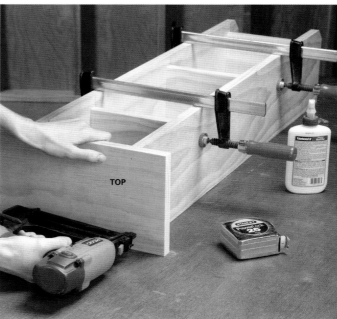

2 Glue and nail the back and shelves between the sides, then add the top. After painting or staining, screw on hooks for the ironing board.

TOP

Double-decker garage shelf

Floor space in most garages is hard to come by—so the best place to find storage space is overhead. This project has a 16-in. top shelf for big items, a 5-in. lower shelf and plenty of hook space. Need different size shelves or more space between them? It's easy to modify this basic design.

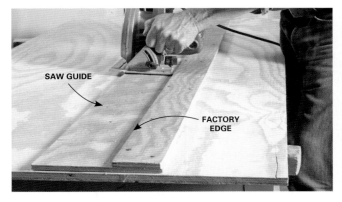

SAW GUIDE

FACTORY EDGE

1 **Rip the plywood top to width.** Use a homemade saw guide and a circular saw, or a table saw, to cut the plywood for the 16-in.-wide top shelf.

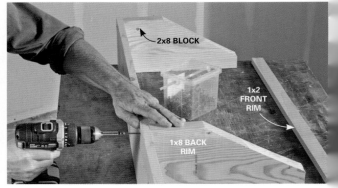

2x8 BLOCK

1x2 FRONT RIM

1x8 BACK RIM

2 **Screw the framework together.** Use all-purpose screws to secure the 1x8 back rim and 1x2 front rim to the 2x8 support block. Space the support blocks every 32 in.

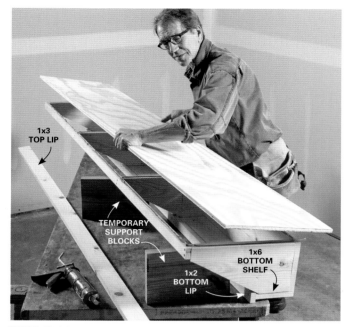

1x3 TOP LIP

TEMPORARY SUPPORT BLOCKS

1x2 BOTTOM LIP

1x6 BOTTOM SHELF

4" SCREW

3 **Finish assembling the shelf.** Install the plywood top, bottom shelf and the 1x2 and 1x3 lips. Use construction adhesive for added strength.

4 **Secure the shelf to the wall.** Use 4-in. lag or construction screws to secure the 1x8 back rim to the wall studs. Drive two screws into each stud—one high, one low.

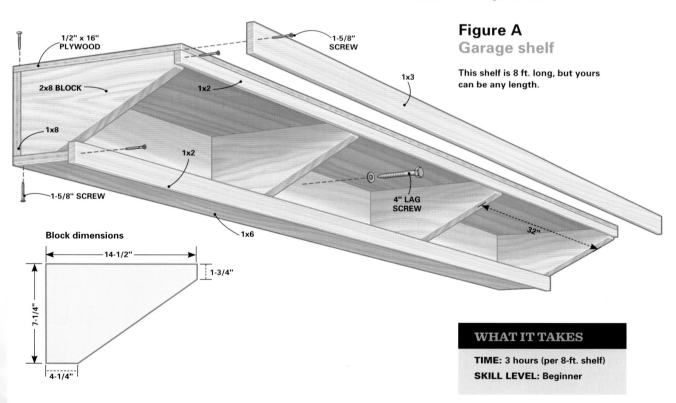

1/2" x 16" PLYWOOD

2x8 BLOCK

1x8

1-5/8" SCREW

1x2

1-5/8" SCREW

1x2

1x6

1x3

4" LAG SCREW

32"

Figure A
Garage shelf

This shelf is 8 ft. long, but yours can be any length.

Block dimensions

14-1/2"

1-3/4"

7-1/4"

4-1/4"

WHAT IT TAKES

TIME: 3 hours (per 8-ft. shelf)
SKILL LEVEL: Beginner

Garage entry storage center

Five easy options for five kinds of clutter

If you have an attached garage, the door to the house is probably a dumping ground for shoes, sports gear, jackets and all kinds of other stuff that you don't have space for indoors. These five cabinets can eliminate that mess so you don't have to walk through an obstacle course to get in the house. Each cabinet is a simple box that has been customized to solve a different storage problem. Build one or all five.

You can build, install and load these cabinets in a weekend. The only power tools you'll need are a drill and a circular saw.

But a table saw and a sliding miter saw are handy for ripping and crosscutting the plywood, and a brad nailer helps tack the cabinets and drawers together before you drive the screws.

Each cabinet requires one sheet of plywood or less and costs about $50, including the hardware and finish. Shown is birch plywood. You could use oak plywood or even MDF. For the pantry cabinet, you'll need 1/4-in. plywood for the drawer bottoms. All the materials are available at home centers, though you may have to shop online for the drawer slides for the pantry cabinet.

WHAT IT TAKES

TIME: 3 hours per cabinet
SKILL LEVEL: Beginner to intermediate

3 hours per cabinet

These cabinets were designed with economy and speed in mind. Here are three tricks to cut costs and assembly time:

- Size all parts to use the plywood efficiently. The sides, for example, are just under 12 in. wide (11-7/8 in.), so you'll get four from a 4 x 8-ft. sheet.
- Eliminate the cabinet backs, saving time and materials. Just be sure to handle the cabinets gently—they're a bit flimsy until they're screwed to the wall.
- Apply the finish before assembly. After you cut the parts to size, sand everything with 120-grit sandpaper and apply a coat of wipe-on poly.

1 Get perfectly straight, accurate cuts with a circular saw using a homemade saw guide. Clamp the saw guide at your mark on the plywood.

SAW GUIDE

2 Clamp the frame parts together, including the screw strip. Drill pilot holes and drive screws.

SCREW STRIP

STUD LOCATIONS

CLEAT

3 Set the cabinets on a cleat, then screw them to the wall at the studs (use tape to mark the stud locations). Drive screws through the cabinet bottoms into the cleat.

Box assembly tips

These cabinets are surprisingly easy to build. The illustrations tell you most of what you need to know. Here are some tips for smooth assembly:

- If you don't have a table saw to rip the plywood, use a saw guide and a circular saw (Photo 1).
- Use a shorter saw guide or a sliding miter saw to get straight, square crosscuts.

- Drill 1/8-in. pilot holes to prevent splitting. Keep screws 1 in. from edges.
- If you have a brad nailer, tack parts together to make drilling easier. But don't rely on brads alone—you still need screws. If you don't have a brad nailer, use clamps (Photo 2).
- If your cuts were slightly off and the top, bottom and sides aren't exactly the same width, don't worry. Just

make sure the front edges of the box are flush.
- Attach the screw strip to the top before attaching the side pieces.
- Attach hardware (drawer slides, shelf standards) to the sides before building the box.
- Screw the top, bottom and any fixed shelves onto one side before attaching the other side.

Wet clothes cabinet

An airy hangout for damp or dirty coats and boots

The wire shelves in this cabinet allow boots to drip dry and air to circulate freely so clothes will dry. The extra-wide screw strip lets you attach coat hooks. To build the cabinet, you'll need 6 ft. of 12-in.-deep wire shelving and coat hooks.

Attach the back cleats flush with the sides. Inset the front cleats 1/4 in. Cut the wire shelves at 22-1/4 in. This gives you 1/8 in. of play on each side. Cut the shelves with bolt cutters or have the home center cut them for you. The metal in the shelves is very tough and hard to cut with a hacksaw.

Place plastic end caps over the shelf ends. Secure the shelves to the front cleats with C-clamps. Fasten two clamps per shelf. Hold the coat hooks in place in the cabinet, drill pilot holes and then drive the screws that came with the hooks to fasten them in place.

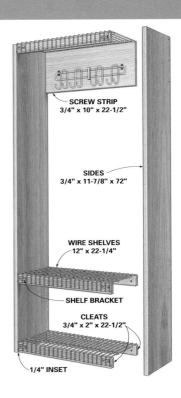

SCREW STRIP
3/4" x 10" x 22-1/2"

SIDES
3/4" x 11-7/8" x 72"

WIRE SHELVES
12" x 22-1/4"

SHELF BRACKET

CLEATS
3/4" x 2" x 22-1/2"

1/4" INSET

Open shelf cabinet

Spacious, adjustable shelves that cut entryway clutter

This open-shelf cabinet needs a fixed shelf in the middle to keep the sides from bowing, but you can make the rest of the shelves adjustable. Install as many adjustable shelves as you want—this cabinet can hold a lot of stuff!

You'll need four 6-ft. shelf standards for this cabinet. Get started by marking the shelf standard locations and the fixed middle shelf location on the two cabinet sides. Cut the shelf standards to length with a hacksaw, then screw them to the sides above and below the fixed shelf marks.

Install the adjustable shelves after you hang the cabinet on the wall.

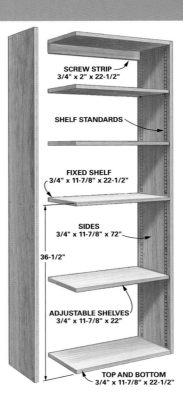

SCREW STRIP
3/4" x 2" x 22-1/2"

SHELF STANDARDS

FIXED SHELF
3/4" x 11-7/8" x 22-1/2"

SIDES
3/4" x 11-7/8" x 72"

36-1/2"

ADJUSTABLE SHELVES
3/4" x 11-7/8" x 22"

TOP AND BOTTOM
3/4" x 11-7/8" x 22-1/2"

Sports gear cabinet

A compact organizer for all kinds of equipment

The cabinet dividers let you store long-handled sports gear, like hockey sticks, bats and rackets. The lip on the top shelf keeps balls from falling off. Nail the lip to the shelf before installing the shelf at any height that suits your needs.

When installing the dividers, cut two 7-in. spacers and place them between the cabinet sides and the dividers to keep the dividers straight as you install the cabinet face.

Measure diagonally from box corner to corner to make sure the cabinet is square before attaching the face. Set the face on the cabinet, leaving a 1/8-in. reveal along both sides and the bottom. Drill pilot holes and screw the face to the sides and the dividers.

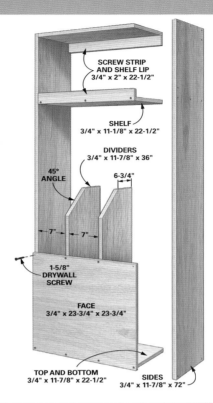

SCREW STRIP AND SHELF LIP
3/4" x 2" x 22-1/2"

SHELF
3/4" x 11-1/8" x 22-1/2"

DIVIDERS
3/4" x 11-7/8" x 36"

45° ANGLE

6-3/4"

7"   7"

1-5/8" DRYWALL SCREW

FACE
3/4" x 23-3/4" x 23-3/4"

TOP AND BOTTOM
3/4" x 11-7/8" x 22-1/2"

SIDES
3/4" x 11-7/8" x 72"

Shoe and boot cabinet

Eliminate the footwear pileup on the back steps

The lower shelves in this cabinet hold boots and shoes, while the cubbyholes at the top are for slippers and sandals. The screw strip is lower in this cabinet than it is in the rest, but it'll still hold the cabinet in place.

Install the lower shelf first, then add the divider and screw on the shelves that fit between the divider and the cabinet sides.

Build the cubbyholes on your work surface, then stick the assembled cubbies into the cabinet. Start by screwing two dividers onto a shelf. Make two shelves this way. Then install a center divider between these two shelves. Add a shelf to the bottom, over the two dividers. Then insert the cubbies inside the cabinet and screw through the sides into the shelves and through the top into the dividers.

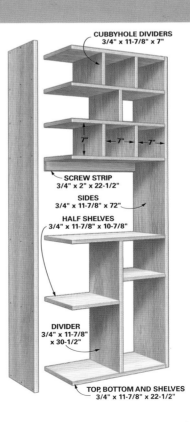

CUBBYHOLE DIVIDERS
3/4" x 11-7/8" x 7"

7"   7"   7"

SCREW STRIP
3/4" x 2" x 22-1/2"

SIDES
3/4" x 11-7/8" x 72"

HALF SHELVES
3/4" x 11-7/8" x 10-7/8"

DIVIDER
3/4" x 11-7/8" x 30-1/2"

TOP, BOTTOM AND SHELVES
3/4" x 11-7/8" x 22-1/2"

Install a 2x2 cleat on the wall for the cabinets to sit on. You'll need 24 in. of cleat for each cabinet. Keep the cleat at least 8 in. above the floor so you can sweep under the cabinets.

Snap a level chalk line on the wall for the cleat (measure down from the ceiling if your floor slopes!). Attach the cleat at the chalk line by driving a 3-in. drywall screw into each stud. Set the cabinets on the cleats. Place a level alongside the cabinet to make sure it's standing plumb and square. Then drill pilot holes through the screw strips and attach the cabinets to the wall with 3-in. drywall screws (Photo 3). Screw adjoining cabinets together by driving 1-1/4-in. drywall screws through the side near the top and the bottom.

NOTE: All cabinets are 11-7/8" deep x 24" wide x 72" tall.

Pantry cabinet

Bulk storage that frees up kitchen space

If you buy groceries in bulk, this is the storage solution for you. The bottom drawers in this cabinet are deep enough to hold two cases of soda. The top drawers are perfect for canned goods or bottled water. The upper shelves are adjustable for more bulk storage. The cabinet faces and door keep everything enclosed.

Inexpensive drawer slides let the drawers open and close easily. You'll also need two 6-ft. shelf standards.

Lay the cabinet sides next to each other and mark the center for each drawer slide. Place a slide over each mark, drill pilot holes (a self-centering drill bit works best) and screw the slides into place. Cut the shelf standards with a hacksaw and screw them to the cabinet sides, above the fixed shelf.

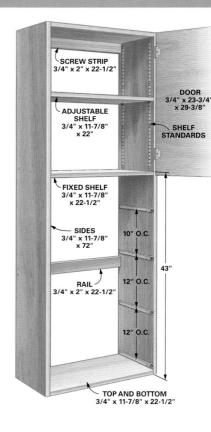

Assemble the drawers with 1-5/8-in. screws. Place the drawer slides on the drawers, drill pilot holes and attach them with screws. Test-fit them in the cabinet. If the cabinet sides are bowed even slightly, attach a 2-in. rail in the back to hold the sides in place so the drawers slide smoothly.

Fasten the faces to the drawers with 1-1/4-in. screws driven from inside the drawers. Build the handles with leftover plywood and attach them with 2-in. screws (driven from the inside).

Attach the door to the cabinet with 1/2-in. overlay hinges, also called half-wrap hinges. They're available at home centers or woodworking stores.

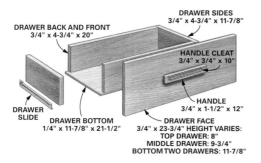

DRAWER BACK AND FRONT
3/4" x 4-3/4" x 20"

DRAWER SIDES
3/4" x 4-3/4" x 11-7/8"

HANDLE CLEAT
3/4" x 3/4" x 10"

HANDLE
3/4" x 1-1/2" x 12"

DRAWER SLIDE

DRAWER BOTTOM
1/4" x 11-7/8" x 21-1/2"

DRAWER FACE
3/4" x 23-3/4" HEIGHT VARIES:
TOP DRAWER: 8"
MIDDLE DRAWER: 9-3/4"
BOTTOM TWO DRAWERS: 11-7/8"

Yard tool slant rack

Stashing stuff in the unused spaces between studs is a smart move; adding these slant boxes to expand the space is smarter yet. They give your tools more "headroom" and give you easier access to long- and short-handled tools.

For the tall unit, use the bottom wall plate for the bottom of your box. Attach the plywood to create a 1-in. gap at the bottom for removing dirt or dropped items. For the shorter slant boxes, install your own blocking to create the bottom; leave a gap at the bottom of the plywood for those, too. We show 48-in. and 16-in. versions; you can make yours any depth or length you want.

Note: If your garage has a short ceiling (or your tools have extra-long handles), create a cutout in the top of the plywood face, as shown in Figure A, to allow more entrance and exit leeway for your tools.

Rip a 2x4 diagonally to create the sides. Screw each wedge to the face of a stud. Install a plywood face and you're ready to store stuff.

Figure A
Slant rack

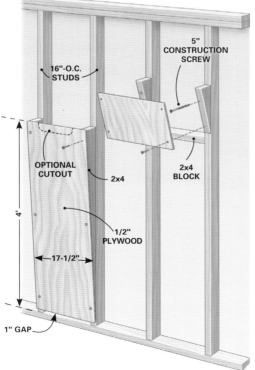

5"
CONSTRUCTION
SCREW

16"-O.C.
STUDS

OPTIONAL
CUTOUT

2x4

2x4
BLOCK

1/2"
PLYWOOD

17-1/2"

4'

1" GAP

WHAT IT TAKES

TIME: 1 hour
SKILL: Beginner

Quick projects for beginners

Between studs shelving

Store smaller containers—spray paint, putty cans, glue bottles—right in the wall! Screw shelf brackets (6-ft. lengths are sold at home centers) to the studs, then install shelves, cut from standard 1x4 boards, on adjustable clips. The boards fit perfectly; there's no need to saw them to width.

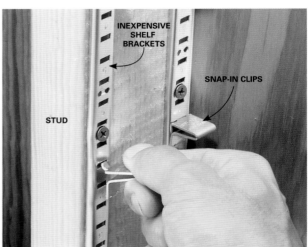

INEXPENSIVE
SHELF
BRACKETS

SNAP-IN CLIPS

STUD

Ceiling-mounted ladder rack

An extension ladder has to be one of the most difficult things to store. When you need to use it, it has to be easy to get to. But there are long stretches when it just gets in the way of everything else in your garage. Here's a good solution: Mount it on your garage ceiling on sturdy racks made of scrap 2x4s that are screwed into the ceiling joists. Use two 3-1/2-in. screws at each joint to make the rack secure. These racks make it easy to slide the ladder out when you need it. Just make sure to position the racks where they won't interfere with your garage door.

8" 11" 28"

Garden/garage tool caddy

Use some leftover wood and plastic lattice to build a caddy for garden shovels, hoes and brooms. Install casters, so it scoots easily into a corner of your garage.

Sports rack

A wall-mounted rack will keep bats and balls from getting lost in the recesses of your garage or basement. Just cut 6-in.-diameter holes in the top 1x10 shelf and 3-in. holes in the bottom 1x6 shelf. Then screw the bottom shelf to the top shelf from below. Attach a 1x2 cleat to the back and screw it to the wall studs. Customize the size and shape to fit your needs.

6" HOLES

1x10

SLOT FOR BATS
OR RACKETS

1x2 CLEAT

1x6 BOTTOM
AND SIDES

3" HOLES

One-day garage storage system

An incredibly easy solution for a cluttered garage

This storage system is made mostly from wire shelving and plastic-coated particleboard (called "melamine"). Those two simple materials, along with some clever engineering, provide three big benefits:

Quick, simple construction. If you can make a few easy cuts (which don't have to be perfect), drive some screws and brush on a little paint, you can build this system in a weekend. If you're an experienced DIYer, you might even be done in a day.

Fits any space. The system is made up of separate units, so you can build just one, cover an entire wall with several units or leave spaces between units.

Versatile storage. Aside from wire shelves, the system includes optional hanging spaces for clothes and outdoor gear, plus oversize upper shelves for bulky stuff. As your needs change, you can easily remove or reconfigure the shelves.

Build the units

To get started, cut all the parts (see Cutting List, p. 93). The coating on melamine tends to chip when you cut it. For cleaner cuts, use a 60-tooth carbide circular saw blade and apply painter's tape over the cut (Photo 1). Melamine is slippery stuff, so clamp it in place before cutting. Set the depth of your saw

WHAT IT TAKES

TIME: 1 or 2 days
SKILL: Beginner

1 **Cut the sides.** Cut one melamine board at a 45-degree angle and use it as a pattern to mark the others for cutting. Mark your cutting line on a strip of painter's tape—the tape reduces chipping as you cut.

PAINTER'S TAPE

2 **Position the shelf supports.** Mark where the edge of each shelf support is located and mark a centerline for screw locations. Drill three 9/64-in. screw holes for each support.

SCREW LINE

1-1/4"

SHELF SUPPORT EDGE

3 **Fasten the shelf supports.** Drive 1-1/4-in. screws through the sides and into the shelf supports. A clamp makes this step much easier.

SHELF SUPPORT

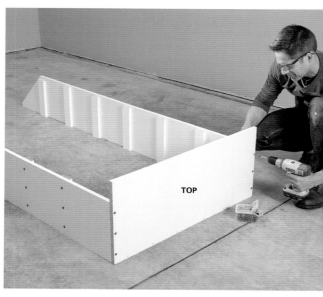

4 **Assemble the unit.** Drill holes in the top, then drive cabinet screws to fasten the top to the sides.

TOP

blade at 1 in. Chipping won't be a problem when you cut the solid wood parts (B and D). When you cut the supports for the lowest shelves (B1), note that they're shorter than the others. To avoid slow, fussy painting later, paint the wood parts before assembly.

Our shelf spacing is 12 in., but any spacing you choose is fine. Lay pairs of sides (A) next to each other when you mark shelf support locations. That way, you can be sure that the supports will match up after assembly. Drill screw holes

(Photo 2) and then fasten the shelf supports (Photo 3).

Pick out a flat spot on the floor and attach the top (C) to the sides (Photo 4). Then tilt the assembly up a few inches and slide wood scraps beneath it so you can add the rails (D) with 2-in. screws (Photo 5).

With the unit completely assembled, sand the exposed cut edges of the melamine using 150-grit sandpaper, then paint them (Photo 6). Finally, hammer on some furniture glides (Photo 7) and the unit is ready for installation.

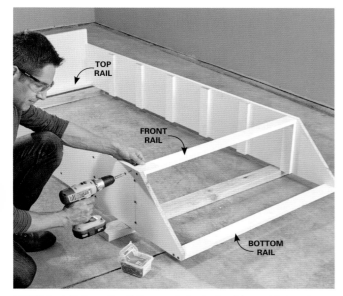

5 **Install the rails.** Drill screw holes in the sides and fasten the three rails. You'll need to raise the unit off the floor in order to screw the top and bottom rails.

TOP RAIL

FRONT RAIL

BOTTOM RAIL

6 **Paint the cut edges.** For looks and moisture protection, apply two coats of paint. If you slop a little paint onto the melamine surface, just wipe it off with a damp rag.

CUT EDGE

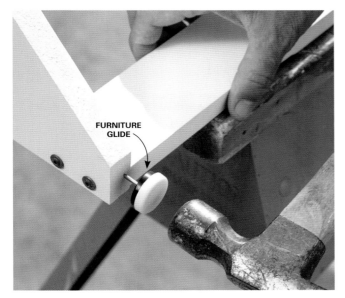

7 **Add glides.** Nail plastic furniture glides to the bottom of the sides to keep them from resting directly on damp surfaces, especially concrete.

FURNITURE GLIDE

Install the units

If you have finished walls, locate the wall studs with a stud finder and mark them with masking tape. Get some help to lift the assembly up to the wall and hold it in place (Photo 8). Our floor had a row of concrete blocks that protruded from the wall about 1-1/2 in., so we rested the glides on them. The blocks were level but the floor had a slight pitch toward the door, so this saved us the hassle of having to allow for the slope of the floor.

8 **Install the first unit.** Mark the stud locations with painter's tape and set the first unit in place. To ensure that the unit is level and square, check both the top and one side with a level.

STUD LOCATION

With the assembly against the wall, you can shim underneath to level it (if necessary) and then plumb the sides with a level. Screw it to the wall studs with 2-1/2-in. screws (Photo 9).

If you're willing to spend some money on a bolt cutter, cutting the wire shelves will be quick and easy (Photo 10). Bolt cutters are sized by length; 24 in. is a good choice. When the shelves are cut, set them in place and "clip" them to the wall (Photo 11). Also secure the shelf fronts with coaxial cable staples (Photo 12), which are available in the electrical aisle at home centers. Remove the nails that come with the staples and use 4d nails instead. To store balls or other items that tend to roll off shelves, install a shelf or two upside-down. The lip on the front of the shelf keeps stuff in place.

9 Add as many units as you like. With the first unit installed square and level, you can simply butt the next unit against it. Screw all units to studs at the top and bottom rungs.

10 Cut the shelves. A bolt cutter is the best tool for cutting wire shelving to length. A hacksaw or a metal-cutting blade in a jigsaw will also do the job.

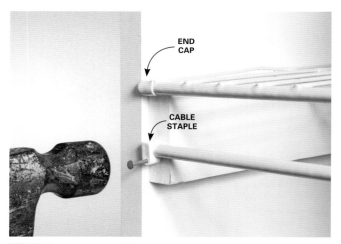

11 Anchor the shelves. Fasten each shelf to the wall with at least two clips. When you want to fasten the clip to a stud, simply cut off the drywall anchor part of the clip and drive a screw through the clip.

12 Fasten the shelf fronts. Lock the shelves in place with coaxial cable staples. End caps give the shelves a finished look.

Choosing screws

We used No. 8 "cabinet" screws throughout this project for three reasons:

■ The large "washer" heads design looks much neater than a bugle head countersunk into the melamine surface.

■ The washer heads won't pull through the particleboard.

■ The coarse threads hold well in particleboard.

Cabinet screws are made by GRK, Spax and other manufacturers.

Figure A
Shelf unit

Overall dimensions: 11-3/4" deep x 37-1/2" wide x 85-1/2" tall (top shelf is 15-3/4" deep)

Materials List
(for one unit)

ITEM	QTY.
3/4" x 11-3/4" x 8' melamine shelf board	2
3/4" x 15-3/4" x 37-1/2" melamine shelf board	1
3/4" x 2-1/2" x 8' pine boards	3
12" x 12' wire shelving	2
Wire shelving wall clips	12
Wire shelving end caps	12
Coaxial cable staples	12
Cabinet screws (1-1/4", 2", 2-1/2"), 4d (1-1/2") nails	1 pkg. ea.
Furniture glides	2
White paint	1 qt.
150-grit sandpaper	

All of these materials are available at home centers.

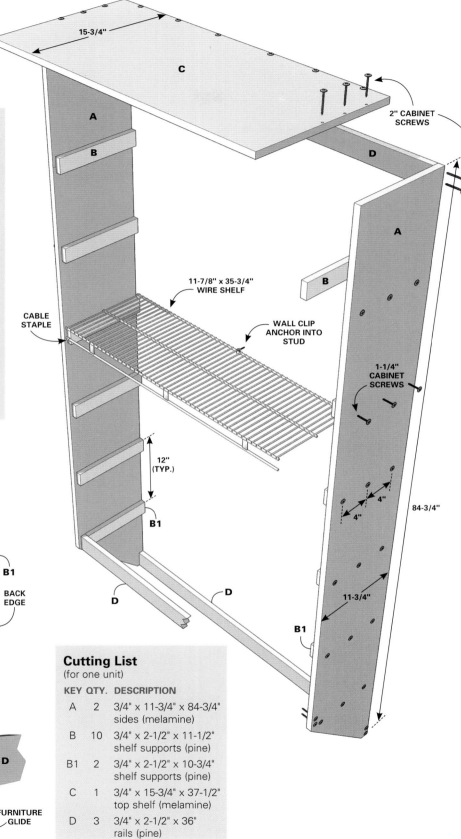

15-3/4"

C

A

B

2" CABINET SCREWS

D

11-7/8" x 35-3/4" WIRE SHELF

WALL CLIP ANCHOR INTO STUD

CABLE STAPLE

B

A

1-1/4" CABINET SCREWS

12" (TYP.)

B1

4"

4"

84-3/4"

11-3/4"

D

D

B1

Figure B
Bottom detail

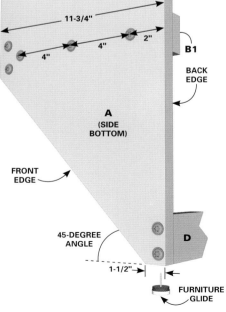

11-3/4"

4"

4"

2"

B1

BACK EDGE

A (SIDE BOTTOM)

FRONT EDGE

45-DEGREE ANGLE

1-1/2"

D

FURNITURE GLIDE

Cutting List
(for one unit)

KEY	QTY.	DESCRIPTION
A	2	3/4" x 11-3/4" x 84-3/4" sides (melamine)
B	10	3/4" x 2-1/2" x 11-1/2" shelf supports (pine)
B1	2	3/4" x 2-1/2" x 10-3/4" shelf supports (pine)
C	1	3/4" x 15-3/4" x 37-1/2" top shelf (melamine)
D	3	3/4" x 2-1/2" x 36" rails (pine)

Compact compressor station...97
Super sturdy drawers...100
Quick tool storage for beginners 106
Mobile tool chest 107
Hardware organizer 108
Quick projects for beginners 111

6 SHOP ORGANIZERS

Compact compressor station

WHAT IT TAKES

TIME: 1 day

SKILL: Beginner to intermediate

Save floor space and get organized with this sturdy compressor stand

You can get your nail guns, fasteners, hose and accessories off your workbench and out of your way by building this wall-mounted compressor station. This easy project requires just one sheet of 3/4-in. plywood; about 8 ft. of 1x2 lumber; and only standard carpentry tools, plus a circular saw and a jigsaw. We used a table saw for most of the plywood cuts, and a miter saw for the trim, but a circular saw and straightedge will give good results too.

Figure A
Compressor station

Overall dimensions:
25-1/2″ wide
20-3/4″ deep
30-1/4″ tall

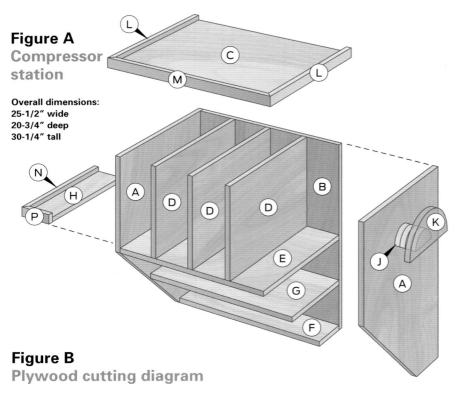

Figure B
Plywood cutting diagram

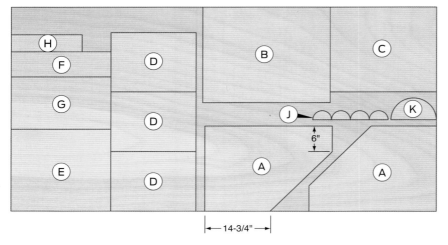

14-3/4″

6″

We spent more for birch plywood and birch 1x2 for this station, but you can cut the cost in half by using less expensive wood. Plan to spend about six to eight hours on this project.

Start by cutting out the plywood pieces according to Figure B. Use a table saw or a circular saw fitted with a sharp carbide-tooth blade to minimize splintering. If you're using a circular saw, clamp a straightedge or a saw guide to the plywood for straight, accurate cuts. Photo 1 shows how to make the diagonal cuts for the sides.

Build the hose holder by marking four half circles with a gallon paint can and a half circle with a 5-gallon bucket on a plywood strip. Cut out the parts with a jigsaw (Photo 2). Glue and clamp the four small half circles together. After the glue dries, use a belt sander to smooth the edges, then glue the half round block to the larger half circle.

Once the parts are cut, assembly is straightforward. Mark the centerline of the shelves (E, F and G) on the sides, and the centerline of the dividers (D) on the top (C) and upper shelf (E). Drill holes and countersinks for screws on

Materials List

ITEM	QTY.
4' x 8' x 3/4" plywood	1
1x2 x 8'	1
1/4" x 3/4" strips of wood (optional)	16'
1-5/8" screws	1 lb.
2" finish nails	1/2 lb.
Wood glue	

Cutting List

KEY	QTY.	SIZE & DESCRIPTION
A	2	3/4" x 20" x 28-3/4" plywood
B	1	3/4" x 22-1/2" x 28-3/4" plywood
C	1	3/4" x 20" x 24" plywood
D	3	3/4" x 14" x 19-1/4" plywood
E	1	3/4" x 19-1/4" x 22-1/2" plywood
F	1	3/4" x 5-1/4" x 22-1/2" plywood
G	1	3/4" x 12-1/4" x 22-1/2" plywood
H	1	3/4" x 4" x 16" plywood

KEY	QTY.	SIZE & DESCRIPTION
J	4	3/4" x 6-1/2" diameter half circles of plywood
K	1	3/4" x 10-1/4" diameter half circles of plywood
L	2	3/4" x 1-1/2" x 21" (miter to fit)
M	1	3/4" x 1-1/2" x 26" (miter to fit)
N	1	3/4" x 1-1/2" x 17" (miter to fit)
P	1	3/4" x 1-1/2" x 5" (miter to fit)

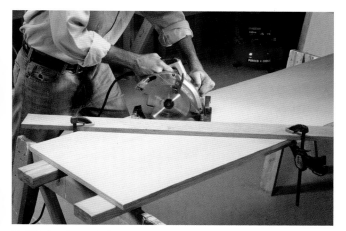

1 Cut the angled sides using a straightedge to guide your saw. Cut the rectangular pieces with a table saw or a circular saw and straightedge.

2 Saw out the hose holder parts with a jigsaw. Trace around one half of a paint can and one half of a 5-gallon bucket to mark the pieces. Glue and screw the half circles together to make the hose holder.

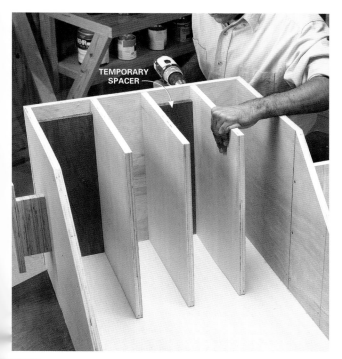

TEMPORARY SPACER

3 Position the dividers with temporary spacers. This eliminates the need for measuring and marking and makes alignment much easier. Use the same spacers again when you install the shelf below the dividers.

ACCESSORY SHELF

4 Wrap the top of the station with a sturdy lip to prevent the compressor from "walking" off. Use both glue and nails for a strong connection.

the centerline of all shelves and dividers. Space screws about 1-1/2 in. from plywood ends and about 8 in. apart.

Start by driving 1-5/8-in. screws through the sides into the back and attaching the shelf and hose holder with screws. Then screw the top to the sides and back and add the dividers (Photo 3). We made the first space 6 in. wide and the three remaining spaces 4-3/4 in. wide to fit our nail guns. Adjust these

dimensions to fit your own tools. Screw the wide shelf (E) to the dividers and then screw through the sides into the three shelves (E, F and G).

Finish the station by adding a 1x2 edge to the top and to the accessory shelf (Photo 4). Align the 1x2s with the plywood so they protrude 3/4 in. above the top and shelf to create a lip. Glue and nail the 1x2s to the plywood. For a more finished appearance, we covered the raw plywood edges with

1/4-in. strips of wood, but screen molding would work fine.

We brushed two coats of clear polyurethane on the station before hanging it on the wall. When you mount the station, be sure to locate wall studs and attach the station firmly to them with four 1/4-in. x 3-1/2-in. lag screws and washers. To reduce noise and compressor movement, cut a rubber mat or piece of carpet to fit under the compressor.

Super sturdy drawers

Super big, super tough, super easy

WHAT IT TAKES

(for four units)

TIME: 2 days

SKILL: Beginner to intermediate

This heavy-duty storage system is modeled after old filing cabinets and works great for storing tools, materials or even old paper records.

For this project, we built six of them and added shelves and a continuous top. The first one took one full day to build and a couple hours to paint and finish, but we built the other five in just two more days. This isn't a project that requires a high-end furniture maker's craftsmanship: If you can build basic plywood boxes, you can build these drawer units.

Getting started

We'll focus on how to build one unit, but you can build as many as you like and arrange them whichever way works best. Refer to the cutting diagram (p. 103), and cut all the plywood components except the back (C), drawer bottoms (D) and hardwood drawer fronts (L, M, N). Cut these parts to size as you need them in case one or more components get a little out of whack. Many home centers will help you cut your plywood so it's easier to haul home, but don't wear out your welcome and expect them to make all the cuts for you.

Cut and install the drawer supports

Lay the two sides (A) next to each other on your workbench. Position them so the surface with the most flaws faces up—this will be the inside and won't be visible once the drawers are installed. Also, determine which of the plywood edges have

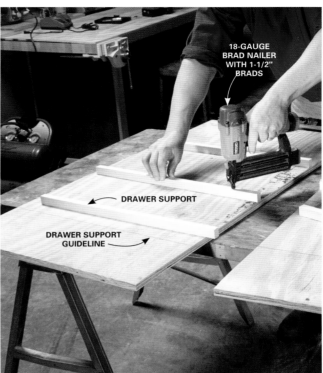

1 **Mount the drawer supports.** Attach the drawer supports to the side panels before assembling the cabinet. Glue each support and tack it down with brads. Then flip the panel over and drive 1-1/2-in. screws into the supports.

18-GAUGE BRAD NAILER WITH 1-1/2" BRADS

DRAWER SUPPORT

DRAWER SUPPORT GUIDELINE

STAY 1-1/2" FROM END

1-1/2" TRIM HEAD SCREWS

2 **Assemble the carcass.** Fasten the sides to the top and bottom with glue and brads, and then add screws. To avoid splitting the plywood, drill pilot holes for the screws and stay 1-1/2 in. from the ends.

the fewest flaws and voids, and arrange the pieces so the best edges face toward the front. Measure up from the bottom on each side 14 in., 26 in. and 38 in., and make a pencil mark near the outside edge of each side. Use a straightedge, and draw a line between your marks and across the face of both sides at the same time. These will be the guidelines for the tops of the drawer supports (P).

Cut 18 in. off the 6-ft. pine 1x4, and set it aside to be used as the center brace (Q). Rip down what's left of the 1x4 into 1-in. strips to be used as the six drawer supports, and cut them to length (see Cutting List on p. 103).

Install the drawer supports with glue and 1-1/2-in. brads (Photo 1). The drawer supports should be 1/2 in. short on the

3 **Add the back.** Use the back to square up the cabinet. Fasten the whole length of one side, and then align the other sides with the back as you go.

4 **Install the center brace.** The brace prevents the sides from bowing in or out. Clamp the brace in place, and then fasten it with 3-in. trim head screws.

front side to accommodate the thickness of the hardwood drawer fronts. Flip the sides over and install three 1-1/2-in. screws in each support. Countersink all the screws a bit on the outside of the entire carcass so the holes can be filled with wood filler before painting.

Assemble the carcass

Apply wood glue and tack on the top or bottom (B) to the sides with three or four brads. Even if you picked the straightest plywood available at the home center or lumberyard, it will probably cup and curl a bit after it's cut up. So whenever you join two pieces of plywood, start on one end and straighten out the plywood as you go.

Secure each joint with three 1-1/2-in. screws before moving on to the next one. Whenever drilling close to the edge of plywood, avoid puckers and splits by predrilling 1/8-in. holes for the screws. And stay at least 1-1/2-in. from the end of the plywood that's being drilled into (Photo 2). If a screw is installed too close to the end, it will just split the plywood instead of burying into it.

Spread glue on the back edge of the carcass and fasten the back with 1-1/2-in. brads along one whole side first. Then use the back as a guide to square up the rest of the carcass (Photo 3). Finish attaching the back with screws every 16 in. or so.

The center brace keeps the plywood sides from bowing in or out. Measure the distance between the drawer runners at the back of the carcass. Cut the center brace that same length.

5 **Build the drawers.** Assemble the drawers just as you built the cabinets: Glue, nail and screw the sides, front and back. Then square up the box as you fasten the bottom.

Install the brace between the two middle runners 4 in. back from the front. Make sure the brace is flush or just a little lower than the drawer supports or the drawer will teeter back and forth on it. Hold it in place with a clamp and secure it with two 3-in. screws through each side (Photo 4). Install a brace at more than one drawer support location if your plywood is particularly unruly.

Assemble the drawers

Lay out each drawer so all the best edges face up. Then, just as you did with the carcass, assemble the drawers with glue, brads and screws. Cut the drawer bottoms after the sides (F, H, K) and fronts/backs (E, G, J) are assembled. That way you can cut the bottoms exactly to size. A perfectly square bottom will ensure your drawers are also square. Make sure the bottom is flush or a little short on the front side of the drawer; otherwise the hardwood drawer fronts won't sit flat on the front of the drawer (Photo 5).

Fasten the drawer fronts

The local home center carried three options of hardwood plywood: oak, birch and one labeled just "hardwood." We went with the generic hardwood, but if you do the same, make sure you get enough to finish your project because the grain and color will vary from one batch to the next.

The drawers may not sit perfectly flat until they are filled with stuff, so before you secure the hardwood drawer fronts, add some weight to the drawer you're working on and the one above it. And center each drawer in the opening before you secure the drawer front.

Start at the bottom, and cut the hardwood drawer fronts to size one at a time. Cut them so there's a 1/8-in. gap between the bottom and the sides and the bottom of the drawer above it. Rest the drawer front on a couple of shims to achieve the gap at the bottom and eyeball the gaps on the side. Glue it and secure it with four brads, one in each corner (Photo 6). There's no need for screws; the handle bolts will sandwich everything together. If you're building several of these storage units and purchased a piece of hardwood plywood larger than 2 x 4 ft., you'll have the option to line up the grain on the drawer fronts the same way it came off the sheet. It's a small detail that can add a lot to the looks of your project.

Build and attach the handles

Rout the edges of the handle with a 1/4-in. round-over bit before cutting the handles (R) to length. Next, cut the dowels for the handle extensions (S) to length.

Build one simple jig to align the dowels on the handles, and to position the handles on the drawer fronts. Cut a 3/4-in. piece of plywood the same width as the drawer fronts and rip it down to 4-3/8 in. Fasten a scrap of 3/4-in. material to the end of the jig. Measure in from each side and mark a line at 2-1/8 in., 3-1/8 in. and 4-3/8 in.

This jig is designed to center the top handle on the top drawer front and keep the others the same distance down from the top on all

HANDLE

the other drawers. If you want all the handles centered, you'll have to build two more jigs or mark center lines on the other drawers.

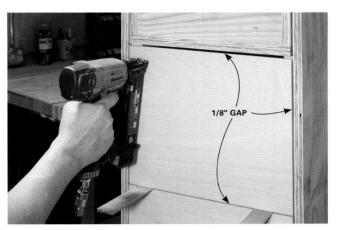

1/8" GAP

6 **Position the drawer fronts.** Slip the drawer boxes into the cabinet. Center the drawer fronts and shim under them to achieve 1/8-in. gaps. Secure the fronts to the drawer boxes with glue and one brad in each corner.

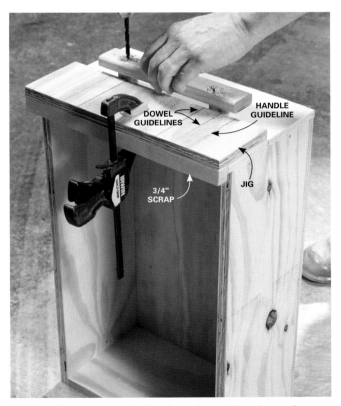

DOWEL GUIDELINES

HANDLE GUIDELINE

3/4" SCRAP

JIG

7 **Add the handles.** Build a simple jig and clamp it onto the drawer front. Hold the handle in place and drill holes for the carriage bolts.

Mark the bottom of each handle extension and the area near the hole on each drawer with the same number so you can install that same handle on the same drawer after you apply the finish.

Build and secure the base

If you're building only one unit, cut the base parts (T) and assemble them with glue and two 3-in. screws that are compatible with pressure-treated lumber. Secure the base to the bottom of the carcass with glue and 1-1/2-in. screws: three on the sides and two each on the front and back.

Finish the components

Patch all the screw holes, brad holes and voids on the carcass with wood filler or wood patch. We painted only the outside and front of the cabinet, and didn't bother painting the wood on the insides, backs or sides that were going to be sandwiched together. Cover the hardwood drawer fronts and edges with two coats of polyurethane, or a similar coating of your choice. Avoid discoloration around the brad hole on the drawer fronts by filling them with matching putty between coats of poly. Stain the oak handles with a medium-tinted stain to make them "pop" a little more before finishing them with two coats of poly.

Install the handles with the carriage bolts, washers and nuts. Seat the carriage bolts with a hammer so they don't spin while you turn the nut, and turn them tight.

Install multiple units

If you're building several units, build the base and then set each unit in place individually (Photo 8). Create a toe space by building the base 4 in. narrower than the units. Our garage floor slants down toward the overhead door, so we had to rip down the base to make the whole thing level. You may just need a few shims to make yours level. Level each storage unit as you go and screw them to the base and to one another with 1-1/2-in.screws. Angle the screws a bit so they don't poke

Figure A
Storage unit

Overall dimensions:
16" wide x 51-1/2" tall
x 24" deep

There are three drawer sizes. See the Cutting List (p. 103) for dimensions.

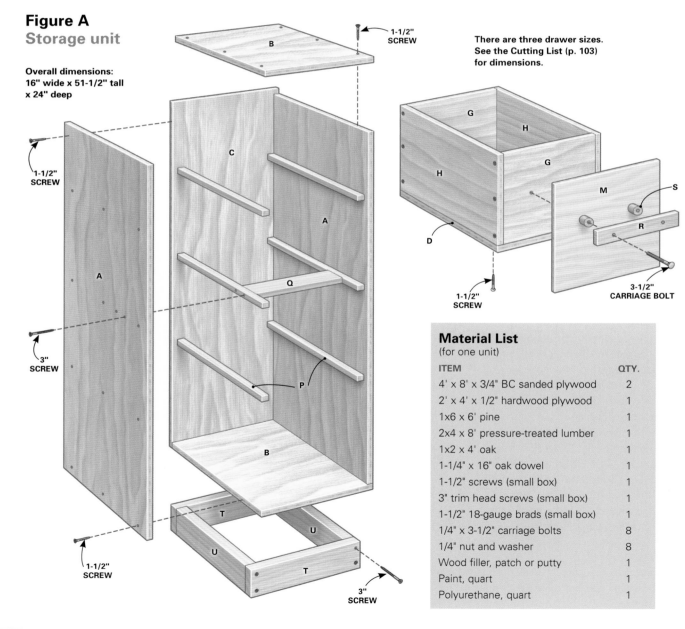

Material List
(for one unit)

ITEM	QTY.
4' x 8' x 3/4" BC sanded plywood	2
2' x 4' x 1/2" hardwood plywood	1
1x6 x 6' pine	1
2x4 x 8' pressure-treated lumber	1
1x2 x 4' oak	1
1-1/4" x 16" oak dowel	1
1-1/2" screws (small box)	1
3" trim head screws (small box)	1
1-1/2" 18-gauge brads (small box)	1
1/4" x 3-1/2" carriage bolts	8
1/4" nut and washer	8
Wood filler, patch or putty	1
Paint, quart	1
Polyurethane, quart	1

Figure B
Cutting diagram

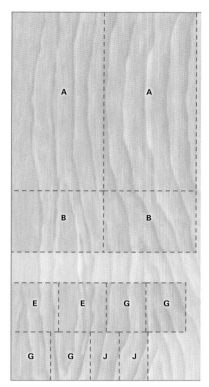

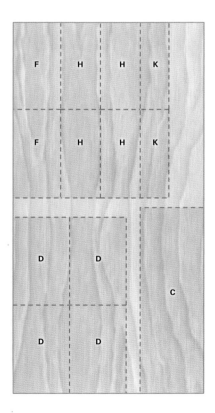

8 Set the carcass on the base. When installing multiple units, build, paint and lay down the base first, and then attach each unit to the base.

9 Hang shelving between units. Install the bottom shelf on the base. Install cleats to support other shelves.

Cutting List
(for one unit)

KEY	QTY.	SIZE & DESCRIPTION
3/4" BC sanded plywood		
A	2	46-1/2" x 23-1/4" sides
B	2	16" x 23-1/4" top/bottom
C	1	48" x 16" back*
D	4	22-3/4" x 14-1/4" drawer bottoms*
E	2	12-3/4" x 12" bottom drawer front/back
F	2	22-3/4" x 12" bottom drawer sides
G	4	12-3/4" x 10" middle drawer front/back
H	4	22-3/4" x 10" middle drawer sides
J	2	12-3/4" x 7-1/4" top drawer front/back
K	2	22-3/4" x 7-1/4" top drawer sides
1/2" hardwood plywood		
L	1	14-1/4" x 13-7/8" bottom drawer front*
M	2	14-1/4" x 11-7/8" middle drawer fronts*
N	1	14-1/4" x 8-3/8" top drawer front*
Cut from 6' pine 1x4		
P	6	22-1/2" x 1" x 3/4" drawer supports
Q	1	12-1/2" x 3-1/2" x 3/4" center brace
Cut from 4' oak 1x2		
R	4	10" x 1-1/2" x 3/4" handles
Cut from 1' oak 1-1/4" dowel		
S	8	1" x 1-1/4" handle extensions
Cut from 8' pressure-treated 2x4		
T	2	16" x 1-1/2" x 3-1/2" base front/back
U	2	17" x 1-1/2" x 3-1/2" base sides

*Cut to fit

through when you screw the units together.

Rip down a couple of cleats and screw them to the sides for the middle shelf to sit on. Leave them a couple inches short of the front so you don't see them. Attach the lower shelf to the base before you install the middle shelf (Photo 9).

Once all the units are in place, attach the top(s) so the seams fall in the middle of one unit. Screw the whole thing to the wall studs last using one screw per unit. The front side of the base may need a few shims to make it sit flush against the wall.

Touch up the exposed screw holes and scuff marks with paint. Now all that's left is to file away all that clutter.

Quick tool storage for beginners

NOTCHES CUT
TO SEPARATE
BLADES

5/8"
DOWEL

ALUMINUM
FOIL

Saw blade roost

Here's a double-duty holder for storing and cleaning table saw and circular saw blades. It features a slotted dowel to keep stored blades spaced apart so the teeth stay sharp.

Using a handsaw, cut notches spaced at 3/8-in. intervals halfway through a 5/8-in. dowel. Glue the dowel in a hole drilled in a 16 x 12-in. piece of 3/4-in. plywood. Frame the sides and lower edge of the plywood with 2-in. strips of plywood and add a lower facing piece to create a basin at the bottom. When a blade needs cleaning, remove the other blades and line the rack with aluminum foil. Then mount the gunked-up blade on the dowel, spray one side with oven cleaner, and flip it over and spray the other side. Any drips go in the basin, and the sides minimize overspray. Let the cleaner work for an hour or so, then use a moistened kitchen scrub pad to scour the dissolved gunk and burned sawdust off the blade. Then throw away the foil and store your blades.

Tool tote

Keep all your hand tools within easy reach in a portable 16-in. pine carton. Build one from a 1x8 x 12-ft. pine board, 1/4-in. plywood and a 3/4-in. oak dowel, and you'll never run back to the garage for a bit, blade, wrench or nail. Here's how:

- Cut and screw together the sides and ends with the ends protruding 1 in. beyond the sides. Drill holes in the top of the ends for a 3/4-in. dowel handle and tap it in the holes before assembling the ends and sides. Drill the 3/8-in. storage holes in the top edges of the sides before assembly.
- Saw 1/4-in. x 1-1/2-in. pine strips for the side slats and screw them to the protruding ends.
- Cut and screw on the 1/4-in. plywood floor.
- Cut 3/8-in. pine partitions and screw them behind the side slats to create custom-width pockets for the tools.

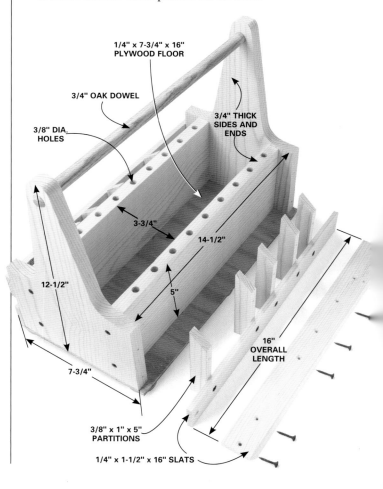

1/4" x 7-3/4" x 16"
PLYWOOD FLOOR

3/4" OAK DOWEL

3/8" DIA.
HOLES

3/4" THICK
SIDES AND
ENDS

3-3/4"

14-1/2"

12-1/2"

5"

7-3/4"

16"
OVERALL
LENGTH

3/8" x 1" x 5"
PARTITIONS

1/4" x 1-1/2" x 16" SLATS

Mobile tool chest

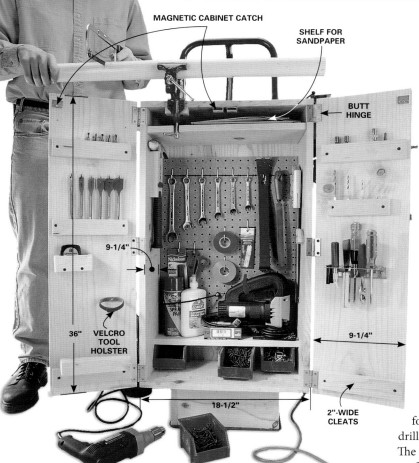

MAGNETIC CABINET CATCH

SHELF FOR SANDPAPER

BUTT HINGE

9-1/4"

36"

VELCRO TOOL HOLSTER

9-1/4"

18-1/2"

2"-WIDE CLEATS

Build this mobile tool chest and take all your tools to the job in just one trip. All you need is a new dolly and some pine boards. If you use 1x10 pine boards, you won't need to cut any boards to width.

Screw the cabinet together with 1-5/8-in. drywall screws after drilling pilot holes. Clamp on the plywood back, check for square, then screw it to the sides, top and floor with 1-5/8-in. drywall screws. Attach the doors with 2-1/2-in. butt hinges.

Pine boards tend to warp, so to keep the doors flat, screw several 2-in.-wide cleats across the inside. The cleats can be drilled to double as great drill and driver bit holders.

To raise the cabinet to a more comfortable height, screw four scrap boards into a frame and attach this base to the dolly's base with lag screws. Next drill holes in the base, then rest the cabinet on the base and attach it with 1-5/8-in. drywall screws through the floor into the base. To attach the upper part of the cabinet to the dolly, drive two 5/16-in.-diameter bolts through a board positioned behind the dolly's frame and into two 5/16-in. tee nuts set in the cabinet back. If this won't work for your dolly or design, use metal strapping or drill a couple of bolt holes through the dolly.

The cabinet's 9-1/4 in. depth provides plenty of space for power and hand tools plus full sheets of sandpaper. Have fun engineering convenient holders for your tools using pegboard, magnets, hooks and shop-fashioned holsters. Be sure to securely store tools so they won't fall or roll around as you cruise to and from the job.

WHAT IT TAKES

TIME: 1 day

SKILL: Beginner to intermediate

Materials List

ITEM	QTY.
36-in.-long 1x10 pine boards (actually 3/4 in. x 9-1/4 in.) for the doors and sides	4
18-1/2-in.-long 1x10 pine boards for the cabinet top and floor	2
18-1/2-in. x 36-in. piece of 1/2-in.-thick plywood for the back	1
Scrap boards for a base	
Assorted fasteners	

BARREL BOLT LATCH

BASE

EXTENSION CORD ABOARD

ATTACH CABINET TO DOLLY WITH 5/16" BOLTS

MOUNTING BOARD

Hardware organizer

Flexible, portable—and possibly free!

DIY isn't just about building and fixing things. It's also about inventory management: maintaining a supply of the stuff you need and knowing where to find it. This simple bin system is the perfect project to get you organized. It's modeled on the systems used in cabinet shops, plumbers' vans and mechanics' garages.

French cleats make it neat. This simple hanging system—made from a 1x4 cut at a 45-degree bevel—lets you grab a bin and take it to the job, or rearrange bins instantly as your needs change.

The materials cost for the bins shown here will depend on the type of plywood you choose. A store-bought light-duty system would cost just a few bucks more, but these homemade bins offer two big advantages: They're far tougher than plastic bins, and you can customize them to suit your stuff. Plus, they make the perfect scrap-wood project because all the parts are small. We built these bins from leftovers and didn't spend a dime.

Mass-produce parts

Begin by measuring the items you want to store. We found that the basic bin (see Figure A) was just right for most stuff: nuts and bolts, construction screws, plumbing and electrical parts. For larger items, we made a few bins wider, but didn't change the bin sides (A). That approach is the most efficient because the sides are the most complex parts and changing them requires more fuss.

Once you've determined the sizes you want, fire up your table saw and rip plywood into strips. If you're following our plan, you'll need strips 1-3/4, 3-1/2 and 6 in. wide. Then cut the strips to length, making parts for one box only. Test-assemble the box to check the fit of

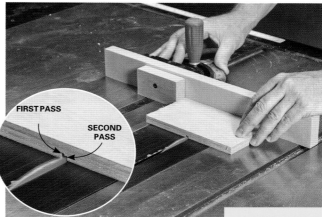

1 Cut the parts. Rip strips of plywood to width on a table saw, then cut them to length with a miter saw. Clamp a scrap of plywood to the saw's fence to act as a stop block. That lets you cut identical lengths from several strips with one chop.

2 Cut divider slots. Mount a fence on your saw's miter gauge and position a stop block on the fence. Run the bin side across the blade. Then rotate the side 180 degrees and make a second pass to widen the slot.

FIRST PASS

SECOND PASS

CAUTION: You have to remove the guard for this step. Be extra careful!

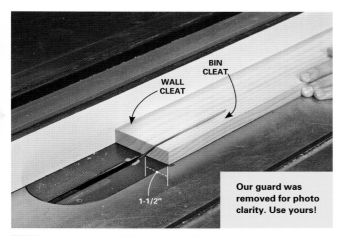

WALL CLEAT

BIN CLEAT

1-1/2"

Our guard was removed for photo clarity. Use yours!

3 Cut the cleats. Tilt the blade to 45 degrees and set the fence so that the bin cleat is 1-1/2 in. wide. Getting the fence positioned may take some trial and error, so cut a test scrap first.

4 Assemble the bins. Join the parts with glue and brads. The glue will provide plenty of strength, so drive only as many brads as needed to hold the parts together while the glue sets.

the parts. **Note:** "Half-inch" plywood is slightly less than 1/2 in. thick, so the bin bottom (B) needs to be slightly longer than 6 in. Start at 6-1/8 in., then trim as needed. When you've confirmed that all the parts are the right size, mass-produce them by chopping the strips to length (Photo 1).

If you want dividers (E) in any of the bins, your next step is to cut the divider slots. Set your table saw blade to a height of 3/16 in. Screw a long fence to your miter gauge and run the fence across the blade to cut a notch on the fence. Position a stop block 3-1/4 in. from the center of the notch. Place a side (A) against the block, run it across the blade,

rotate it and cut again (Photo 2). Check the fit of a divider in the slot and reposition the block slightly to adjust the width of the slot. It may take two or three tries before you get the width right.

Materials List

To build an organizer similar to the one shown, you'll need:

ITEM	QTY.
4' x 8' x 1/2" plywood	1
2' x 4' x 1/8" hardboard	1
1x4 x 8' pine	3
1" brads, 2-1/2" screws, wood glue and Danish oil	

Cutting List

KEY	QTY.	SIZE & DESCRIPTION
A	2	3-1/2" x 6-1/2" (sides)
B	1	4" x 6" (bottom)
C	1	3-1/2" x 4" (back)
D	1	1-3/4" x 5" (front)
E	1	3" x 4-5/16" (divider)
F	1	3/4" x 1-1/2" x 5" (cleat)

Dividers are hardboard. Cleats are pine. All other parts are plywood.

When you're done cutting slots, it's time to clip off one corner of each side. Set your miter saw 45 degrees to the right. Clamp on a stop block and "gang-cut" sides just as you did when cutting

Mount the wall cleats. Mark the stud locations with tape and screw on the lowest cleat. Then work your way up the wall, using spacers to position each cleat.

parts to length (similar to Photo 1). Remember this: Slotted sides require left/right pairs. For every side that you cut with the slot facing up, cut another with the slot down.

Next, cut the cleats (Photo 3). The 45-degree bevel cuts will leave sharp, splintery edges, so crank the table saw blade back to zero degrees and shave 1/8 in. off each cleat before cutting them to length.

Assemble them and hang them up

Assembly is fast and easy with glue and an 18-gauge brad nailer. First, tack the back (C) to the bottom (B), then add the sides (A), the front (D) and finally the cleat (F). After assembly, we wiped on two coats of penetrating oil finish to keep the wood from absorbing greasy fingerprints and oils from hardware.

When mounting the wall cleats, start at the bottom. Make sure the bottom cleat is level and straight. Then cut spacers at least 1-3/4 in. tall and use them to position the remaining wall cleats (Photo 5). Larger cleats will create more space between rows of bins, making it easier to reach in and grab stuff. Bins filled with hardware put a heavy load on the cleats, so drive a screw into every wall stud.

Figure A
Basic bin

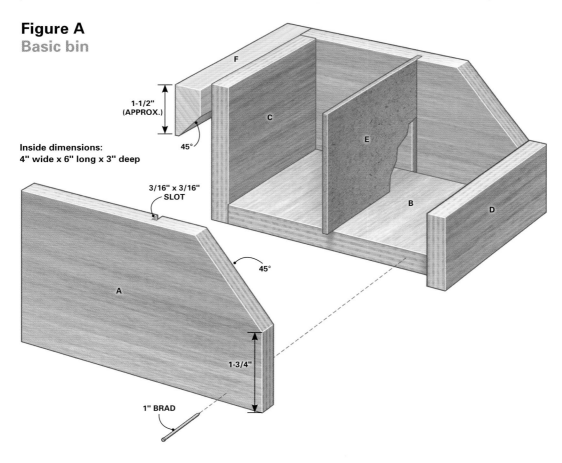

1-1/2" (APPROX.)

45°

Inside dimensions:
4" wide x 6" long x 3" deep

3/16" x 3/16" SLOT

1-3/4"

1" BRAD

Quick projects for beginners

Chisel pockets

Here's a neat tabletop chisel storage idea that's a snap to build from scrap boards. It angles the handles toward you for easy reach.

Start with a 4-in.-wide board. Using your table saw, cut stopped slots to match the width and depth of each chisel (plus some wiggle room). Screw or glue on another board to create the pockets, then run the lower edge of the doubled board through a table saw with the blade set at 15 degrees. Now cut three triangular legs with 75-degree bottom corners and glue them to the pocket board.

If you like, drill a few holes through the boards for pegboard hooks so the holder is easy to store on the wall.

75°

VARIED WIDTH SLOTS FOR CHISELS

3-1/2" TO 4"

Shop-made parts boxes

Have you priced those plastic parts bins? Too expensive! Instead, make your own out of scrap. The trick is to keep them modular. Make the front, back and bottom from 3/4- or 1/2-in. material, and the sides from 1/4-in. plywood. Nailed and glued together, they're plenty tough. The ones shown here are 12 in. front to back (to fit in old kitchen upper cabinets), 3 in. tall, and either 3-1/2 in. or 7 in. wide. Save up some scrap and you can make a couple dozen in an hour or so.

Tape caddy

Keep your tape rolls in one place and easy to use with this plywood dispenser. When you run out of tape, just lift the dowel out of the notches, reload and slide it back in the notches. You'll need:

- Two 5-in. x 6-in. side pieces of 3/4-in. plywood
- One 5-in. x 12-in. plywood base
- One 1-in. x 13-1/2-in. hacksaw blade support
- One 14-in. x 1-1/2-in.-diameter dowel rod
- An 18-tooth, 12-in. hacksaw blade

Notch the sides to the dimensions shown and screw them to the base, along with the hacksaw blade support.

Saw the dowel ends to fit in the notched sides and screw the hacksaw blade on the support, positioning it so the saw teeth extend a little beyond the edge of the plywood. That's it. Load up with tape and you'll never go hunting for stray rolls again.

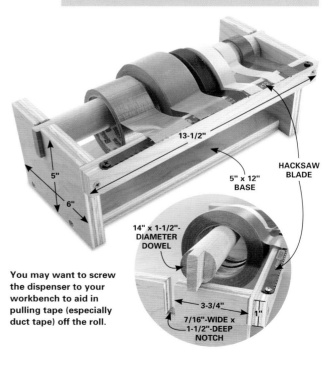

13-1/2"

5"

6"

5" x 12" BASE

HACKSAW BLADE

14" x 1-1/2"-DIAMETER DOWEL

You may want to screw the dispenser to your workbench to aid in pulling tape (especially duct tape) off the roll.

3-3/4"

1"

7/16"-WIDE x 1-1/2"-DEEP NOTCH

Build a cutting grid 113
Hinged sawhorses 114
Channels add versatility to sawhorses 115
Basic bench and miter saw table................................ 116
Quick projects for beginners...........................117
Stackable sawhorses 119

7 SAWHORSES & STANDS

Build a cutting grid

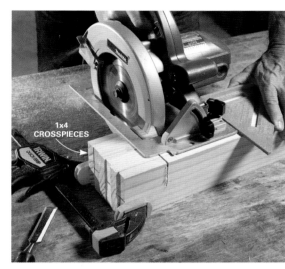

1x4 CROSSPIECES

You can lay a few 2x4s across a pair of horses, but that's not as good as a grid, especially if you're cutting flimsy or small stuff.

For this version, you'll need five knot-free oak or pine 1x4s, 8 ft. long. The secret to building it: Clamp the crosspieces together and "gang-cut" the notches (photo, top right). Do the same for the stretchers. Don't fasten the grid parts with glue or screws. Slip them together so they can be disassembled for easy storage.

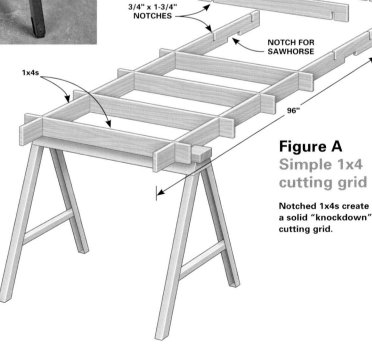

40"

3/4" x 1-3/4" NOTCHES

NOTCH FOR SAWHORSE

1x4s

96"

Figure A
Simple 1x4 cutting grid

Notched 1x4s create a solid "knockdown" cutting grid.

Hinged sawhorses

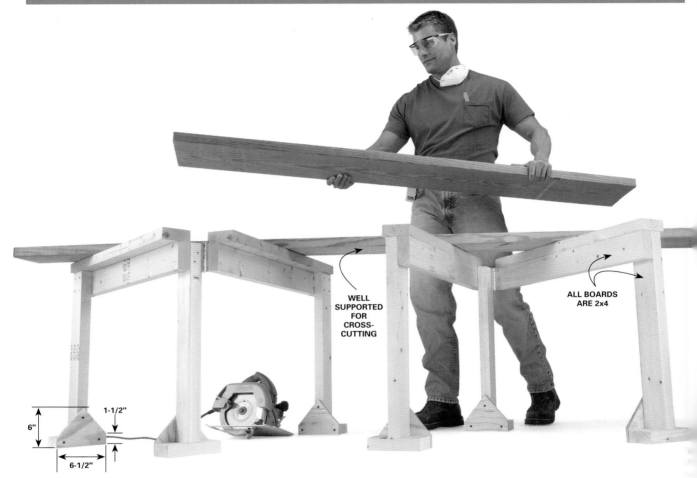

WELL SUPPORTED FOR CROSS-CUTTING

ALL BOARDS ARE 2x4

6"

1-1/2"

6-1/2"

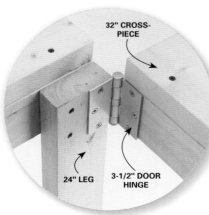

32" CROSS-PIECE

24" LEG

3-1/2" DOOR HINGE

Want more versatility than standard sawhorses can deliver? With these, you can support both long and short lumber at the same time or large sheets of plywood. When you're done, just fold them up for storage.

To build these sawhorses, you'll need five 8-ft. 2x4s, a couple of pieces of scrap 1/2-in. plywood, 2-1/2 in. and 1-5/8 in. drywall screws, and a pair of 3-1/2 in. door hinges.

First, cut the 2x4s into eight 32-in. crosspieces, six 24-in. legs and six 6-1/2 in. pieces for the feet. Cut six triangles from the plywood, making them 6-1/2 in. on two sides.

Next, screw the horizontal pieces into two angle iron–shaped crosspieces, then screw a leg on each end of two crosspieces, positioning the legs on opposite sides so the two crosspieces will meet edge to edge when closed. Finally, screw one leg on the remaining crosspieces, then screw on the feet and triangles and attach the crosspieces with the hinges. That's it. Now you can saw, sand or rout those unwieldy workpieces in comfort.

WHAT IT TAKES

TIME: 1/2 day
SKILL: Beginner

Channels add versatility to sawhorses

You gotta screw lumber to the top of a folding metal sawhorse anyway, so why not build a simple channel and turn your horse into a multi-trick pony?

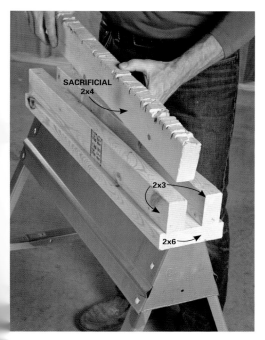

For normal use, keep a "sacrificial" 2x4 in the slot. When it gets too "kerfed up," flip it over and use the opposite edge until it's time to replace the whole thing. Drop a longer 2x4 into the channel to support bigger projects. Change working heights by simply slipping a different-size board—a 2x4, 2x6, 2x8, 2x10 or 2x12—into the channel.

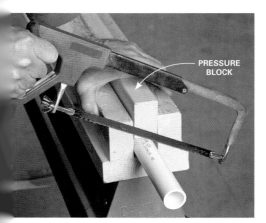

Hold round or small items while cutting. A 2x3 "pressure block" locks your work in place while the square end of the channel guides your saw and gives you a square cut.

Create an instant work support for your miter saw or an outfeed table for your table saw. To get the height right, just slip in a board of the correct width.

Basic bench and miter saw table

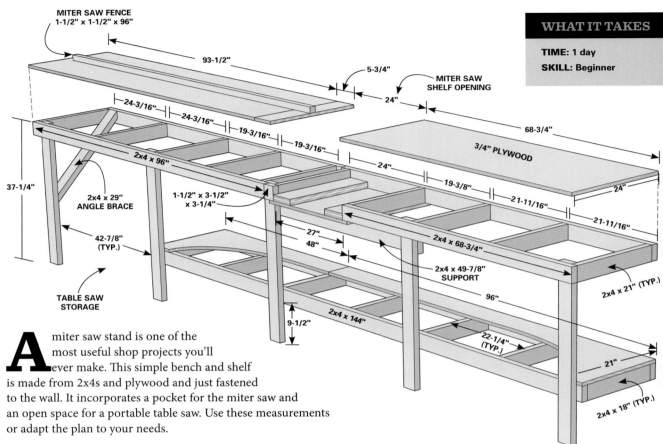

MITER SAW FENCE
1-1/2" x 1-1/2" x 96"

93-1/2"

5-3/4"

MITER SAW
SHELF OPENING

24"

24-3/16"

24-3/16"

19-3/16"

19-3/16"

2x4 x 96"

68-3/4"

3/4" PLYWOOD

37-1/4"

2x4 x 29"
ANGLE BRACE

1-1/2" x 3-1/2"
x 3-1/4"

24"

19-3/8"

21-11/16"

24"

21-11/16"

42-7/8"
(TYP.)

27"
48"

2x4 x 68-3/4"

2x4 x 49-7/8"
SUPPORT

2x4 x 21" (TYP.)

TABLE SAW
STORAGE

9-1/2"

2x4 x 144"

96"

22-1/4"
(TYP.)

21"

2x4 x 18" (TYP.)

A miter saw stand is one of the most useful shop projects you'll ever make. This simple bench and shelf is made from 2x4s and plywood and just fastened to the wall. It incorporates a pocket for the miter saw and an open space for a portable table saw. Use these measurements or adapt the plan to your needs.

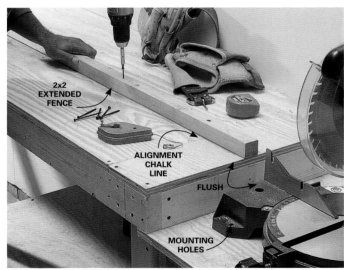

2x2
EXTENDED
FENCE

ALIGNMENT
CHALK
LINE

FLUSH

MOUNTING
HOLES

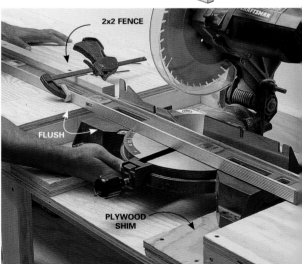

2x2 FENCE

FLUSH

PLYWOOD
SHIM

1 After building the frame, place the miter saw in its permanent position and measure the distance from the front of the fence to the wall. Measure and mark that distance from the wall and snap a chalk line on the left table to align the extended fence. Screw an 8-ft. long 2x2 into every 2x4 crosspiece with 3-in. screws, holding the right end even with the edge of the miter saw bay.

2 Cut wood shims to bring the miter saw table up flush with the bench top. Use a straightedge to line up the miter saw fence with the extended fence. Then mark the locations of the miter saw mounting holes and drill 5/32-in. pilot holes. Set the saw with two 3-in. x 1/4-in. lag screws with washers.

Quick projects for beginners

Multipurpose T-bars

These are wonderfully simple, versatile shop aids. Use them to raise a project off the bench for clamping, or clamp or even screw parts to them to keep things flat. You can make these from 5-in.-wide strips, with a double thickness on the upright. A little masking tape on the top edge makes them easy on finished surfaces and keeps glue from sticking.

Clamp holders

Anything that gives you more control when gluing is a good thing. These simple-to-build clamp bars, made of 2x4s, will keep clamps from tipping, and can be set up on a couple of sawhorses to free up space on your bench. Screw the two 2x4s together so you can cut the notches on both at the same time.

CLAMP BAR

World's handiest "bench"

This cool little bench can be used to stand on, cut on, store tools in and, of course, to sit on during lunch! It's built from 3/4-in. plywood and the bench only takes a couple of hours to cobble together. Give it a whirl; you'll use it more than you think.

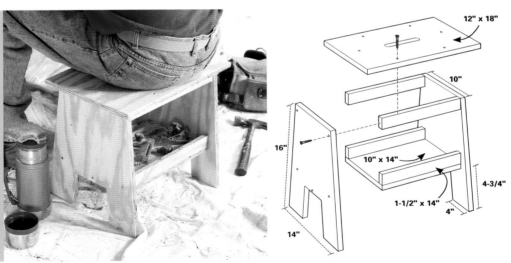

12" x 18"

10"

16"

10" x 14"

1-1/2" x 14"

4-3/4"

4"

14"

NOTCH

Instant stand and outfeed

With a few minutes, a couple of 2x4s, a slab of plywood and a pair of sawhorses, you can build a stand for a benchtop saw, plus a long outfeed table. On the version shown here, the 2x4s are notched so that the saw table is flush with the plywood. Screw the plywood to the 2x4s and the 2x4s to the horses. Also screw or clamp the saw to the 2x4s.

Finishing stand-offs

These simple little contraptions are immensely useful for staining and finishing. Make them from scrap, but be careful to countersink all the screws to the same depth so their points all protrude the same length. For many projects, you can stain or finish both sides at once. The little mark left by the screw tip won't be detectable.

Ladder caddy

For some projects, you need to constantly switch between tools. If you're tired of changing back and forth and running up and down the ladder, try this caddy. Find a scrap of 3/4-in. plywood (10 in. x 24 in.) and cut an opening in it to fit over the stepladder (7 in. x 14 in.). Then make cutouts to hold a drill and a driver or whatever tools you use. Wedge a scrap piece of 2x4 between the ladder top and the holder to stabilize it when one tool is in use.

Stackable sawhorses

These sawhorses are strong, yet they stack compactly. Build them from construction-grade 1x4s (for the legs) and 1x6s (for the top), glue and a handful of screws.

The legs are 32 in. long, which puts the horse height at about 30 in., the height of a standard table. Adjust the leg length to your own comfort level. The top 1x6 is 32 in. long, but again, adjust its length to fit your needs.

The trickiest part is cutting the sharp (15-degree) angle on the top of each leg. The best method is to clamp at least four 1x4s together and cut them on edge (Photo 1). Mark the cutting line on all sides because you have to flip the 1x4s over to complete the cut. A standard Speed Square has angle marks that'll help you measure the 15 degrees. Then cut the legs to length at a 75-degree angle (15-degree saw setting) so they rest flat on the floor.

If you don't have a table saw, screw the cleat stock to your workbench using spacers (Photo 2). That'll keep the piece stable while you cut the angles with a circular saw. Note that the narrow side of the cleat is 2-1/8 in. wide. Make sure the legs are perpendicular to the 1x6 when you assemble them (Photo 3).

1 Clamp four 1x4s together, mark the 15-degree angle along their edges and cut them all at once. Flip the bundle over and finish the cut from the opposite side.

2 Temporarily screw a 1x4 to your workbench and mark the cleat cuts. Set your saw to 15 degrees and cut the angles. Unscrew the board and cut off 5-in.-long cleats.

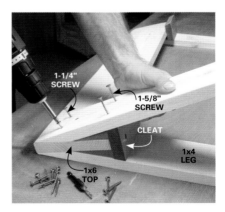

3 Center and screw the cleats to the 1x6. Predrill, then spread glue and screw the legs to the 1x6 and cleats. Keep the edges flush.

Quick router jigs for beginners...................................... 121
A classic workbench 122
Instant workbench 127
Build a rolling shop cart.. 128
One-day workbench... 130
Magic miter sled 134
Workshop stool 137
Easiest add-on drawers 138
Table saw guide box 139
Floor lamp for the shop.. 139

8 WORKBENCHES & WOODWORKING EQUIPMENT

120

Quick router jigs for beginners

Jig for routing dadoes

When you build a cabinet, it's a good idea to use dadoes to ensure that shelves and partitions are spaced correctly. To make a strong joint, the width of the dadoes must exactly match the thickness of the plywood. That can be a challenge because few pieces of plywood are precisely 3/4 in. thick. They're usually 1/32 in. or so less than the "nominal" thickness. We designed this jig to rout perfect-fitting dadoes for any piece of 3/4-in. plywood regardless of its actual thickness.

We use a special top-bearing trim router bit (shown below) with the jig. The bit is 1/2 in. wide, 1/2 in. long and has a bearing mounted above the cutter. The bearing is flush with the bit's cutting edges.

TOP-BEARING BIT

The routing jig has two long, parallel guides made from 1/2-in. MDF. When you rout the dado, ride the bearing along one guide, then make a second, return pass and ride the bearing along the second guide. This way, the space between the guides determines the width of the dado.

Setting up the guides is easy. One guide is fixed to the jig's 3/4-in. cross members; the other is loose and adjustable. Take two small pieces of the plywood you're using and place them against the fixed guide. Then slide the adjustable guide against the pieces and clamp the guide to the cross members. Done!

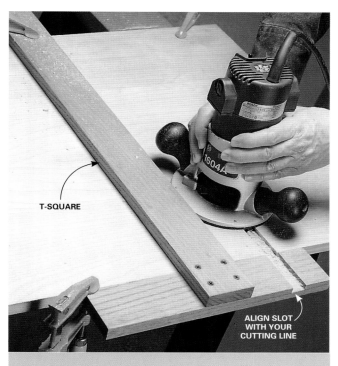

T-SQUARE

ALIGN SLOT WITH YOUR CUTTING LINE

T-square router fence

If you need to cut dadoes or grooves across the sides of a cabinet, this tool is the way to go. Build the T-square for one particular router and one particular bit, and test it on a scrap. Once the "head" of the T-square has been cut, you can use that cut to perfectly position the rest of the cuts.

1 **Perfect dadoes made easy.** Use this jig to rout a dado that perfectly fits any piece of 3/4-in. plywood. Take two passes with a 1/2-in. top-bearing bit.

OFFCUT

2 **Goof-proof setup.** Set up the jig using scrap pieces of your plywood to space the guides. It's foolproof!

A classic workbench

A *timeless design that's* simple and strong

If this workbench looks familiar, it's probably because you've seen one a lot like it in your father's or grandfather's shop. Variations of this design have been around for decades, and for good reason: The bench is strong, practical and super easy to build. You can run to the lumberyard in the morning, grab a few boards, and by noon you'll have a perfectly functional workbench.

The workbench isn't fancy—it's built from standard construction lumber. But you can easily customize it with drawers or other features now or later.

If you can cut a board, you can build this bench. And you don't need any fancy tools either. In addition to a small square and a tape measure, you'll need a circular saw to cut the parts and a drill to drive the screws.

WHAT IT TAKES

TIME: 1 day
SKILL LEVEL: Beginner

Getting started

You'll find all the materials at a lumberyard or home center (see Materials List on p. 122). Choose lumber that's straight and flat, and that doesn't have too many gouges, slivers or cracks. We used Torx-head screws with self-drilling tips. But you can substitute any construction screw. If you're not using screws with self-drilling tips, drill pilot holes to avoid splitting the wood.

> **Tip:** If your car is too small for the long boards, you can ask to have the boards cut to length. Just remember to take the Cutting List with you to the store.

Cut the parts according to the Cutting List on p. 123. We used a miter saw, but a circular saw will work fine. Mark the 2x4s with a Speed square or combination square. Then carefully cut the boards to length. If you plan to stain or paint the bench, now is the time to sand the parts. And to really simplify your job, you could also stain or paint the parts before you assemble the bench.

Start by building the top and shelf frames

We used an old door propped up on sawhorses as a work surface, but the floor will work too. Lay the 2x4s for the front and back of the top and shelf on the work surface and mark the centers. Remember, if you're not using self-drilling screws, drill pilot holes for the screws. Photo 1 shows how to assemble the frames. Set the top frame aside and screw the shelf boards to the shelf frame (Photo 2).

Build and attach the leg assemblies

Photo 3 shows how to build the leg assemblies. You'll notice that the leg assemblies are 1/8 in. narrower than the inside dimension of the top. That's so you can install the legs without binding, which would cause the pegboard to bow. Also, if the only pegboard you can find is thinner than the 1/4-in. pegboard specified, add the difference to the front

1 **Build the frames.** Use 3-in. screws to assemble the frames that support the top and the shelf. To avoid splitting the 2x4s, either drill pilot holes or use self-drilling screws. Build both frames and set the top frame aside.

2 **Attach the shelf boards.** Attach the outside boards first. Then position the two remaining boards to create equal spaces between them and screw them to the frame. Before driving screws, drill pilot holes with a countersink bit.

3 **Assemble the legs.** Drill five holes about 2 in. from the edge of the pegboard with the countersinking bit. Spread a bead of construction adhesive on the legs and attach the pegboard with 1-1/4-in. screws. If glue oozes through the holes, wait for it to dry. Then shave it off with a sharp chisel.

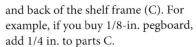
TOP FRAME

4 **Screw the legs to the top frame.** Apply construction adhesive where the legs contact the top frame. Then attach the legs with screws.

SHELF

BOTTOM OF PEGBOARD

5 **Add the shelf.** Rest the bench on one end. Slide the shelf between the legs and line it up with the bottom of the pegboard. Screw through the shelf into the legs.

TRIM SCREW

2" OVERHANG

6 **Mount the top boards.** Starting at the back, align the first 2x6 flush to the back and measure for the 2-in. overhang on the side. Attach the 2x6 with trim screws. Attach the rest of the boards the same way. The front 2x6 will overhang the frame about 2 in.

7 **Install the backboard.** Attach the 1x4 shelf to the 1x10 backboard. Then add a 2x4 block at each end. Rest the backboard assembly on the workbench and drive screws through the back to hold it in place.

and back of the shelf frame (C). For example, if you buy 1/8-in. pegboard, add 1/4 in. to parts C.

The pegboard is useful for hanging tools, but its real function is to stabilize the workbench as a brace. We added the construction adhesive to make sure the assemblies stayed strong and rigid. Be aware, though, that some of the adhesive will be visible through the holes.

The pegboard holes are a little too big to use as screw holes, so use a No. 6 countersink bit to drill pilot holes and make countersinks for the screws. Secure five evenly spaced 1-1/4-in. screws into each leg.

The next step is to attach the legs to the top frame. Apply construction adhesive to the top 3 in. of the legs. Then attach the leg assemblies with 3-in. screws (Photo 4).

Add the shelf and top

Stand the workbench on one end. Then it's simple to slide the shelf into place and line it up with the pegboard (Photo 5). Drive 3-in. screws through the shelf frame into the legs to support the shelf.

The top of this bench is 2x6s, placed tight together. The boards overhang the frame 2 in. on the sides and front. The overhang makes it easier to use clamps on the edges of the workbench. Photo 6 shows how to get started. We attached the 2x6s with trim screws, but you could substitute 16d casing nails.

Materials List

ITEM	QTY.
2x4 x 8' pine	6
2x6 x 10' pine	2
2x6 x 8' pine	1
1x10 x 10' pine	1
1x6 x 10' pine	2
1x4 x 6' pine	1
2' x 4' x 1/4" pegboard	1
3" self-drilling screws	42
2" self-drilling screws	50
1-1/4" self-drilling screws	20
2-1/2" trim screws	30
Tube of construction adhesive	1

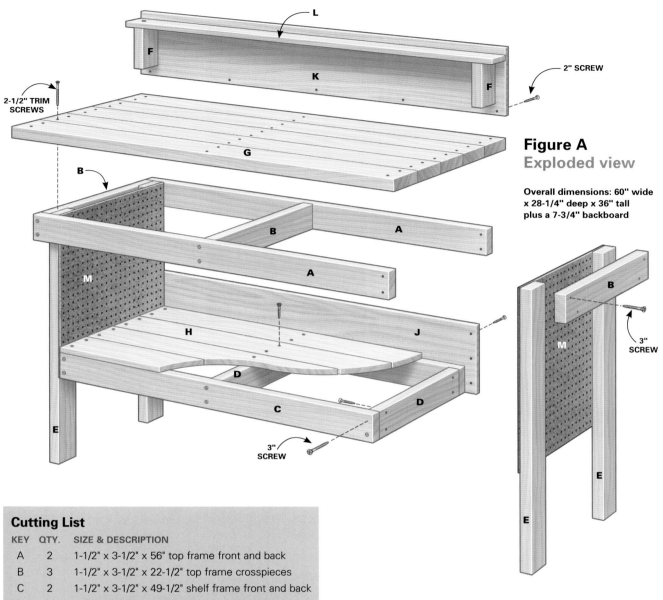

Figure A
Exploded view

**Overall dimensions: 60" wide
x 28-1/4" deep x 36" tall
plus a 7-3/4" backboard**

2-1/2" TRIM
SCREWS

2" SCREW

3"
SCREW

3"
SCREW

L

F

F

K

G

B

M

A

B

A

H

J

D

D

C

E

B

M

E

E

E

Cutting List

KEY	QTY.	SIZE & DESCRIPTION
A	2	1-1/2" x 3-1/2" x 56" top frame front and back
B	3	1-1/2" x 3-1/2" x 22-1/2" top frame crosspieces
C	2	1-1/2" x 3-1/2" x 49-1/2" shelf frame front and back
D	3	1-1/2" x 3-1/2" x 19-1/2" shelf crosspieces
E	4	1-1/2" x 3-1/2" x 34-1/2" legs
F	2	1-1/2" x 3-1/2" x 6" back shelf supports
G	5	1-1/2" x 5-1/2" x 60" top boards
H	4	3/4" x 5-1/2" x 49-1/2" shelf boards
J	1	3/4" x 9-1/4" x 53" back brace
K	1	3/4" x 9-1/4" x 60" backboard
L	1	3/4" x 3-1/2" x 60" backboard shelf
M	2	22-3/8" x 22-3/8" x 1/4" pegboard leg braces

Attach the back brace and backboard

The 1x10 back brace keeps things from falling off the back of the shelf, but it also stiffens the bench to prevent side-to-side rocking. Apply construction adhesive before attaching the brace with 2-in. screws.

The backboard is a 1x10 with a 1x4 shelf attached. On the side of the 1x10 you want facing out, draw a line the length of the board, 1-3/4 in. down from the top. This is where you'll align the bottom of the 1x4. Draw a second line 1-3/8 in. from the top. Drill pilot holes with the countersink bit every 8 in. along this line. Now ask a helper to hold the 1x4 on the line while you drive 2-in. screws into the shelf through the pilot holes. After the shelf and 2x4 blocks at each end are attached, screw the backboard to the workbench (Photo 7).

You can modify your bench to fit your space and work style. We mounted an inexpensive woodworking vise on the front of the workbench and drilled holes in the 1x4 shelf to hold screwdrivers. If you've got a pint-size carpenter in the family, check out the mini version of the bench on p. 124. It would make a great project to build with your kids or grandkids.

Mini-classic for mini DIYers

Here's a plan for a downsized version of the workbench. All of the construction steps are the same; it's just smaller to fit the young carpenter in your family. The height is about right for a 42- to 48-in.-tall DIYer, but you can easily increase the height just by making the legs longer.

Materials List
(small workbench)

ITEM	QTY.
2x4 x 8' pine	4
2x6 x 8' pine	2
1x8 x 8' pine	1
1x6 x 10' pine	1
1x4 x 4' pine	1
2' x 4' x 1/4" pegboard	1
3" self-drilling screws	42
2" self-drilling screws	40
1-1/4" self-drilling screws	16
2-1/2" trim screws	24
Tube of construction adhesive	1

Cutting List
(small workbench)

KEY	QTY.	SIZE & DESCRIPTION
A	2	1-1/2" x 3-1/2" x 45" top frame front and back
B	3	1-1/2" x 3-1/2" x 17-1/2" top frame crosspieces
C	2	1-1/2" x 3-1/2" x 38-1/2" shelf frame front and back
D	3	1-1/2" x 3-1/2" x 14-1/2" shelf crosspieces
E	4	1-1/2" x 3-1/2" x 22-1/2" legs
F	2	1-1/2" x 3-1/2" x 4" back shelf supports
G	4	1-1/2" x 5-1/2" x 48" top boards
H	3	3/4" x 5-1/2" x 38-1/2" shelf boards
J	1	3/4" x 7-1/4" x 42" back brace
K	1	3/4" x 7-1/4" x 48" backboard
L	1	3/4" x 3-1/2" x 48" backboard shelf
M	2	17-3/8" x 17-3/8" x 1/4" pegboard leg braces

Figure B Small bench

Overall dimensions: 48" wide x 22-3/4" deep x 24" tall plus a 5-3/4" backboard

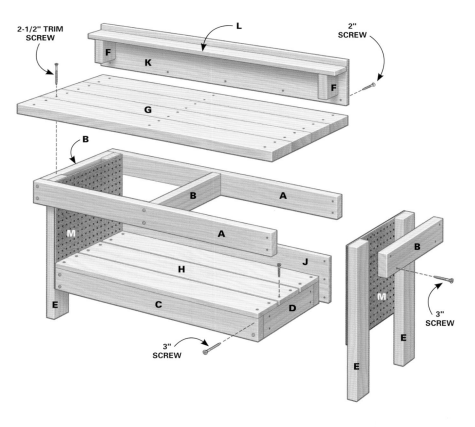

Instant workbench

G o on, take an hour to build this sturdy, simple workbench from a single sheet of 3/4-in. plywood. Then spend only a couple of seconds tapping it together whenever you need it. It can hold heavy power tools, large project assemblies or even that old outboard motor you're overhauling.

Saw 4-in. x 3/4-in. notches in the legs and stretchers, spacing them 3 in. in from the edge on the legs and 4 in. in from the ends on the stretchers. Tap them together to create an interlocked base. Lay the top upside down on the floor, then position the base so the top overhangs all four sides equally. Screw cleats on the top so they will fit just inside the base. Position them slightly away from the base to make assembly easy. Stand everything right side up and put your instant workbench to work!

Cutting List

QTY.	ITEM
2	38" x 8" stretchers
2	27-1/2" x 23" legs
1	48" x 30" top
2	26" x 3/4" x 3/4" side cleats
2	12" x 3/4" x 3/4" end cleats

WHAT IT TAKES

TIME: 1–2 hours
SKILL LEVEL: Beginner

8"
4"
4"
STRETCHER
38" x 8"
4"
3"
LEG
27-1/2" x 23"
3/4" THICKNESS

TOP
48" x 30"
CLEATS

Build a rolling shop cart

Whether your shop is big or small, it's sure handy to have a cart or two for moving stacks of parts from planer to table saw to drill press to sander, and on and on.

Constructing this cart is simple—all the parts are just glued and screwed or nailed together. You'll need one full sheet of 3/4-in. plywood and a box of 1-1/4-in. screws.

You can use the cart to support table saw work, so build it the same height as your saw. Buy the casters for your cart before cutting any parts to size. (We recommend using casters that are at least 2-1/2 in. in diameter.) Then measure the total height of one caster and alter the lengths of the cart's legs as needed.

We've laid out the parts so you can crosscut your plywood into three 32-in. pieces before having to cut anything to exact size. It's OK if these crosscuts are rough; a jigsaw or circular saw would work fine. After this, it's best to use a table saw for ripping the parts and a miter saw or table saw for cutting them to length.

After breaking down the plywood into manageable sizes, cut all the leg pieces (A and B). Glue them together, using nails or screws to hold them together while the glue dries. Make sure their ends are even.

Cut the parts for the upper and lower boxes (C, D, E and F) and glue and screw them together. Next, cut the shelf and bottom (G) to fit the boxes and glue and screw these pieces into place. (Adding a bottom to the upper box makes it easier to clamp things to the top of the cart. Without a bottom, you'd only have a narrow 3/4-in. edge to clamp to.) Make sure the shelf and bottom don't overhang each box or the legs won't fit correctly. To avoid any overhang, you could cut the shelf and bottom 1/16 in. smaller all around.

Fasten the legs to the boxes, using three screws at each corner. Finally, cut the caster supports (H) and top (J) to size and add them to the cart. Fasten the casters using 3/4-in. No. 14 sheet metal screws.

Figure A
Rolling shop cart

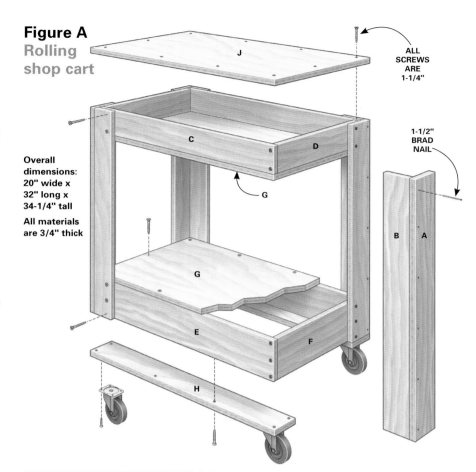

ALL SCREWS ARE 1-1/4"

1-1/2" BRAD NAIL

Overall dimensions:
20" wide x
32" long x
34-1/4" tall

All materials are 3/4" thick

Cutting List

KEY	QTY.	DIMENSIONS	NAME
A	4	3/4" x 4" x 29"	Wide leg pieces
B	4	3/4" x 3-1/4" x 29"	Narrow leg pieces
C	2	3/4" x 3-1/2" x 30-1/2"	Upper box, long sides
D	2	3/4" x 3-1/2" x 17"	Upper box, short sides
E	2	3/4" x 5" x 30-1/2"	Lower box, long sides
F	2	3/4" x 5" x 17"	Lower box, short sides
G	2	3/4" x 18-1/2" x 30-1/2"	Shelf and bottom
H	2	3/4" x 4" x 32"	Caster supports
J	1	3/4" x 20" x 32"	Top

ROUGH CROSSCUTS

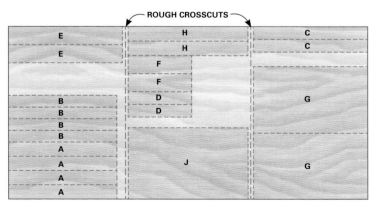

One-day workbench

WHAT IT TAKES

TIME: 1 day
SKILL LEVEL: Beginner
to intermediate

Like a traditional woodworker's bench, this workbench offers a large, rock-solid work surface and plenty of storage space below. But because it's built mostly from ready-made components, constructing this bench doesn't take much time or skill. If you have a little experience with simple hand and power tools, you can complete it in an afternoon.

You'll find everything you need for this project at home centers. You can use any combination of cabinets that add up to a width of less than 80 in. (the length of the door used for the top). Shown here is a 60-in. sink base cabinet and an 18-in. drawer unit. Buy a solid-core door rather than a flimsy hollow-core door for the top. Although the cabinets shown here are oak, a mahogany (lauan) door was used. If you choose

unfinished rather than prefinished cabinets, and construction-grade plywood rather than oak for the back, your cost will be about $400. That's not exactly cheap, but you'd have to spend at least twice as much to buy a workbench of comparable size, storage capacity and durability.

Assemble the base

Set the cabinets on their faces on a drop cloth and cut off the pedestal that forms the toe-kick under the cabinet (Photo 1). Pull the front toe-kick off. Make sure that the cut leaves at least a 3/4-in. space for the 1x4 filler strips that the plywood is attached to so that the weight of the workbench is carried by the sides of the cabinets. We removed the pedestal mostly to

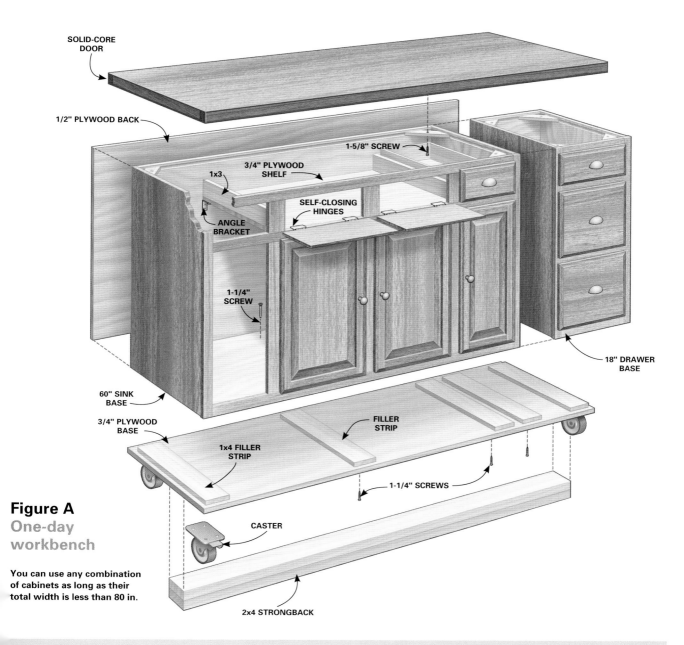

SOLID-CORE DOOR

1/2" PLYWOOD BACK

1-5/8" SCREW

3/4" PLYWOOD SHELF

1x3

SELF-CLOSING HINGES

ANGLE BRACKET

1-1/4" SCREW

18" DRAWER BASE

60" SINK BASE

3/4" PLYWOOD BASE

FILLER STRIP

1x4 FILLER STRIP

1-1/4" SCREWS

Figure A
One-day workbench

You can use any combination of cabinets as long as their total width is less than 80 in.

CASTER

2x4 STRONGBACK

Materials List

ITEM	QTY.	ITEM	QTY.
60" unfinished oak kitchen sink base	1	200-lb.-capacity locking caster wheels	2
18" unfinished oak drawer base	1	Drawer pulls (optional)	11
2' 8" x 6' 8" solid-core door (work top)	1	1-1/4" screws	1 lb.
4' x 8' x 3/4" plywood for base	1	1-5/8" screws	1 lb.
4' x 8' x 1/2" plywood for back	1	1/4" x 1" lag screws (for attaching casters)	16
1x4 x 10' pine for filler strips	1	2-1/2" screws (for joining cabinet stiles)	2
2x4 x 10' stud for strongback	1	No. 8 x 3/4" pan head screws	1 box
200-lb.-capacity caster wheels (3" wheels for a 36-1/4"-high workbench, 4" for 37-1/4")	2	Self-closing cabinet hinges	2 sets
		1-1/2" angle brackets	8

1 Cut the back and sides of the cabinet to remove the pedestal under the cabinet box. Break off the toe-kick beneath the front of the cabinet.

PEDESTAL

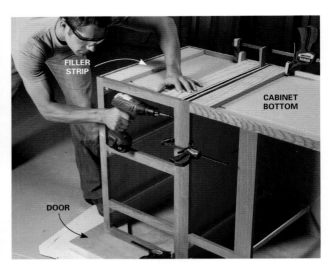

2 Align the cabinets and screw their face frames together. The door you'll use for the top provides a perfectly flat surface to set the cabinets on.

FILLER STRIP

CABINET BOTTOM

DOOR

3 Screw a plywood base to the undersides of the cabinets and add a double 2x4 "strongback" to prevent the workbench from sagging in the middle.

STRONGBACK

4 Glue and screw a plywood back to the cabinets. The back strengthens the workbench and provides a fastener surface for shelves, hooks or other hardware.

5 Fasten the top with screws only—no glue. After years of wear, you can simply flip the top over to get a flawless new work surface.

keep the height of the workbench at about 36 in. You can skip this step if the workbench stays in one place or you don't mind a high workbench.

Lay the door on cardboard or a drop cloth and set the two cabinets upside down on top of it so you can join them on a perfectly flat surface. Shim any low spots under the door so it stays flat. Attach the filler strips under the cabinets, predrilling and screwing up through the base with 1-1/4-in. screws (see Figure A). Align the cabinet stiles, then screw the cabinets together with 2-1/2-in. screws at the top and bottom (Photo 2).

Use a shim and a clamp to hold the cabinet sides parallel (Photo 2). Cut a 3/4-in. plywood base the same length as the assembled cabinets but 1/2 in. wider. Mount the base flush with the front of the cabinets and overhanging the back by 1/2 in. (This provides a lip for the back to rest on.) Predrill and screw on the casters with lag screws 1 in. back from the edges, placing the locking wheels in front. Glue and screw two 2x4s to the plywood behind the farthest turn of the front wheels to keep the center of the workbench from sagging (Photo 3).

Tip the base upright and lock the wheels. Set the plywood back on the base's lip (Photo 4) and fasten it to the cabinets with 3/4-in. pan head screws from inside (cabinets with thicker backs may require a different size screw). The plywood back strengthens the workbench and provides a base for shelving and hooks.

Add the top

Set the solid-core door on top of the base. Center the door from side to side, then leave a 1-1/2-in. overhang in front to create an edge for clamping.

Attach the workbench top at the corner braces as shown in Photo 5. Screw on additional angle brackets to the front and back if needed for more strength.

Sand any rough edges on the door, then add shelves to the sides and back. If you need to compensate for an uneven garage floor, jam shims or wedges under the bench after you roll it into position.

SHELF

SELF-CLOSING HINGE

Save money with a sink cabinet

A 60-in. sink base cabinet was chosen for this project because it cost much less than two 30-in. cabinets. The downside of a sink base is that it has false drawer fronts instead of drawers. To make use of that space, install a shelf in the cabinet and mount the drawer fronts on hinges. This creates a perfect cubbyhole for bar clamps and other long tools. Mark the drawer front positions with tape before you remove the fronts and attach the hinges.

The ideal wheel

Swiveling casters often come with built-in locks. No surprise there, but did you know that there are two different kinds of locks?

A standard lock prevents the wheel from turning but doesn't stop the caster from rotating around its plate or stem. A cart or machine with these casters won't roll away when locked, but it will jiggle when pushed. If you put them on a cabinet supporting a tool, a workbench or anything else that has to lock down solid, you'll be sorely disappointed.

A double lock, shown at left, totally freezes the caster. The wheel won't turn and the caster won't rotate. Put a set of 3-in. double-lock casters on a heavy cabinetmaker's bench, and you'll be very pleased with the results. When you're working, the bench will hardly wiggle at all. Locked, it's stable; unlocked, it's mobile. That's the best of both worlds.

Magic miter sled

A simple jig for your table saw makes miters easy and perfect!

Anybody can cut a 45-degree miter by using a miter saw. But how about cutting eight precise 45-degree miters to create a perfect picture frame? If you've ever tried it, you know that task can be ticklish, frustrating and difficult.

One way to accomplish this seemingly impossible feat is to build a miter sled for your table saw. You can build this simple sled using nothing more than a half sheet of 3/4-in. plywood, particleboard or MDF, a few squirts of wood glue and a couple of full paint cans for glue-up weights. After you throw it together, you'll be cutting perfectly matched miters for frames, furniture or trim in no time, without muss or fuss.

WHAT IT TAKES

TIME: 2 hours, including time standing around waiting for glue to set.

SKILL LEVEL: Intermediate

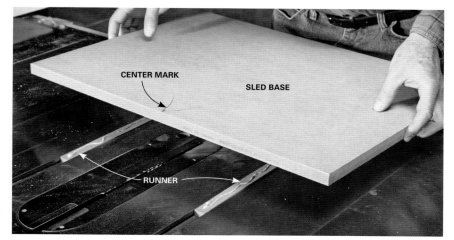

CENTER MARK

SLED BASE

RUNNER

1 **Mount the base on the runners.** Mark the center of the base. Add a thin line of glue to the runners and rest the base on the strips, aligning the center mark with the saw blade. Keep the runners and the miter base flush with the back of the saw table.

MITER GAUGE SLOT

RAFTER SQUARE

2 **Square the base.** Rest two paint cans on the table and use a rafter square and the miter gauge slots to square the miter table to the table saw. Let the glue set up for 20 minutes or so. Then give the sled a test slide. If it binds at all, flip it over, clean off any glue squeeze-out and use a sanding block to knock down the edges of the runners.

How it works

Here's the beauty of the system. We show you how to position the fence so it's very close to perfect. But if it's a little off, the jig is self-correcting. That's because you cut one miter on one side of the jig and its matching miter on the other side. So if your jig cuts at 46 degrees on the first side, it'll cut at 44 degrees on the other. Even though one of the miters will be a little longer than the other, it's easy to sand off the excess so the difference will be imperceptible. But try to build the jig as accurately as you can. This self-correcting business only goes so far!

Safety tip

Try to use your fence whenever you can. We left ours off, mostly for photo clarity. If you simply can't use your fence, the next best thing is to take advantage of the 1-1/2-in.-thick fence by keeping the blade below the top. That way it's impossible to catch your fingers on an exposed blade.

Figure A Miter sled

The sled base is nothing more than a slab of MDF cut into a 24 x 18-in. rectangle as shown. The fence is just a 16 x 16-in. square of MDF. Since the factory corner is 90 degrees, mounting it diagonally gives you accurate 45-degree angles for cutting the miters. After the square is glued on top (Photo 4), cut it in half (Photo 5) and stack the waste on top (Photo 6) so the edge of the fence becomes 1-1/2 in. thick and more suitable for cutting thicker material.

The only tricky part is cutting the runners to a width such that they don't wiggle or bind in the slots, and to a thickness so they project about 1/8 in. above the table (Photo 1). Rip them so they glide smoothly in the slots without binding or slop. Spend time on them. They're one of the main ingredients of an accurate sled.

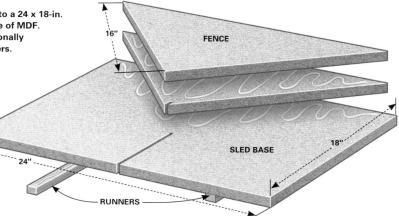

16"

FENCE

24"

18"

SLED BASE

RUNNERS

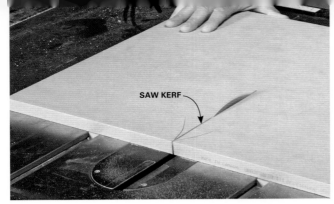

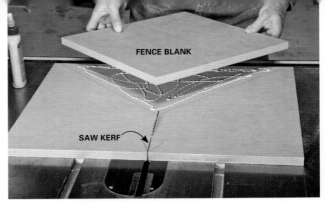

FENCE BLANK

SAW KERF

SAW KERF

3 **Cut a centerline.** Cut a saw kerf about one-third of the way through the miter table. Turn off the saw and let the blade come to a stop. You'll use the kerf to line up the fence for the next step.

4 **Glue on the first fence layer.** Apply some glue to the fence blank and sled base. Line up the tip of the blank with the saw kerf and the two other corners with the back edges of the table. Clamp it in place with a paint can for 15 minutes.

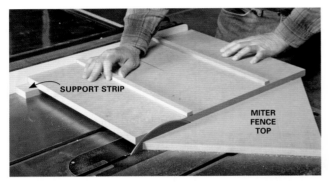

SUPPORT STRIP

MITER FENCE TOP

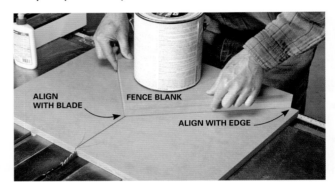

ALIGN WITH BLADE

FENCE BLANK

ALIGN WITH EDGE

5 **Cut off the fence.** Lift the sled out of the miter slots and turn it 90 degrees. Adjust the fence so it cuts off the overhanging fence. Use a strip of waste to support the edge of the sled, and cut off the overhanging triangle.

6 **Top off the fence.** Spread some glue on the fence and square up the edges, holding it down with another gallon can of paint until it sets up. After 15 minutes, you'll be ready to cut a perfect picture frame!

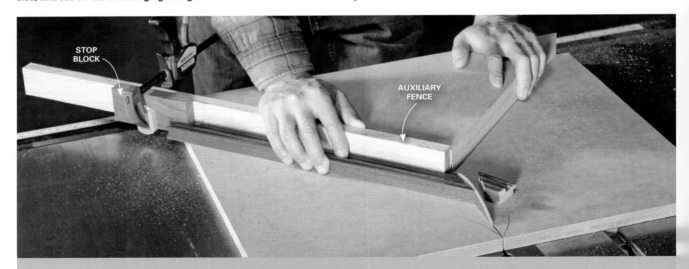

STOP BLOCK

AUXILIARY FENCE

Identical cuts every time

If you're cutting miters for windows or other house trim, you can get close enough just by careful measuring and cutting. But if you're building a picture frame or any other frame that calls for maximum precision, attach an auxiliary fence to the right or left side of the triangle fence. Screws or hot glue works well. The fence should be long enough so there's room for a stop block behind the longest piece you're cutting.

For the first piece, cut the first miter. Mark the length and cut the miter at the other end, from the opposite side of the sled. When you're satisfied with the length, use the piece as a guide to place a stop block on the auxiliary fence. Now when you cut the matching, opposite side of the frame, the lengths will be identical.

Workshop stool

Flip the top down and you have a stool for sitting or working; flip it up and you have a small stepladder for reaching. Build two of them and you have sawhorses for supporting sheets of plywood or long boards when working.

Begin by building the two side ladders using the spacing shown in Figure A. Use a square to ensure each "rung" is square to the leg, then secure each using glue and 1-1/4-in. screws (Photo 1). Use a 1/4-in. round-over bit to soften the outer edges of each leg. Stand the two ladder sides facing each other and install the two steps and the back brace. Predrill the holes to prevent splitting.

Cut the two top boards to length and round over the top edges. Secure the two top edges to each other using 2-1/2-in. no-mortise hinges; regular hinges will also work but will leave a slightly wider gap. Position the hinged-together top boards so they overhang the sides of the legs by about 3/4 in. and the front and back by about 3/8 in. Attach one of the top boards to the top "rungs" of the ladder using 2-in. screws.

WHAT IT TAKES

TIME: 2 hours
SKILL LEVEL: Beginner

Figure A
Workshop stool

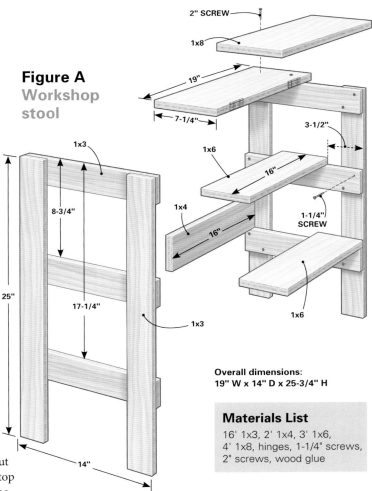

Overall dimensions:
19" W x 14" D x 25-3/4" H

Materials List
16' 1x3, 2' 1x4, 3' 1x6,
4' 1x8, hinges, 1-1/4" screws,
2" screws, wood glue

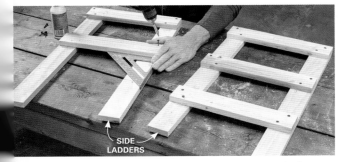

1 **Build the two side ladders.** Cut the pieces to length, then glue and screw the crosspieces to the legs. Use a square to ensure the assemblies are square.

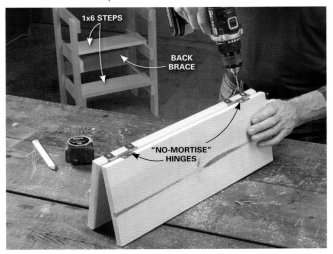

2 **Put it all together.** Attach the two steps and the back brace to the ladder sides. Use hinges to join the two top pieces, then secure one of the boards to the top "rungs."

Easiest add-on drawers

WHAT IT TAKES

TIME: 1/2 day
SKILL LEVEL: Beginner

These roll-out drawers are easy—you don't even have to mount them to the bench. They're just sturdy boxes that ride on 2-in. casters. Measure from the floor to the bottom shelf of your workbench and subtract 3-1/4 in. to figure the height of the boxes. Then subtract 3/4 in. from this measurement to determine the height of the drawer front, back and sides. Next, decide how many drawers you want and calculate the widths. Allow for a 1/2-in. space between drawers.

Cut the parts and screw them together. Then measure the width and length of the box and cut the bottom. Screw on the bottom and cut a handhold in the front of the drawer with a jigsaw. Finish up by screwing 2-in. fixed (not swiveling!) casters to the bottom of the drawer as shown.

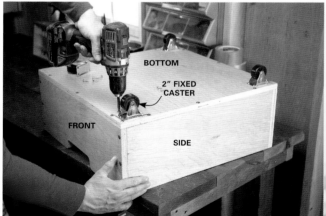

Build basic plywood boxes and screw on the casters. Carefully align the casters parallel to the box sides so the drawers roll smooth and straight.

Table saw guide box

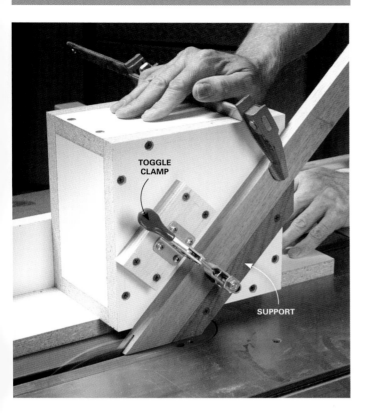

TOGGLE CLAMP

SUPPORT

When you have to stand boards on end to machine them on your table saw, you can use this simple box. It steadies the wood so you get a straight cut. The box is made of melamine and measures 8 in. square and 5-1/2 in. deep. It's screwed to two optional runners that are 12 in. long.

Here, we're cutting slots into the ends of each part of a picture frame so we can join them with spline (thin pieces of solid wood). You couldn't do this using the table saw's fence alone because the fence doesn't offer enough support—it's not tall enough. Using this box, you're sure to get an absolutely straight cut.

The picture frame piece is supported by a block that's screwed to the box. If you need to support pieces at 90 degrees—for cutting tenons, for example—just remove the 45-degree support and screw on another.

To ensure a straight cut, clamp the workpiece to the box. Use a toggle clamp to hold the frame's lower end because it's difficult to get a regular clamp down there. The table saw's fence gets in the way. You can buy a toggle clamp at a woodworking store or online.

WHAT IT TAKES

TIME: 2 hours

SKILL LEVEL: Beginner to intermediate

Floor lamp for the shop

This lightweight, height-adjustable pole lamp will instantly illuminate every tool or project in your shop. You'll need:

- A 68-in. piece of 1-1/4-in.-diameter wood closet rod
- Two 16-in.-long pieces of 2x4
- Two 4-in.-long pieces of 2x4
- A clamp light

Overlap the two long 2x4s to make an X-shaped base, securing it with 3-in.-long screws. Then screw the 4-in. pieces under the upper piece to level the base. With a spade or Forstner bit, drill a hole in the center of the base for the closet rod. Check the diameter of the rod before drilling. If the diameter is between 1-1/8 and 1-1/4 in., use a 1-1/8-in. drill bit and file and sand the hole for a snug fit.

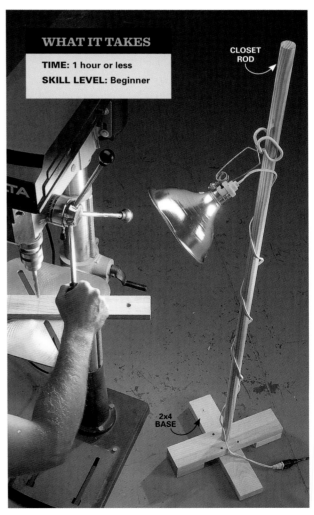

WHAT IT TAKES

TIME: 1 hour or less

SKILL LEVEL: Beginner

CLOSET ROD

2x4 BASE

Pegboard palooza 141
Quick projects for beginners 146

9 ORGANIZATION AROUND THE HOUSE

Pegboard palooza

Ordinary material—extraordinary possibilities

Take a look around you next time you're out shopping and you'll start noticing pegboard everywhere—panels, hooks, doodads, you name it. Every hand tool in the hardware store is probably hanging on pegboard. Every bag of bolts, roll of duct tape and pack of Tic Tacs at the checkout counter—pegboarded. Even the pegboard hooks are hanging on pegboard hooks.

But that should come as no surprise. Retailers want a display system that's sturdy, easy to rearrange and adaptable—the same qualities we need in our work spaces at home.

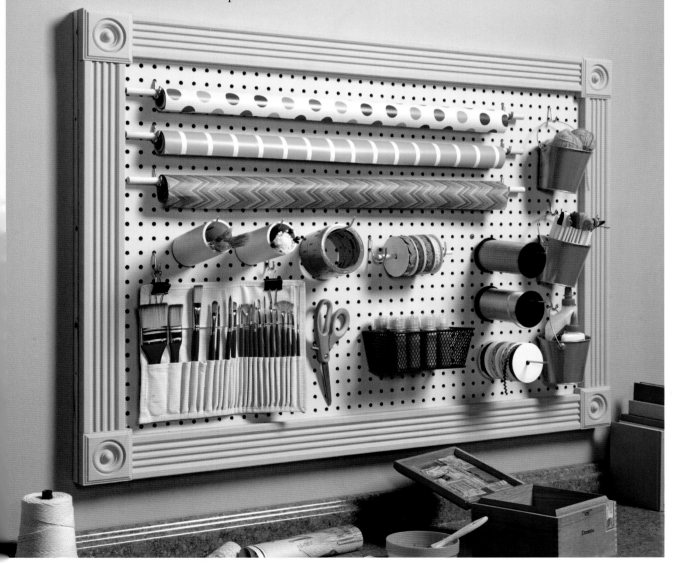

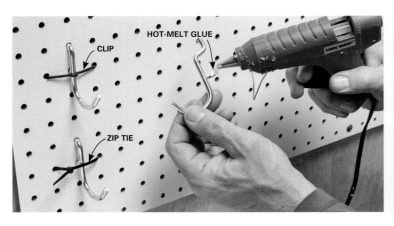

Pegboard specs

All pegboard has holes with 1-in. spacing, but there are two thicknesses and two hole sizes available.

■ "Small hole" pegboard is usually 1/8-in.-thick hardboard with 3/16-in.-diameter holes. The holes will accommodate only the smaller 1/8-in. pegs. This thickness is good for small projects (like our cabinet door panel) and for hanging lighter weight stuff. But for heavy tools—and longevity—go with the thicker board.

■ "Large hole" pegboard is usually 1/4-in.-thick hardboard with 1/4-in.-diameter holes that will accept both 1/8-in. and 1/4-in. hooks. This is the type you need for workshops, garages and other heavy-use areas. Some come with a melamine coating on one side.

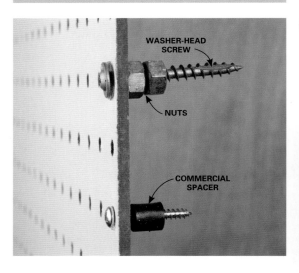

WASHER-HEAD SCREW

NUTS

COMMERCIAL SPACER

Hefty standoffs

Pegboard needs about 1/2 in. of "standoff" space behind it so the hooks can be inserted. Plastic and metal pegboard panels have this space built in, created by the L-shape flanges at the edges. But you can also create this standoff space in several ways:

■ Install screw-in standoffs with spacers (see photo). The store-bought versions often have short screws with small heads and wimpy plastic spacers. Make your own using beefier washer-head screws and nuts for spacers. On larger panels, install standoffs in the center to maintain space and add support. Tip: Use hot-melt glue to hold these mid-panel spacers in place before you install the pegboard.

■ Create a frame for the back of the panel using 1x2s or 1x3s (see photo, p. 143). For panels wider than 3 ft., add a 1x2 rib to the back every 2 ft. to support the weight of the tools and take the flex out of the panel.

Lock 'em in

The No. 1 complaint about pegboard? Hooks falling out when you remove a tool. The solution? Lock 'em in place. Zip ties are an inexpensive, sure-shooting way to go—but you need to have access to the back of your pegboard (or plan ahead and install the pegs and zip ties before you mount the board). Pegboard clips have small barbs that lock into holes on both sides of the hook to keep them in place. Another approach is to add a dab of hot-melt glue to the lower leg before slipping the peg into the hole. The glue will hold well enough to keep the hook in place, but it will be removable later with a light tug.

CLIP

Make hooks hold more

Some items won't hang directly on pegboard hooks. But with a little ingenuity, you can make hooks hold just about anything. Here are three ideas:

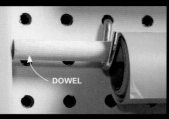

Hooks and 1/2-in. wood dowels organize wrapping paper—no more digging through a stack of unraveling rolls.

DOWEL

BINDER CLIP

Binder clips grab items that can't hang on hooks. The clip shown here, for example, holds a canvas tool pouch.

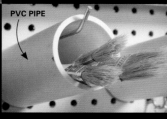

PVC PIPE

A section of PVC pipe slipped over a long hook is a great nook for skinny stuff: pencils, brushes, zip ties....

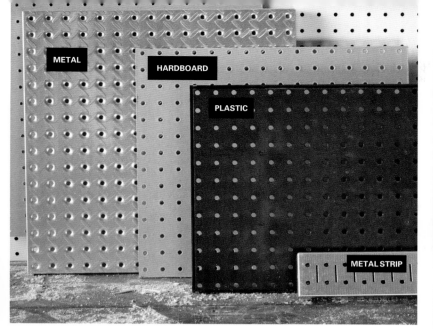

METAL

HARDBOARD

PLASTIC

METAL STRIP

Beyond hardboard

Most home centers carry only hardboard pegboard, but you'll find other materials by searching online for "metal pegboard" or "plastic pegboard." Prices run from 5 to 15 times the cost of ordinary 1/4-in. pegboard.

■ Metal pegboard has 1/4-in. holes and L-shape edge flanges that create built-in standoffs. The panel sizes are normally in 16-in. and 24-in. increments. Metal pegboard has a cool industrial look and is darn near indestructible.

■ Metal pegboard strips are ideal for situations where you need a single, sturdy strip of pegboard—like in the garage for hanging long-handled tools. The strips have 1/4-in. holes and built-in edge flanges for standoffs, and they're outrageously sturdy.

■ Plastic pegboard has 1/4-in. holes, folded edges to create standoffs and center ribs for rigidity. Many systems come with slide-in connectors for joining panels. It's at least as sturdy as hardboard pegboard.

CIRCULAR SAW SHELF

CORDLESS DRILL HOLDER

PEGBOARD BIN

Go hookless

You can craft your own hooks using stuff from the hardware aisle. Clip the tips from No. 6 hollow wall anchors, drive them into 1/4-in. pegboard holes, then secure your custom tool holder by driving screws into the anchors. Short 5/16-in.-diameter lag bolts fit snugly into 1/4-in. holes to create inexpensive hangers for lightweight objects.

WALL ANCHOR

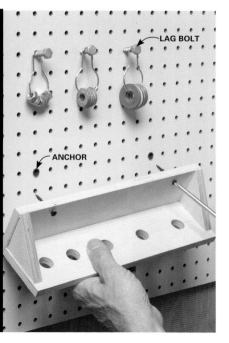

LAG BOLT

ANCHOR

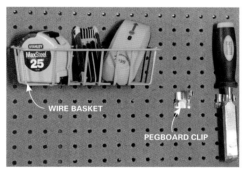

WIRE BASKET

PEGBOARD CLIP

Hang anything

Most hardware stores and home centers carry standard hooks for basic hand tools, but specialized hangers are available too. The circular saw shelf, cordless drill holder, wire basket, bins and other doodads can help organize hard-to-hang tools. Search online for "pegboard" followed by the type of hanger you're looking for, such as "pegboard circular saw shelf."

Custom shelving

Standard pegboard hooks can accommodate most tools—but sometimes you need a special place for special stuff.

Drill 1/4-in. holes in the backs of homemade shelves, then use those holes to slide the shelves over L-hooks. Or use cable staples to attach plywood shelves to standard pegboard shelf brackets. The staples allow you to slide the shelf back and forth so you can easily fit the shelf bracket "legs" into the holes.

CABLE STAPLE

1/4" HOLE

RABBET BIT

RABBET

Storage behind closed doors

Pegboard is great for organizing kitchens, laundry rooms and bathroom cabinets. Rout a groove in a 1x2 frame using a rabbet bit, attach the pegboard with glue and brads, then mount it to the door. The frame helps support the edges of the pegboard and creates a 1/2-in. space behind the board so pegs can be inserted.

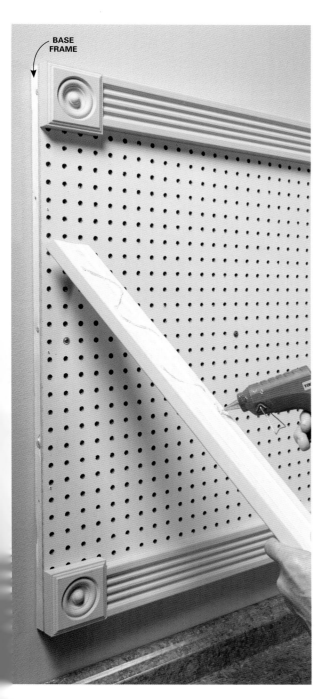

BASE FRAME

1x3 STRIP

Pegboard walls

Create pegboard walls by running 1x3 strips horizontally at the top and bottom of the panel and every 16 in. or 24 in. between. Use 1/4-in. pegboard and attach it to the strips with washer-head screws. The strips will also allow you to mount screw-on hooks to the wall for very heavy items like bikes and wheelbarrows.

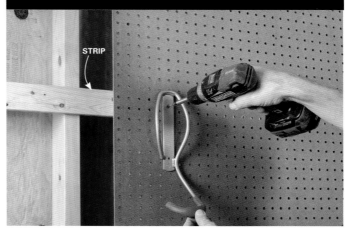

STRIP

Dress it up

Most pegboard comes in two colors—boring white and boring brown. But it doesn't have to stay that way. Roll on a coat of primer followed by gloss or semigloss paint (glossy paints are easier to wipe clean). Apply light coats so you don't clog the holes. Then snazz it up with a frame. After we attached our pegboard to a 1x3 frame, we added corner blocks and trim with hot-melt glue—no fancy miter cuts or fasteners needed.

Quick projects for beginners

Ski and pole organizer

Keep your skis up and easy to find with this simple 2x4 rack. Drill 3/4-in.-diameter holes spaced 3/4 in. apart. Glue 4-1/2-in. lengths of 3/4-in. dowel into the holes and then mount the 2x4 to the wall studs. Space the groupings about 8 in. apart to make room for ski bindings. Now you'll spend less time looking for your skis and more time on the trails.

Drawer dividers

Here's a fast, inexpensive way to organize a messy drawer.

Cut standard dentil molding the width and length of your drawer, aligning the dentil slots on opposite sides. Glue or brad-nail the strips into place—one strip for dividers up to 2 in., two strips for larger dividers. For dividers, use oak or pine mull strip (sometimes called lattice) or rip 1/4-in. plywood.

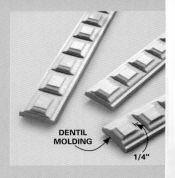

DENTIL MOLDING

1/4"

Dentil molding and 1/4-in.-thick mull strip are available at most home centers and lumberyards. Sand the mull strip smooth with fine sandpaper, then wipe off all the dust. The wood can be left unfinished, or finished before it's installed in the drawer.

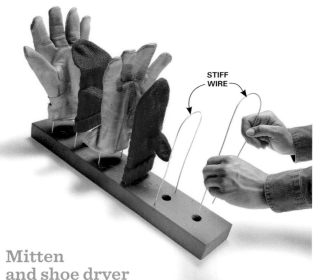

STIFF WIRE

Mitten and shoe dryer

Drill pairs of 1/8-in. holes in a scrap of 2x4 and insert U-shaped pieces of galvanized 14-gauge wire (sold at home centers). If you have forced-air heat, drill 1-in. holes between the pairs of 1/8-in. holes using a spade bit, and set the rack on a register for fast drying.

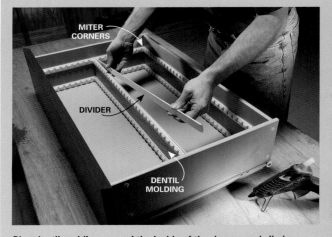

MITER CORNERS

DIVIDER

DENTIL MOLDING

Glue dentil molding around the inside of the drawer and slip in dividers. Use additional molding to divide the space further.

Sleek coat and hat rack

Organize your hallway or mudroom with this simple, attractive coat and hat rack. You just cut the boards to fit your space, paint them, outfit them with different kinds of hooks to suit your needs and then screw them to the wall. Shown are 6-ft.-long 1x4s, but use whatever length works for you and the space available. Shown is poplar, which is the best choice if you want a painted finish. If you're after a natural wood look, choose any species you want.

Finish the boards first and then attach your hooks. Shown here are drawer pulls down the middle and a robe hook near the top to hold backpacks and larger items. You'll find hooks in a tremendous range of styles, colors and prices at hardware stores and online retailers.

Attach the boards to studs, or to the drywall with screw-in drywall anchors. Drive three screws in each board: one at the top, one in the middle and one at the bottom.

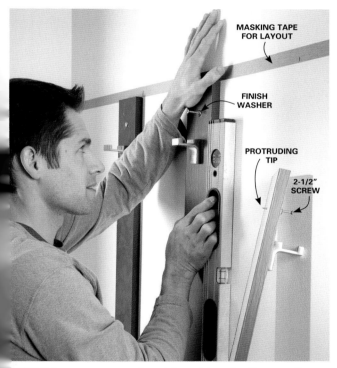

MASKING TAPE FOR LAYOUT

FINISH WASHER

PROTRUDING TIP

2-1/2" SCREW

1 Drive your screws partway into each board so the screw tips poke out the back. Place the boards where you want them, and press hard to mark the spots for your drywall anchors.

SCREW-IN DRYWALL ANCHOR

2 Screw your anchors into each marked spot and then attach the boards.

Storage bench 149
Remote garden storage 154
Garden tool cabinet 155
Rustic garden toolbox 161

10 OUTDOOR STORAGE

Storage bench

FOAM WEATHERSTRIP

A lift-up lid gives you tons of storage inside the bench. Foam weatherstrip keeps the interior fairly dry.

WHAT IT TAKES

TIME: 1 day
SKILL LEVEL: Beginner

Stash your stuff in this easy-to-build project

You can never have enough storage space, especially on a deck or patio, where there are no closets or cabinets. Although this bench won't be the answer to all your outdoor storage needs, it sure will help!

It's a place to tuck a bag of charcoal, stick a pair of work shoes, hide an extension cord or watering can and hey, you can even sit and take a breather on it, too.

Even if you've never taken on a woodworking project, you can build this bench. There is no fancy joinery holding it together, and you don't need special tools. The sides are 1x4s with sheet metal sandwiched between. The 1x4s intersect at the legs to create a strong joint. Drop in a plywood bottom and a hinged top, and you've got a sturdy attractive storage bench. It only takes about a day to build.

The tools are basic

You'll need a power miter saw (a circular saw with a speed square works, too), a jigsaw and a cordless drill. Clamps

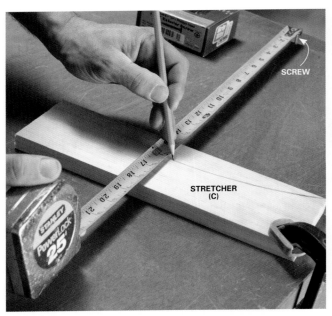

1 Draw an arc on each side stretcher by hooking a tape measure on a screw driven into the work surface. Draw the arcs on the legs using a compass or coffee can, then cut out all the arcs with your jigsaw.

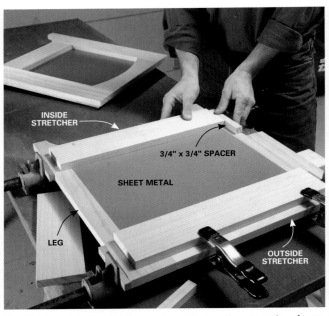

2 Clamp together the legs and outside stretchers to make a frame. Lay the sheet metal on it, then position the inside stretchers. Use a spacer to get the stretchers centered, then screw them on to lock everything together.

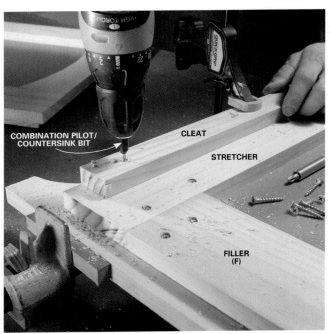

3 Screw filler pieces between the stretchers, then add cleats to hold the bottom. Be sure to predrill and countersink all screws.

aren't necessary, but they're very helpful. They'll hold the joints tight while you screw them together, and they provide an extra hand when you need it. If you don't have clamps, now might be the time to invest in a pair. The holes for the screws need to be predrilled and countersunk. A combination bit works best (Photo 3). Also have a nail set on hand (Photo 4).

Materials

This project is made primarily of 1x4s, and you can use just about any type of wood. Cedar, cypress or pine are great choices, but you'll need them smooth on all four sides. We used clear pine because it's straight and easy to work with, but it will need an annual coat of exterior stain, wood preservative or paint to protect it from the elements.

Sheet metal is used for the panels. Purchase it from a sheet metal shop or home center. You will need metal shears to cut it to size. We selected 24-gauge pre-finished steel ("Uniclad"), which is commonly used for flashing on buildings and is available in an array of colors. We used a copper color. If you prefer, cut the panels with tin snips from copper or galvanized roll flashing (available at home centers). Plywood forms the bottom and top of the bench. And 2- by 4-ft. sheets fit in a car better than full-size sheets.

Your first step: assemble the panels

Assemble all four sides in the same manner. Here's how:

Cut the legs and outside front stretchers to size from the Cutting List. Good square ends are essential, so if you're using a circular saw, use a speed square as a guide.

Lay out arcs (Photo 1) on the legs and outside stretchers (C), then cut out the curved pieces with a jigsaw. If you don't have a jigsaw or want a simpler look, cut a 60-degree angle on the legs and eliminate the arc on the stretchers.

Clamp the stretchers between the legs. Use a scrap piece of wood between the clamps and the legs to avoid denting your wood. Lay the sheet metal on the clamped boards, flush with the bottom and centered.

Figure A
Storage bench

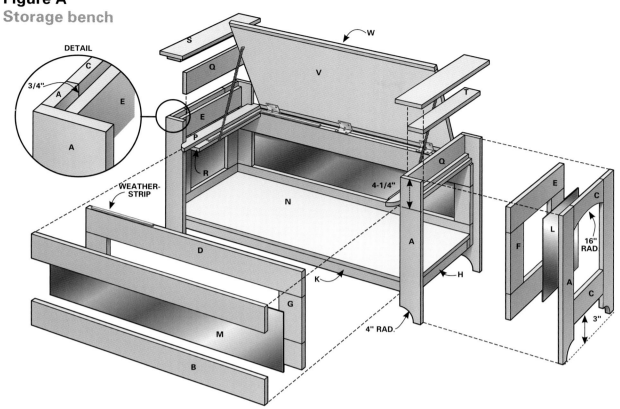

DETAIL

3/4"

WEATHER-STRIP

4-1/4"

4" RAD.

16" RAD

3"

Cutting list

Overall Dimensions: 22-3/4"H x 50"W x 23"D

KEY	NAME	QTY.	DIMENSIONS	NOTES
A	Legs	8	1x4 x 22"	Cut arcs in feet
B	Outside front & back stretchers	4	1x4 x 41"	
C	Outside side stretchers	4	1x4 x 12-1/2"	Cut arcs in two of them
D	Inside front stretchers	4	1x4 x 46-1/2"	Measure from bench
E	Inside side stretchers	4	1x4 x 18"	Measure from bench
F	Inside side fillers	4	1x4 x 11-1/4"	Measure from bench
G	Inside front & back fillers	4	1x4 x 7-3/4"	Measure from bench
H	Side cleats	2	1x2 x 16-1/4"	Measure from bench
K	Front & back cleats	2	1x2 x 44-3/4"	Measure from bench
L	Side panels	2	17-3/4" x 18"	24 gauge sheet metal
M	Front & back panels	2	46" x 14-1/2"	24 gauge sheet metal
N	Bottom (1/2" plywood)	1	45" x 18"	Measure from bench
P	Arm supports	2	1x4 x 21-1/2"	Cut notches and round corners
Q	Arm fillers	2	1x4 x 19-1/2"	
R	Lid supports	2	1x4 x 18"	Measure from bench
S	Arms	2	1x6 x 23"	
T	Cleats	2	1 x 19-1/2" x 2"	Rip to fit, measure from bench
V	Lid (3/4" plywood)	1	20-1/4" x 37-3/4"	Measure from bench
W	Molding	2	3/4" x 3/4" x 37-3/4"	Measure from bench

Materials list

1   roll of galvanized steel flashing (12' x 18" wide)

Wood

10   1x4 - 8'
1   1x6 - 6'
2   1x2 - 8'
1   2'x4' 1/2" BC plywood
1   2'x4' 3/4" BC plywood
1   3/4" x 3/4" square molding

Hardware

1 lb   1-1/4"x #8 exterior screws
1 lb   2" galvanized casing nails
3   3" butt hinges
4   small eye screws
4'   lightweight chain
12'   1/2" weatherstrip
     Exterior glue

4 Nail the front, back and sides together. Predrill for each nail, and drive the nail heads slightly below the surface with a nail set. For additional strength, run a bead of glue along each joint before assembling.

NAIL SET

FLUSH HERE

ARM SUPPORT (P)

5 Mark the notches for the arm supports directly from the bench. Cut out the notches with a jigsaw, then round off the protruding corners.

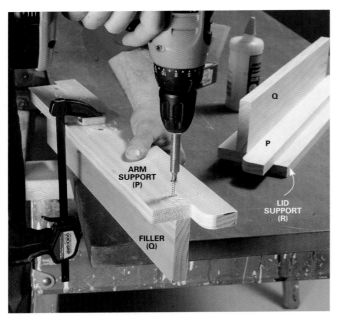

ARM SUPPORT (P)

Q

P

LID SUPPORT (R)

FILLER (Q)

6 Clamp the arm support to the filler piece, screw them together, then add the lid support.

Cut one inside stretcher, then lay it on top of the clamped-together frame, as shown in Photo 2. Center it on the frame; it will be narrower than the width of the frame. It's important that the gap at each end equals the thickness of your wood plus the sheet metal. Adjust the length if necessary and cut the remaining inside stretchers. Screw them all in place, remembering to keep the inside stretchers on the sides 3/4 in. from the top edge (see Figure A, detail). The lower stretcher is flush to the bottom. Use 1-1/4-in. deck screws, predrilled and countersunk. Position the screws so they're sure to catch the front 1x4s; because of the offset, it's easy to miss.

Add filler pieces (F) between stretchers, then add the 1x2 cleats (H and K) that'll hold the bench bottom (Photo 3). Repeat this process for the other three panels.

Nail the panels together

The toughest part of nailing the panels together is holding them in place. Here's where a clamp really helps. Clamp a side panel inside the front and back panels, flush up all the edges and gently tighten the clamp. This is a bit of a juggling act, so you may want to call for someone to help. Place a piece of wood or cardboard between the jaws and the legs to avoid denting the wood (Photo 4). Predrill 3/32-in. holes, then glue and nail the corners with 2-in. galvanized finish nails. Reposition the clamp as you nail to keep the joints tight. Repeat at the other end.

Measure the bottom and cut a piece of plywood to fit. When you drop in the bottom, it will square up the bench. Predrill, countersink, glue and screw the bottom to the cleats.

The arm assembly

This assembly looks a little complicated, but it's really not. It's made up of three pieces, which are measured from the bench (Photo 5) and cut to fit. After you notch the arm supports, round off the front ends shown in Photo 7 (so they won't catch a pant leg), then temporarily set them in place. Hold the lid supports (R) in place underneath the arm supports and mark. Fit and nail the two assemblies to the bench.

Fastening a cleat to the bottom of each arm (Photo 8) lets

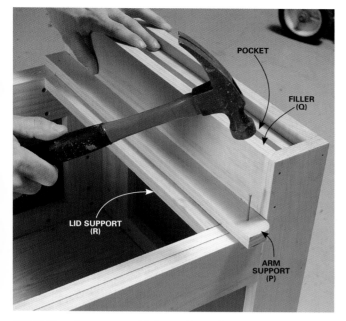

LID SUPPORT (R)
POCKET
FILLER (Q)
ARM SUPPORT (P)

7 Place the arm assembly in position and nail it to the legs and stretcher. There will be a pocket formed at the top where the arm cleat will go (see next photo).

CLEAT (T)
ARM
45°

8 Attach a cleat to the underside of each arm, using diagonal lines to center it. Place the arms on the bench and nail through the cleats to secure them.

you hide nails on the sides of the bench when you attach them. Measure the width of the opening of the arm and rip (cut the long way) the cleat (T) to fit. Although not the quickest, your jigsaw is the safest tool for this cut. Attach the cleats to the arms (Photo 8), then nail the arms to the bench.

The lid

Installing the lid can be a bit awkward. Here are a few techniques that'll make it go easier:

Cut the plywood 1/4 in. shorter than the width of the opening, so the lid closes easily. Then glue and nail two pieces of molding (W) to cover the exposed edges of the plywood. Place the lid on the workbench and attach the hinges to the lid. We used no-mortise hinges, but any butt hinge will work.

Flip the bench on its back with its arms overhanging each side of your workbench (Photo 9). Put a couple of 1-in. blocks under it to raise it to the level of the lid, center it, then screw on the hinge.

A few remaining details

Install a pair of screw eyes and attach a chain to keep the lid from falling back. Then place a band of foam weatherstrip around the perimeter to help keep out the rain. Finally, bore a dozen 3/8-in. ventilation holes in the bottom.

Seal the bench with a coat of deck stain and preservative. If it's used outdoors, the bench will need a fresh coat annually. And if you're like most folks, you'll have to clean it out once a year, too, because it's sure to fill up fast.

LID

9 Fasten the hinges to the bench. Rest the bench on its back, on top of 1-inch blocks, center the lid in the opening, then screw it on. Give the whole bench a once-over with sandpaper, and you're ready to finish!

Remote garden storage

Figure A
Exploded view

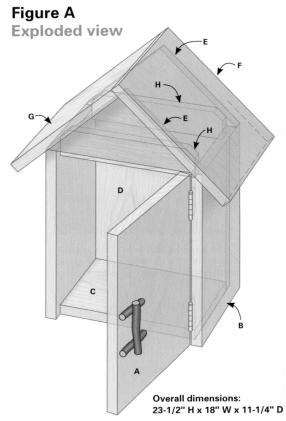

Overall dimensions:
23-1/2" H x 18" W x 11-1/4" D

WHAT IT TAKES

TIME: 3 hours
SKILL LEVEL: Beginner

Keep tools and supplies right next to your garden with this small storage house. It only takes a few hours to build, and can be made with pine or rough-sawn cedar as shown here.

Cut flat, dry 1x12s to the sizes in the Cutting List. Nail and glue the sides, base and back together, then attach the rafters and gables.

Fasten the shorter roof panel on one side, leaving 7/8-in. overhangs in the front and back. Caulk the top edge, then nail the long panel on.

Cut the hinge mortises into the door and side, and hang the door. Stain or paint the wood inside and out to seal it. Use green branches for the handle, nailing them in place.

Make a rustic door handle from a tree branch. Nail the crosspieces to the door with brad nails, then notch the back of the handle so it sits flat on the crosspieces and nail it in place.

Cutting list

KEY	QTY.	SIZE & DESCRIPTION
A	1	11" x 15-3/4" door
B	2	9-1/2" x 15-7/8" sides
C	1	11-1/4" x 8" bottom
D	1	11-1/4" x 15-7/8" back
E	2	12-3/4" x 6-1/2" gables
F	1	11-1/4" x 12-3/4" long roof panel
G	1	11-1/4" x 12" short roof panel
H	2	11-1/4" x 2-1/2" rafters

Note: All dimensions are for 3/4"-thick wood.

Materials list

QTY.	ITEM
2	1x12 x 8' cedar or pine
1	4x4 x 8' post
1 pr.	2" x 2" mortise hinges
1	Magnetic catch
1 lb.	1-1/2" galvanized finish nails

Garden tool cabinet

WHAT IT TAKES

TIME: 1 weekend
SKILL LEVEL: Intermediate

Give your garden tools their own home so they're easy to find

I magine this: You drive home with a carload of new plants and flowers. You open your new outdoor garden tool cabinet and grab your shovel, bulb planter, trimmer or whatever you need—and it's all there in plain view! This scenario doesn't have to be a dream. You can build this cabinet in one weekend and paint and organize it the next.

This cabinet is compact, but it can store all of your garden hand tools and still have room for boots, fertilizers and accessories. Most gardeners set aside a tiny spot in their garage for their tools, which often end up tangled in a corner. Now your garden tools can have a home of their own, outside the garage. The design is flexible, so you can customize the interior to suit your needs and add a lock if you wish.

Here you'll learn how to assemble the cabinet in your garage and then wheel it out and mount it on your garage wall. And you don't have to be a crackerjack carpenter or own special tools to build it.

Besides being good looking, this project is designed to last. The shingled roof will keep the rain out. And if moisture does get in, the slatted bottom and

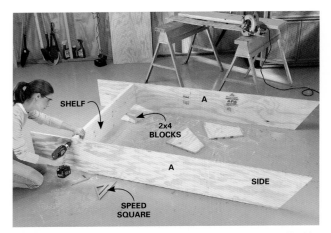

1 Cut the plywood sides and 2x10 shelf, prop up the shelf with 2x4 blocks and fasten the sides into the shelf with 2-in. deck screws.

2 Turn the assembly over and screw the back to the sides and center shelf. Use a level or straightedge to mark the shelf location on the back side of the plywood.

3 Cut the subrails (D) and the roof supports (H), then screw them into place. Use 2-in. screws for the subrails and 3-in. screws for the roof supports.

4 Glue and nail the 1x2 cleats (E and F) to the sides, back and subrail (D) and then screw the 1x4 floor slats (G) to the cleats. Start with the center slat and leave 7/16-in. gaps.

4-in.-diameter vents near the top allow enough air circulation to dry everything out. This storage cabinet was mounted on the outside of a garage, but you can easily mount it to the back of your house or to a shed.

The 4-ft. by nearly 8-ft. cabinet is made from exterior plywood with pine trim. All the materials are available at home centers and lumberyards. You can find a huge variety of tool mounting clips and retainers at hardware stores for hanging rakes, shovels, clippers and everything else. Just let your imagination solve the need. So what are you waiting for? Get the materials, read the photo sequence, examine the detailed drawings and text instructions, and get started.

Assemble the main box

Exterior-grade plywood is the basic building material for this project. Unfortunately, you'll never find *absolutely* flat pieces of plywood at a home center or lumberyard, but the flatter you can find them, the better this project will turn out. Choose a BC grade

5 Mount the 1x2 roof trim to the 3/4-in. plywood roof, then center it and mark the position. Then temporarily screw it to the roof supports with a pair of 2-in. screws on each side.

Figure A Garden tool cabinet

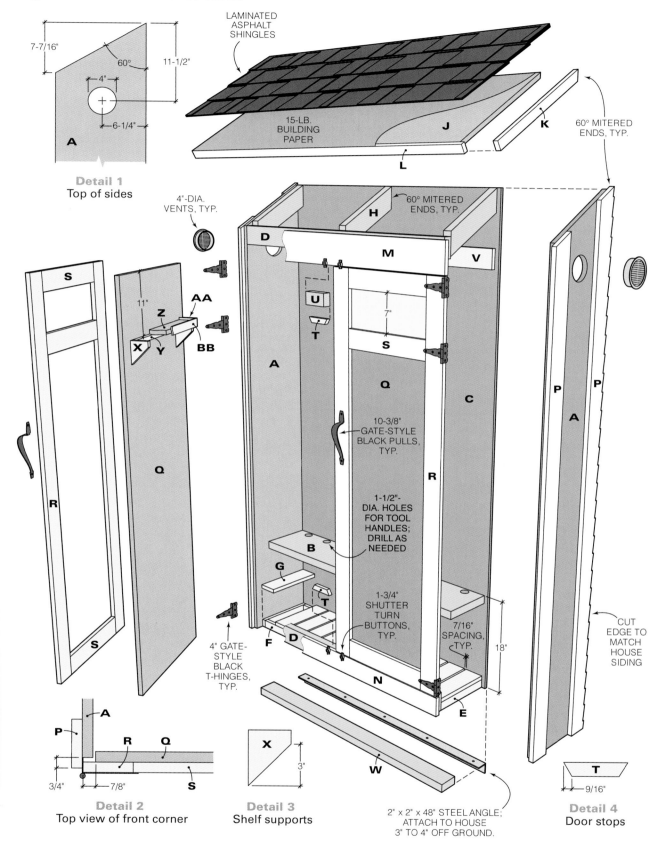

Detail 1
Top of sides

7-7/16"
60°
11-1/2"
4"
6-1/4"
A

LAMINATED
ASPHALT
SHINGLES

15-LB.
BUILDING
PAPER

J

L

K

60° MITERED
ENDS, TYP.

4"-DIA.
VENTS, TYP.

60° MITERED
ENDS, TYP.

H

D

M

V

U

T

7"

S

AA
Z
X Y
BB
11"

S

A

Q

S

Q

R

P A P

10-3/8"
GATE-STYLE
BLACK PULLS,
TYP.

C

R

1-1/2"-
DIA. HOLES
FOR TOOL
HANDLES;
DRILL AS
NEEDED

B

G

T

1-3/4"
SHUTTER
TURN
BUTTONS,
TYP.

CUT
EDGE TO
MATCH
HOUSE
SIDING

7/16"
SPACING,
TYP.

18"

4" GATE-
STYLE
BLACK
T-HINGES,
TYP.

F D

N

E

Detail 2
Top view of front corner

A
P
R Q
3/4" 7/8" S

Detail 3
Shelf supports

X
3"

Detail 4
Door stops

T
9/16"

W

2" x 2" x 48" STEEL ANGLE;
ATTACH TO HOUSE
3" TO 4" OFF GROUND.

of plywood. This will ensure you have one good side "B" that'll look good on the outside, and the "C" side can go inside.

Once you get the plywood home, keep it out of the sun or your flat panel will turn into a tortilla chip in no time. It's best to cut the pieces in the shade or in your garage. A long straightedge cutting guide for your circular saw will help you get nice straight cuts if you don't have a full-size table saw. Look at the Cutting List below and cut all the parts to size except the door stiles, rails and trim pieces, which are best cut to fit once you've constructed the main plywood box.

Choose the flattest sheet of 3/4-in. plywood for the door cores. As you lay out all the pieces, choose the best-looking side of the plywood for the painted parts. The sides of the cabinet form a 30-degree slope for the roof. Use a Speed square (see Photo 1) to mark the angled roof supports (H) and ends of the trim pieces that follow the roofline. It's easier to cut accurate slopes on the larger side pieces (A) by first measuring each side, marking a diagonal line from point to point and then cutting along the mark. Assemble the main box of the cabinet as shown in Figure A and Photos 1 – 5. Drill pilot holes for all screws with a No. 8 combination countersink and pilot bit. Use 2-in. galvanized deck screws to fasten the sides to the shelf and 1-5/8-in. screws to fasten the back to the sides.

Cut the roof panel (J) and trim pieces (K and L), then glue and nail the trim to the front and side edges of the roof panel. Center the panel (Photo 5) and temporarily screw it to the roof supports so you can install the side trim (P) and the upper rail (M). Note: You'll need to remove the roof and the doors after assembly to make the project light enough to move to your site.

Keeping critters out

Cut a piece of 1/4-in. hardware cloth to fit under the floor slats of the cabinet. This wire mesh will keep furry critters from making your tool cabinet into a cozy winter home.

6 Glue and screw the 1x4 side trim to the plywood sides, keeping the trim pieces 3/4 in. proud at the front. Cut the 4-in.-diameter side vents.

Materials list

ITEM	QTY.
3/4" x 4' x 8' BC plywood	2
1/2" x 4' x 8' BC plywood	1
2x10 x 4' pine	1
2x4 x 8' pine	2
1x6 x 8' pine	1
1x4 x 8' pine	12
1x2 x 8' pine	3
2x4 x 8' treated wood	1
12" x 48" hardware cloth (1/4" grid)	1
Bundle of asphalt shingles	1
3' x 5' strip of 15-lb. building paper	1
1-5/8" galv. screws	2 lbs.
2" galv. screws	2 lbs.
3" galv. screws	1 lbs.
4" T-hinges	6
Shutter turn buttons	4
4" round vents	2
1-1/4" finish nails	1 lb.
1/4" x 3" galv. lag screws and washers	9
2" x 2" steel angle	1
7/8" shingle nails	1 lb.

Cutting list

KEY	QTY.	SIZE & DESCRIPTION
A	2	3/4" x 12-7/8" x 90" plywood sides
B	1	1-1/2" x 9-1/4" x 46-1/2" pine shelf
C	1	1/2" x 48" x 90" plywood back
D	2	1-1/2" x 3-1/2" x 46-1/2" pine subrails
E	2	3/4" x 1-1/2" x 11-3/8" pine bottom cleats
F	2	3/4" x 1-1/2" x 45" pine bottom cleats
G	12	3/4" x 3-1/2" x 11-3/8" pine bottom slat
H	3	1-1/2" x 3-1/2" x 15-1/8" pine roof supports
J	1	3/4" x 21-7/8" x 60" plywood roof
K	2	3/4" x 1-1/2" x 21-7/8" pine roof trim
L	1	3/4" x 1-1/2" x 61-1/2" pine roof trim
M	1	3/4" x 5-1/2" x 48" pine upper rail
N	1	3/4" x 3-1/2" x 48" pine lower rail
P	4	3/4" x 3-1/2" x 91" pine side trim
Q	2	3/4" x 23" x 72-3/4" plywood doors
R	4	3/4" x 3-1/2" x 72-3/4" pine door stile
S	6	3/4" x 3-1/2" x 16-7/8" pine door rail trim
T	2	3/4" x 1" x 4-1/2" pine door stop
U	1	1-1/2" x 2-7/16" x 4-1/2" pine door stop support
V	1	3/4" x 3-1/2" x 46-1/2"pine hang rail
W	1	1-1/2" x 3-1/2" x 48" treated mounting board
X	1	3/4" x 3" x 4" pine shelf supports
Y	1	3/4" x 3/4" x 16-1/2" pine shelf-mounting cleat
Z	1	3/4" x 3" x 20" pine shelf
AA	2	1/4" x 1-1/2" x 3" pine shelf edging
BB	1	1/4" x 1-1/2" x 20-1/2" pine shelf edging

7 Countersink the holes in the inside of the hinge flaps to accept the tapered heads of the mounting screws.

8 Position the flaps of the hinges against the plywood sides at the centers of the door rail locations. Drill pilot holes and drive the screws into the side trim to secure the hinges.

Add trim and assemble the doors

Make sure to extend the front edge of each side. Set the trim (P) 3/4 in. beyond the front edge of the plywood side (Photo 6). Next cut and nail the front upper rail (M) and the lower rail (N) to the subrails. Both ends should butt tightly to the side trim.

Even though the doors are made mainly from plywood, the rail and stile trim boards glued and screwed to the front side give the doors a handsome frame-and-panel look. Be sure to lay the doors out on a flat surface and then glue and nail the rails (short horizontal pieces) and stiles (long vertical pieces) to the plywood surface. The stile on each hinge side must hang 3/4 in. past the plywood (see Photo 10 inset).

You'll need to alter the factory T-hinge for the inset design of the doors. The hinge flap is screwed to the side trim (P) as shown in Photo 8. If you were to use the factory-supplied pan head screws, the door would bind on the screw heads. To solve this problem, taper the edges of the existing holes with a countersink bit. Remove just enough steel (Photo 7) so the head of the tapered No. 8 x 3/4-in. screw fits flush with the hinge flap surface.

Cut the small doorstops with a handsaw and then glue and nail them to the edges of the subrails. With the doorstops in place, set the doors into the opening. Make sure you leave a 1/8-in. gap at the top and bottom and a 3/16-in. gap between the doors. You may need to plane or belt-sand the door edges to get a good fit. Note: Because the flaps of the hinge that fasten to the side trim are about 7/8 in. wide instead of 3/4 in., your doors will sit about 1/8 in. proud of the side trim.

Mount the cabinet to the wall

Fasten a 4-ft. 2x4 to the top flange of a 4-ft.-long piece of steel angle (Figure A). At a hardware store, you can usually find steel angle that measures 1-1/2 in. x 1-1/2 in. with holes drilled every in., but any steel angle that's 1/8 in. thick or larger will do.

Locate the exact position of your cabinet on the wall at least in. above grade and then fasten the angle to the wall with 4-in. galvanized lag screws. It must be level. You may need to cut a course or two of siding to get the angle to lie flat. This

garage slab was several inches off the ground, so holes were drilled into the side of the slab, lag shields were installed and the angle was fastened. If your slab is too close to the ground, you can fasten the angle farther up into the wood studs of the garage. The weight of your cabinet rests entirely on this steel angle. It's not necessary to fasten the bottom of the cabinet to it.

Measure the locations of the wall studs and transfer these to the cabinet back. Locate three 1/4-in.-diameter pilot holes in the hang rail (V) and another three holes 4 in. up from the bottom at the stud locations.

Now, strap your cabinet to a furniture dolly (with the doors and roof removed to reduce the weight) and wheel it over to the steel angle. Set the bottom of the cabinet onto the steel angle, center it and temporarily brace it against the wall. Drill 5/32-in.-diameter pilot holes into the wall studs using the existing pilot holes as a guide. Drive the 3-in. lag screws (including washers) and snug the cabinet to the wall.

Finishing touches

Lay the side trim (P) against the siding. You may need to trim it with your jigsaw to conform (Photo 12). Screw the roof panel to the cabinet. Staple a layer of 15-lb. building paper to the roof panel and shingle the panel using 7/8-in. roofing nails. Avoid driving shingle nails through the overhangs where the points might show. When you get to the last course, trim the shingles to fit and run a bead of matching caulk at the siding to seal the edge.

Rehang the doors and then mount the door handles and the catches at the top and bottom of the door. Wait to add your vents until you've finished painting. The vents shown here were spray-painted to match the color of the sides.

Take a trip to the hardware store and shop for a variety of fasteners, from angle screws to rake and broom holders. Once you finish organizing the cabinet, prime it and then paint it to match your siding.

9 Glue and nail the door rail and stile trim to the 3/4-in. plywood core. Overhang the stile on the hinge side of each door 7/8 in. See Figure A for the exact placement.

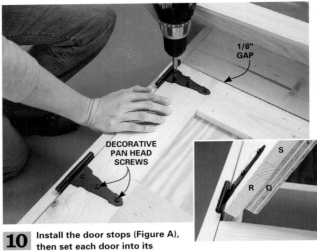

10 Install the door stops (Figure A), then set each door into its opening. Use the decorative pan head screws provided by the manufacturer for the long decorative flap on the door surface.

11 Fasten a steel angle to the foundation with a 2x4 attached to its top (Figure A). Lift the cabinet into place and stabilize it with an 8-ft. 2x4 brace against the ground, forcing the cabinet back against the wall.

12 Scribe the 1x4 side trim to fit the siding. Cut the notches with a jigsaw. Nail it to the cabinet side. Screw on the roof panel and shingle it.

Alternate siding materials

If you have vinyl, aluminum or steel siding, here's how to prevent the siding from deforming as you tighten the cabinet to the wall. Instead of tightening the lag screws one at a time, gently tighten them alternately to even out the pressure as you go.

Rustic garden toolbox

Figure A

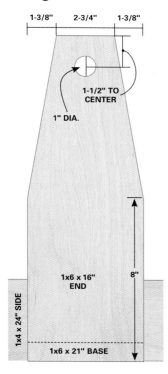

- 1-3/8"
- 2-3/4"
- 1-3/8"
- 1-1/2" TO CENTER
- 1" DIA.
- 8"
- 1x6 x 16" END
- 1x4 x 24" SIDE
- 1x6 x 21" BASE

WHAT IT TAKES

TIME: 4 hours
SKILL LEVEL: Beginner

This simple gardening toolbox gets its natural charm from the branches used for the sides and handle. When you're searching for branches, choose green, freshly cut ones for strength and flexibility. The only tools required are a saw and a drill and maybe a knife to whittle the handle ends.

Along with three 25-in.-long branches, you'll need a 6-ft. 1x6, a 4-ft. 1x4 and a short length of 1/4-in. wood dowel, exterior wood glue and a handful of 1-5/8-in. deck screws. We used clear pine, but No. 2 pine or cedar will work fine too.

Cut the parts using Figure A as a guide. Then screw the box together (Photo 1). Whittle the handle ends to fit the holes. You'll have to bend the handle to slip it into the second hole.

Cut away any knobs on the branches for the sides. Then attach them, keeping the screws at least an inch from the ends to avoid splits (Photo 2). Finally, drill 1/4-in. holes through the handle ends and drive in the dowels to hold the handle in place (Photo 3).

- 1-1/2" INSET
- 1-5/8" DECK SCREW

1 Screw the box together with deck screws. Predrill and countersink the screws to avoid splitting.

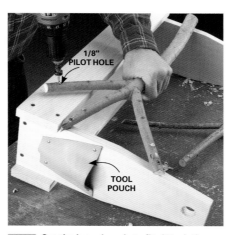

- 1/8" PILOT HOLE
- TOOL POUCH

2 Cut the branch ends to fit. Attach the pieces to the sides of the toolbox with screws or nails. Predrill to avoid splitting.

- 1/4" x 1-1/2" DOWEL

3 Drill 1/4-in. holes through the handle ends and drive in the dowels to hold the handle in place.

Privacy trellis with planters 163
Bamboo planter & trellis 164
Make a bamboo teepee 169
Hardy street-side planter 169
Arched planter 170

11 GARDEN PLANTERS

Privacy trellis with planters

WHAT IT TAKES

TIME: 1 day
SKILL LEVEL: Beginner

For privacy and more greenery, build a trellis with removeable planter boxes. You can adapt this design to fencing (or a section of fencing), the side of a deck, an arbor or pergola. Or you can make a stand-alone trellis in your yard.

The trellis shown here is adapted to an existing pergola, and is built from 1x4s and a center 2x4. The boards are screwed to the 2x4 and the sides with 1 5/8-in. deck screws. The planter boxes are sized to hold four 6-in. plastic pots. Build as many as you want and just hang them from the 1x4s.

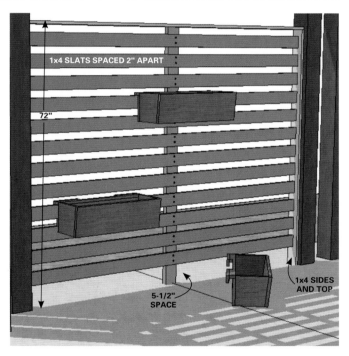

Figure A
Privacy trellis

1x4 SLATS SPACED 2" APART

72"

5-1/2" SPACE

1x4 SIDES AND TOP

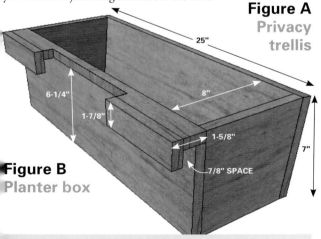

Figure B
Planter box

25"

6-1/4"

8"

1-7/8"

1-5/8"

7"

7/8" SPACE

Cutting list: Privacy trellis

KEY	QTY.	SIZE & DESCRIPTION
A	2	3/4" x 3-1/2" x 71-1/4" (vertical sides)
B	1	3/4" x 3-1/2" x 92" (horizontal top)
C	1	1-1/2" x 3-1/2" x 71-1/4" (center support)
D	12	3/4" x 3-1/2" x 90-1/2" (horizontal slats)

Materials list: Privacy trellis and planter box

ITEM	QTY.
1x4 x 8' treated pine	15
2x4 x 8' treated pine	1
1x8 x 10' cedar (per planter box)	1
No. 8 x 1-5/8" self-drilling exterior screws	50
1-3/4" galvanized nails (for planter box assembly)	1 box
Exterior construction adhesive (for planter assembly)	1 tube

Bamboo planter & trellis

Bring flowers and foliage to your deck or patio

I f you're wishing for wisteria or craving clematis, you can plant them just steps away in this planter and trellis for your deck or patio. And if you build a pair of them, you can create a privacy screen or provide shade from the late afternoon sun.

In one weekend you can build this planter/trellis combination for less than half the cost of a similar one—made of wood or plastic—at a garden center.

To build this planter, you'll need standard woodworking tools like a table saw and a miter saw. If you want to round the edges of the wooden parts as we did, you'll also need a router and two round-over bits (1/4- and 1/2-in. radius). Your cost for materials will depend mostly on the wood you choose for the planter box. We built our planter from "select-grade" pine boards. If you don't mind a few knots, use construction-grade pine, which costs less. If you live in a damp climate, consider rot-resistant choices like cedar or teak. Pressure-treated lumber is another good choice because it costs about the same as construction-grade pine and lasts practically forever. The drawback is that you may have to let it dry for a month before you start building.

Small-diameter bamboo for the planter box slats and lattice is in stock at most home centers and garden centers. The bamboo we used was labeled "3/4 inch." To find 1-1/2-in.-diameter bamboo for the trellis posts and header, visit a large garden center or shop online (search for "bamboo poles"). Select straight poles for the trellis posts and header. You'll find lower prices online, but those savings may be offset by shipping charges.

Master a new material

Bamboo is one of the world's greatest building materials. It's incredibly strong, good-looking and cheap. And if you're a weekend woodworker, you already have the tools to work with it. But bamboo doesn't behave exactly like wood, so you'll also need some new tricks up your sleeve. We'll show you how to build with this hard and brittle, irregular and hollow material.

1 **Build four frames. Glue together** the frames that form the sides of the planter box. Clamp a framing square to your workbench to help align the parts.

BACK OF FRAME

2 **Mask the frames. Line the backs of** the frames with wide masking tape. When you finish the wood later, the tape will keep stain off the bamboo.

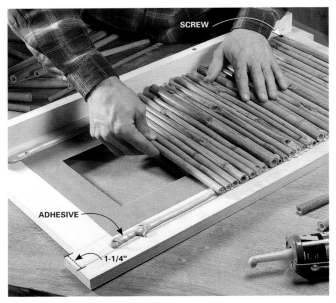

3 **Glue on the bamboo.** Fill the frames with bamboo slats. Screw the first slat in place and set the rest in heavy beads of construction adhesive.

4 **Assemble the planter box.** First screw the frames together at the corners. Then screw on the legs from inside the box and add the floor and top rim.

5 **Build the lattice on a frame.** Screw the first layer of bamboo poles directly to the frame, using spacer blocks to position them. Drill a pilot hole for every screw; bamboo splits easily.

6 **Wire the lattice together.** Tie the second layer of bamboo to the first with wire ties. Twist until the looped ends snap off. Then bend the remaining wire flat against the bamboo.

Build the planter box

To get started, rip four 8-ft.-long 1x6s into strips on your table saw. You'll need two 2-3/4-in.-wide strips for the top rim, two 1-3/4-in.-wide strips for the cleats and legs, and four 2-1/2-in.-wide strips for the legs, rails and stiles. Glue the rails and stiles together to make frames (Photo 1). Sand the frames and round the inside edges with your router and a 1/4-in. round-over bit. Then mask around the frames (Photo 2).

You'll need to cut about 120 slats to fill the frames. To avoid measuring them all, clamp a stop block next to your miter saw. With the slats cut, mark guidelines 1-1/4 in. from the top and bottom of the frames and glue the slats between them (Photo 3). Place the best side of each slat face down. Alternate thin and thick slats,

and the direction of the tapers—one narrow end up, the next down.

While you're waiting for the adhesive to harden, glue together the planter legs. Round the edges with a 1/2-in. round-over bit.

Assemble the planter box (Photo 4). Take diagonal corner-to-corner measurements to make sure the box is square before you screw the pressure-treated

Figure A
Bamboo planter & trellis

Overall dimensions: 40 in. wide x 18 in. deep x 72 in. tall. All wood parts are 3/4 in. thick.

Bamboo parts vary in diameter from 3/8 to 3/4 in. unless otherwise noted.

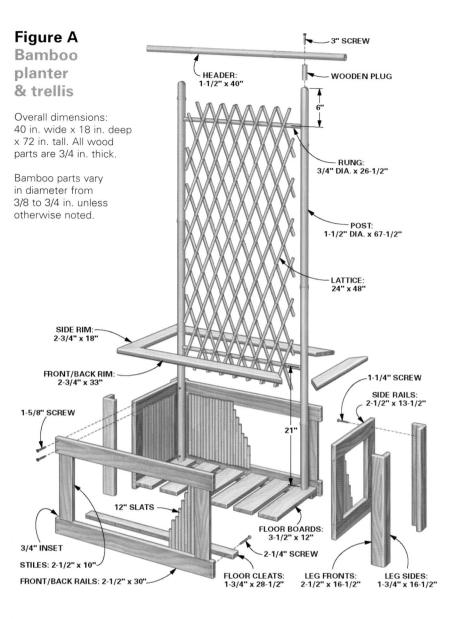

3" SCREW

HEADER: 1-1/2" x 40"

WOODEN PLUG

6"

RUNG: 3/4" DIA. x 26-1/2"

POST: 1-1/2" DIA. x 67-1/2"

LATTICE: 24" x 48"

1-1/4" SCREW

SIDE RAILS: 2-1/2" x 13-1/2"

SIDE RIM: 2-3/4" x 18"

FRONT/BACK RIM: 2-3/4" x 33"

1-5/8" SCREW

21"

12" SLATS

FLOOR BOARDS: 3-1/2" x 12"

2-1/4" SCREW

3/4" INSET

STILES: 2-1/2" x 10"

FRONT/BACK RAILS: 2-1/2" x 30"

FLOOR CLEATS: 1-3/4" x 28-1/2"

LEG FRONTS: 2-1/2" x 16-1/2"

LEG SIDES: 1-3/4" x 16-1/2"

Materials list

All the tools and materials for this project—except the 1-1/2-in. bamboo—are available at home centers.

- Four 8-ft. 1x6s
- One 8-ft. 1x4 (treated)
- 16 lin. ft. of 1-1/2-in.-diameter bamboo
- 200 lin. ft. of 3/4-in.-diameter bamboo
- 2 tubes of construction adhesive
- 150 wire ties
- Exterior wood glue, 2-in. masking tape, 3-in. pan-head screws, construction screws (1-1/4, 1-5/8 and 2-1/4 in.), exterior wood filler, furniture glides and a wire twister tool.

We finished our planter with semitransparent exterior stain.

floor boards to the cleats. Top off the planter box with rim boards, mitered at the corners and screwed to the frames. We rounded the edges of our rim material with a 1/4-in. round-over bit before cutting it to length. The rim over hangs the inside of the box by 1/2 in.

Build the trellis

To assemble the lattice, first grab any 1x4s or 2x4s you have handy and build a 1x4 frame with inner dimensions of 2 x 4 ft. Take diagonal corner-to-corner measurements to make sure the frame is square. Lay the first pole across the frame from one corner to the other and screw it to the frame. Then add more poles, screwing each to the frame (Photo 5). Although it's time-consuming, you must drill a pilot hole for every screw—otherwise, the bamboo will split.

Attach the second layer of bamboo with wire ties and a "twister" tool (Photo 6). Wire ties are designed to connect the rebar that reinforces concrete, so you'll find them and a twister in the masonry aisle at home centers. For a neat, tight connection, pull upward on the twister as it spins. When the lattice is done, cut it out of the frame (Photo 7).

Next, build the bamboo frame that will hold the lattice. Start by cutting kerfs in the posts and header (Photo 8). Bamboo can develop wide cracks as it dries out. Cutting a kerf creates a single, straight opening and prevents random splitting. Then cut the tops of the posts

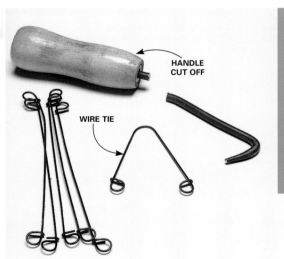

HANDLE CUT OFF

WIRE TIE

Using wire ties

Wire ties are simple to use: Bend each tie in half and slip it over the bamboo. Then hook the looped ends with the twister tool and spin. For faster twisting, cut the handle off the tool and chuck it into a drill (Photo 6).

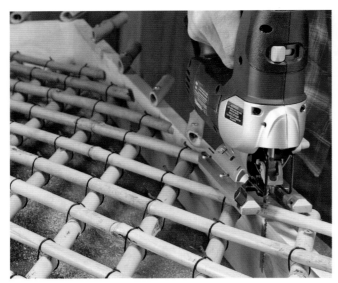

7 **Cut out the lattice.** Trim the completed lattice off the frame by guiding a jigsaw or reciprocating saw along the inner edge of the frame.

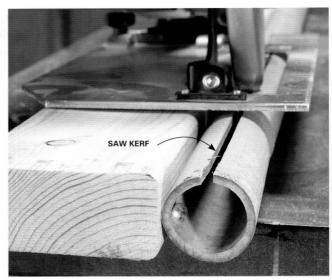

8 **Prevent cracks with kerfs.** Cut saw kerfs in the posts and header. This prevents random cracks from developing later. To cut safely, screw the bamboo to a 2x4.

SAW KERF

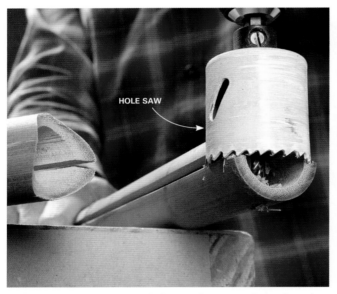

9 **Cut "saddles" with a hole saw.** Create rounded ends on the trellis posts to hold the header. For a clean cut, run the drill at high speed and apply light pressure.

HOLE SAW

10 **Screw on the header.** Screw the header to the posts. Drill pilot holes to avoid splitting the bamboo. Attach the lattice to the rungs using wire ties.

POST

RUNG

PLUG INSIDE

HEADER

using a 1-1/2-in. hole saw (Photo 9). Glue 4-in.-long 3/4 x 3/4-in. wooden plugs into the posts to provide anchors for the screws that fasten the header. The plugs don't have to fit tight; just use lots of construction adhesive.

Drill the posts with a 3/4-in. hole saw to create sockets for the rungs. Don't use a spade bit; the bamboo will split. Insert the rungs and measure the spread of the posts. To fit into the planter box, the spread must be no more than 27-1/2

in. Cut the rungs a bit shorter if needed and then glue them into the posts with construction adhesive. Attach the header (Photo 10). Leave the trellis frame on a flat surface until the adhesive hardens, then attach the lattice to the rungs. When you screw the completed trellis to the planter box, insert wooden blocks behind the bottom ends of the posts. Bamboo isn't perfectly straight, so you'll have to experiment with blocks of different thicknesses to make the posts plumb.

We finished our planter box with deck stain. When you're done finishing, slice the masking tape around the box frames with a utility knife and peel off the tape. Add plastic furniture glides to the legs to keep the wood from soaking up moisture. To hold soil, we used a 12-1/2-in. x 27-in. plastic planter. You could use two or three smaller pots instead.

Make a bamboo teepee

Climbing plants add an attractive third dimension to gardens. And the good news is that they don't care if their support is a pricey architectural statement or a couple of sticks.

A "teepee" made of bamboo stakes fits right in with a country flower or vegetable garden. It's cheap and simple to build and store. All you need are twine and some 3/4-in.-dia. bamboo stakes. Plunge the stakes (three or more, depending on how big you want it) into the soil so they form a teepee when the tops are bound together with twine as shown. Annual vines from beans and peas to morning glories will scramble up just about any support and quickly cover it up (inset photo), so if this bamboo doesn't look attractive to begin with, just wait a few weeks.

WHAT IT TAKES

TIME: 30 minutes
SKILL LEVEL: Beginner

Hardy street-side planter

Life on the street is tough on plants, too. They must survive exhaust fumes, heat and light reflected from the pavement, cramped roots, and winter road salt. In these areas, start with street-tough plants such as salvia, ornamental oregano, cranesbill geranium and sedum. But even these plants benefit from some extra attention.

Enriching the soil quality is essential. Do this by elevating the bed with timbers and adding a 3-in.-thick layer of mulch to conserve soil moisture and protect roots. Water these plants frequently and deeply. Also, hose off the foliage to remove dust, soot and salt, being sure to spray even the underside of the leaves.

WHAT IT TAKES

TIME: 4 hours
SKILL LEVEL: Beginner

3" LAYER OF SHREDDED WOOD MULCH

4x4 LANDSCAPE TIMBER

6x6 LANDSCAPE TIMBER

Arched planter

Bend wood to create this graceful plant stand. You can make it with only two boards!

With this elegant curved deck planter, you can have a splash of garden anyplace you like. Deck it out with flower pots and accent your patio, deck or front steps.

Here, we'll show you how to build the whole project in a leisurely weekend. Bending wood strips into laminated arches may seem challenging, but we'll walk you through the process step by step. After you build your first planter, you'll have the hang of it, and the next one will be a cinch to build. The key, as you'll see, is a simple plywood "bending" jig that you can use over and over again.

You can complete this project if you're handy with basic carpentry tools. However, you'll need a table saw equipped with a thin-kerf blade for ripping the strips and other parts. Sorry, but a circular saw just won't do the job no matter how steady you are. But you'll still need a circular saw, as well as a belt sander and at least four 3-ft. pipe or bar clamps (Photo 4).

Select wood with small, tight knots

You only need two 8-ft.-long 2x8s for the entire project. Our planter is made from western red cedar, chosen for its beauty and natural decay resistance. But any wood you choose will be fine as long as you select straight boards with small, tight knots. The long thin strips will break at large knots during the bending process. You'll be using nearly every inch of each board, so pick ones without splits or cracks at the ends. It may take some sorting at the home center, but the effort's worth it.

While you're at the home center, pick up 2 qts. of exterior woodworking glue along with a mini paint roller (Photo 6), a 4 x 8-ft. sheet of 3/4-in. plywood and a 10-ft. x 20-ft. roll of "painter's" plastic (3 mil). Also buy a small box of galvanized 1-in. brads if you intend to hand-nail. Or, if you have an air nailer (Photo 11), get brads for your nail gun.

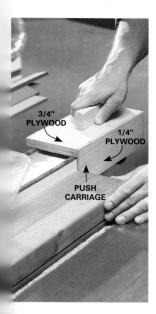

1 Cut the 2x8s to length following Figure A. Rip 5/16-in.-wide strips for the arches and the slats. Build a push carriage sized to fit your fence to safely cut thin strips.

3/4" PLYWOOD · 1/4" PLYWOOD · PUSH CARRIAGE

6' x 5/16" ARCH STRIPS

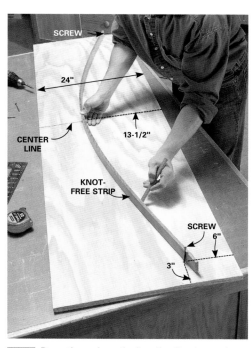

SCREW · 24" · 13-1/2" · CENTER LINE · KNOT-FREE STRIP · SCREW 6" · 3"

2 Draw the arch on the bending jig plywood using one of the knot-free strips of wood and a pair of 3-in. screws.

Figure A Build the whole planter from two 8-ft.-long 2x8s

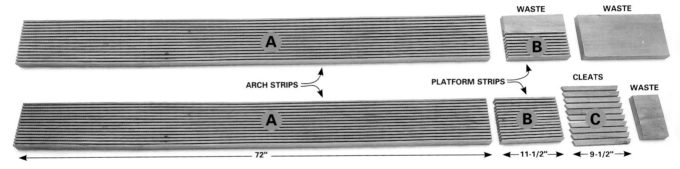

WASTE   WASTE

ARCH STRIPS   PLATFORM STRIPS

CLEATS   WASTE

A   B   C

72"   11-1/2"   9-1/2"

Cut the parts

Cut each 2x8 to the lengths called for in Figure A and then start the ripping process. Ripping 5/16-in.-wide strips can be hazardous, so be sure to use a push carriage (Photo 1). Make your carriage from 1/4-in. and 3/4-in. plywood, custom-sized to match the height of the table saw fence. We were able to cut 15 strips from each board, but you may get fewer depending on the thickness of your blade. Don't worry if you wind up with fewer or unusable ones; you can build each arch with as few as 13 strips. Just make sure to use the same quantity for each arch so they'll match. If any of the strips break at knots, keep the pieces together, because you can still use them (more on this later).

Rip the platform slats next and then the 1/2- x 3/4-in. platform cleats. Rip the pieces first to 3/4 in. wide from a chunk of 2x8, then turn the 1-1/2-in. strips on their sides and rip them into 1/2-in. strips. Cut the cleats to length with decorative 22-degree angles on the ends.

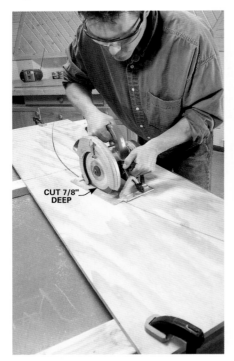

CUT 7/8" DEEP

GAP

3/4" SPACER

3 Set the blade of the circular saw to cut 7/8 in. deep and cut the curve. Clamp the plywood to the workbench and hold your saw with both hands.

4 Clamp 15 strips in the bending jig and re-mark the top curve with a 3/4-in. spacer block. Then remove the strips and recut that curve only.

5 Screw together three clamping cauls, adding blocks as needed so they'll be even with the top of the laminating strips (see Photo 7).

Make the bending jig

Cut the plywood for the bending jig to size (Photo 2) and use one of the knot-free strips to form the curve. Use 3-in. screws partially driven into the plywood at the locations we show and push the center of the strip 13-1/2 in. out from the edge while you scribe the curve. Don't beat yourself up striving for a perfect curve; small variations won't be noticeable. It may seem odd to make this curved cut with a circular saw (Photo 3), but it's surprisingly easy and safe on a gentle curve like this. The curve will be smoother than any you can achieve with a jigsaw. Just make sure to set your blade depth at 7/8 in. Any deeper and the blade may bind and kick back.

The two curves on the two sections of the jig are slightly different, and you'll have to recut the top part of the jig to match the bottom. To find this difference, lay 15 strips in the jig and tighten the clamps until the arch is completely formed (Photo 4). You'll have to tighten the clamps in "turns" as the strips gradually bend; that is, tighten two clamps until they run out of threads. Then leave them in place while you completely unscrew the other two, slide those jaws tight to the jig and continue tightening those. Work on pairs, tightening the outer two, then the inner two. You'll get the feel for the clamping process on this "glue-less" dry run and it'll make the actual glue-up easier. When the clamps are tight, the strips will be tight to the jig at the bottom and there'll be a gap between the arch and the jig at the top. Trace around the top with a

6 Roll glue onto both sides of each strip (one side of top and bottom strips) and position them, keeping the jig and strip center lines aligned.

7 Pull the jig together as far as possible and snug up the clamps. Then screw the cauls down and finish tightening the clamps.

3/4-in. spacer to re-mark the top curve (Photo 4). Then unclamp everything and recut that part of the jig.

Block up the cauls and glue up the arches

During glue-up, the strips have a tendency to lift away from the clamps while the glue is wet and slippery because of the stresses in the curves. "Cauls" are simply blocks of wood that hold the strips flat and prevent this. Make the cauls from six 2x4s (three on both the bottom and the top) and space them evenly with blocking sized so the cauls will be flush with the top of the arch (Photo 7). Have these ready to go before the glue-up—you won't have time to spare later.

Mark a center line on the strips and

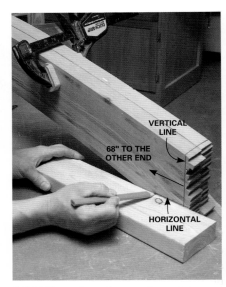

8 Remove the cauls after one hour and scrape off the excess glue from that side. Remove the clamps after three hours and scrape the glue from the other side.

PAINT SCRAPER

9 Belt-sand both sides of the arch flat with 60-grit paper, then 80-grit. Smooth the surface with a random-orbital sander with 100-grit paper.

10 Clamp the arches together and draw vertical lines just short of the ends. Then scribe the bottom horizontal lines with a 2x4 spacer. Cut the ends with a circular saw.

VERTICAL LINE

68" TO THE OTHER END

HORIZONTAL LINE

CLEAT MOUNTING TEMPLATE

FLUSH WITH ARCH BOTTOM

CLAMP

TEMPORARY SPACER

1/2" SPACE

EVEN WITH END OF CLEAT

11 Lay the cleat-mounting template (Figure B) flush with the arch bottoms. Then glue and nail the end cleats. Rest the template over the first set of cleats and mount the next two cleats, then move it again to mount the top cleat.

12 Space and clamp the arches. Then glue and nail the platform strips on the cleats, keeping them even with the cleat ends and spacing them 1/2 in. apart.

keep them aligned with the bending jig center line when you start gluing later (Photo 6). Lay painter's plastic directly below the jig to keep your workbench and clamps clean and then start gluing the strips. A mini paint roller greatly speeds up the process, and time is of the essence. Glue both sides of each strip and push the glued surfaces lightly together to delay glue setup. Slip in any broken strips near the middle of the arch, matching

up the breaks after they're coated with glue. Use flawless strips for the first and last strips of each arch. After you spread the glue, pull the jig together, bending the strips as far as you can while a helper slides the clamps closed. That'll speed up the clamping process. Then lay plastic over the caul locations, screw the cauls into place, screw the top 2x4s into place and tighten the clamps. Again, work on pairs, progressively tightening

Figure B Cleat template

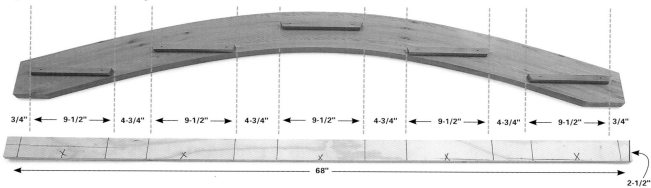

3/4" ← 9-1/2" → 4-3/4" ← 9-1/2" → 4-3/4" ← 9-1/2" → 4-3/4" ← 9-1/2" → 4-3/4" ← 9-1/2" → 3/4"

68"

2-1/2"

them. Work quickly. If you still see gaps between any strips, close them by driving a wedge between the jig and the arch or add more bar clamps from above. Ignore the clamping instructions on the glue bottle—leave the clamps in place for at least three hours.

You don't have to wait until you've removed the clamps to start cleaning up glue and flattening the arch. As the glue starts to "gel up" (dry to the touch but gooey beneath the surface, about one hour into clamping), remove the cauls (leave the clamps tightened) and start scraping away the glue from the top side of the arch. A paint scraper works great for most of it; use a small chisel or screwdriver to get into the crevices. The key is to remove as much glue as possible. Hardened glue is nearly impossible to remove and any leftover glue will clog and ruin sanding belts in no time. After you've scraped off the glue, wipe off any other glue smears with a damp (not wet!) rag. Don't worry about the bottom side yet; you can get it after the three-hour clamping period. The glue there will stay softer longer because it's against the plastic.

Flatten the arches and cut the ends

Start belt-sanding diagonally with 60-grit belts to knock off the high spots (Photo 9). After the surface is flat, remove cross-grain sanding marks by sanding following the curve. Then belt-sand with 80- and then 100-grit belts. Finish up with 100-grit paper in a random-orbital sander. Remove the arch from the jig, scrape off the glue, and flatten and sand the opposite side. Then repeat the whole process for the other arch.

If you have a benchtop planer, use it for the whole flattening process. Feed in one end and you'll be able to gently push the arch sideways and follow the curve as it goes through the machine. Make sure all the glue on the surface is removed. Hardened glue will dull the cutting knives.

Mark and cut off the bottom and ends as we show in Photo 10. Cut one end first, then measure over 68 in. and cut the other end. Ease the sharp edges of each arch with a round-over router bit or sandpaper.

Mount the cleats and the platforms

We show you an easy way to mount the cleats on both arches using a mounting template made from plywood (Photo 11 and Figure B). Cut it to 68 in. and lay out the cleat positions as shown. Then position and fasten the cleats (Photo 11).

Separate the arches with temporary platform strips and lightly clamp the arches together (Photo 12). Make sure the arch ends are even, then glue and nail the platforms to the cleats.

If you'd like a finish on your planter, use any stain designed for exterior siding. To further protect your planter against rot, spread exterior wood glue on the feet of each arch.

Sturdy deck planter.. 177
Stair-step plant display................................. 180
Patio planters... 182
Rot-proof window-planter............................. 187

12 DECK & WINDOW PLANTERS

Sturdy deck planter

WHAT IT TAKES

TIME: 4 hours
SKILL LEVEL: Beginner

This easy-to-make flower box sits on almost any deck rail ... or can even stand alone

Looking for a planter box that fits in just about anywhere? Then this sturdy and attractive planter box is what you need.

Its clever design means it can rest securely on a 2x4 or 2x6 deck railing or sit on a patio, porch or deck floor without tipping. Plus, it can be made just about any length you want. If that's not enough to get you building, it's easy to make, even for first-time woodworkers. You won't need a boatload of tools, either. A table saw is a must, but if you don't have one, perhaps a neighbor or friend can help. Spend a few extra dollars on cedar, redwood or cypress. These woods hold up better to the moisture they'll face from watering flowers.

Figure A
Deck planter

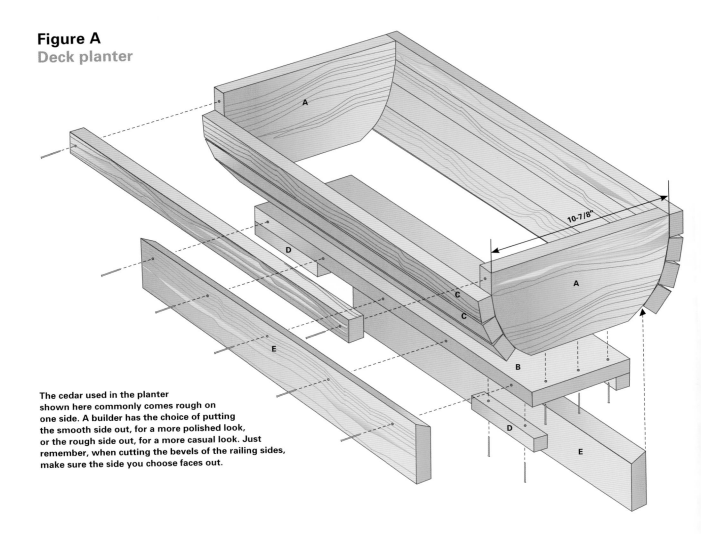

10-7/8"

A

A

D

C

C

B

D

E

E

The cedar used in the planter shown here commonly comes rough on one side. A builder has the choice of putting the smooth side out, for a more polished look, or the rough side out, for a more casual look. Just remember, when cutting the bevels of the railing sides, make sure the side you choose faces out.

Here's how to build it

Enlarge the end pattern (Figure B on p. 35) to exactly 10-7/8 in. Cut two boards to a length of 12 in. and tape or glue the patterns onto the boards. With a jigsaw or band saw, cut each end (A) using the pattern as a guide (Photo 1).

Mark the length of your box on the boards four times, for parts B, C and D, avoiding knots at the ends; cut to length. The planter box shown is 24 in. long.

On a table saw, cut the bottom board (B), slats (C) and railing spacers (D) to width. See the Cutting List.

Cut the railing sides (E), putting a 35-degree bevel along one edge. Be careful here—remember one side is rough and the other smooth. You can have either side facing out, but be sure to cut the angles the proper direction so the finish you prefer faces out.

Stand each end with the top edge down on your workbench and space them apart the length of the bottom board. Center the bottom board on each end and drill pilot holes to avoid splitting the wood. Use waterproof

Materials list

*	1x8 x 10' rough cedar, redwood or cypress (for 24" planter)
1 box	1-1/2" galvanized finishing nails
1 tube	Waterproof construction adhesive
1 qt.	Clear sealer or deck stain (optional)

*Quantity is determined by the length of your box

Cutting list

KEY	QTY.	SIZE & DESCRIPTION
A	2	Enlarge Figure B to 10-7/8" wide (ends)
B	1	5-5/8" x 24"* (bottom)
C	8	1-3/8" x 24"* (slats)
D	4	1" x 5-1/2" (spacers)
E	2	3-3/8" x 24"* (railing sides)

*Length should be adjusted equally on pieces B, C and E.

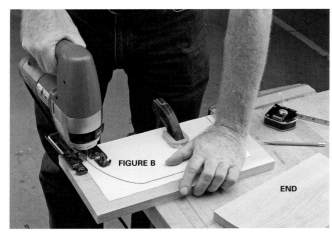

1 Cut out the ends using a jigsaw. Use a fine-tooth blade and follow the paper pattern attached to each end board with tape or glue.

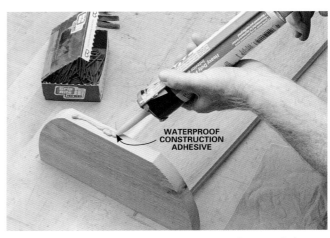

2 Glue the joints so your deck planter will last for years. Before attaching the bottom to the ends, drill pilot holes first so that you don't split the wood when nailing.

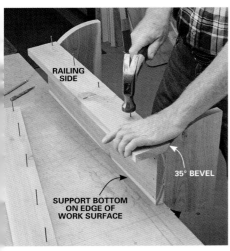

3 Attach railing sides to the bottom. The beveled edge allows the sides to fit snugly against the curved bottom of each end.

4 Nail side slats starting from the top of the box, working your way toward the bottom. Remember, pilot holes are a must when nailing close to the ends of these pieces.

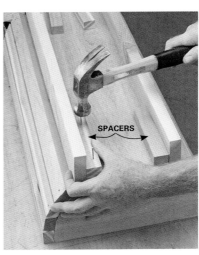

5 Add rail spacers to the inside of each railing side. These clever additions allow this box to sit snugly atop a 2x6 or 2x4 railing.

Figure B End pattern

Enlarge approx. 400%, to 10-7/8". If drawing, use a 1" grid.

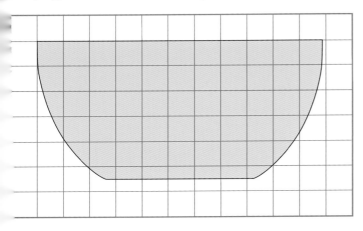

construction adhesive on all joints (Photo 2) before nailing pieces in place.

Nail the railing sides to the bottom as shown in Photo 3. The bevel fits the curve of the end boards nicely.

Working from the top to the bottom (Photo 4), predrill and attach the side slats on both sides of the box.

The spacers should be attached to the inside of each railing side as shown in Photo 5. These spacers strengthen the railing sides and also allow the box to snugly hold onto a 2x4 deck rail.

If you're applying a stain or sealer to help protect the wood, allow the adhesive to dry 24 hours.

In the meantime, go to the garden center for some potting soil and colorful flowers to brighten up your deck, patio or porch.

Stair-step plant display

WHAT IT TAKES

TIME: 4 hours
SKILL LEVEL: Beginner

Show off your favorite plants with this simple cedar stand.

We tend to buy plants first and worry about good spots for them later. So unfortunately, many of the prettiest plants get lost in the corners of a deck and sunroom and don't get the attention (or the light) they deserve.

To help solve this problem and to spotlight some favorite plants, we came up with this simple display stand. It's made from cedar 1x2s that are cut into just two lengths, stacked into squares and nailed together. We used western red cedar with the rough-sawn side exposed. Assembly is simple and fast, because

there's nothing to measure as you build—just keep everything square and use the wood pieces themselves for spacing and alignment.

Here's what you'll need

For supplies, you'll need seven 8-ft.-long cedar 1x2s, exterior glue, a few dozen 4d galvanized finish nails, and some 100- or 120-grit sandpaper. You'll also need a hammer, a tape measure and a framing square, plus a saw that can cut the 1x2s to a consistent length. A power miter saw is great for this (you can rent one) but you could also use a handsaw in a miter

box. An exterior finish for the wood is attractive, but not really necessary.

Begin by trimming any rough or out-of-square ends from your 1x2s. Almost all the ends will show, so they need to look good. Cut the 1x2s into sixteen 20-in. pieces and twenty-seven 10-3/4-in. pieces. It's important that the two groups of pieces are consistent in length, so rather than measuring each one, clamp a "stop block" to your bench the appropriate distance from the blade of your saw, and push the 1x2 up against it for each cut.

How to build it

Begin making your stand by arranging the lowest two layers without nails or glue (Photo 1). Lay out the bottom three 20-in. pieces against a framing square,

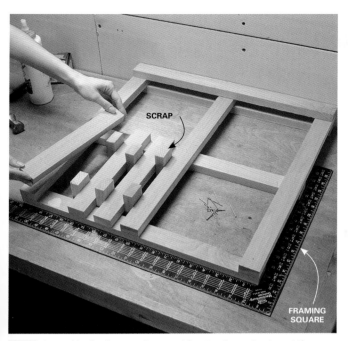

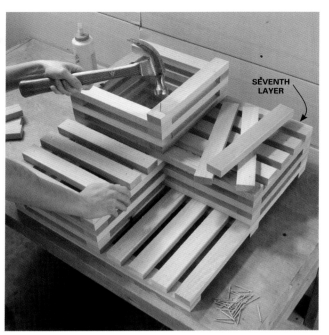

1 Assemble the first two layers without nails or glue to get the spacing right and to make sure everything is square. Use scrap pieces of 1x2 as spacers. Once everything is square, glue and nail all the intersections.

2 Build up the stand "log-cabin style" until you get to the seventh layer, which has two platforms. When that's nailed down, continue until the 12th layer, which has the final platform.

then lay three more 20-in. pieces and three 10-3/4-in. pieces on top of them as shown in Photo 1.

Adjust the spacing, using scrap pieces to create the gaps, and make sure everything is square. The second layer should have a plant platform in one corner and nothing in the other three. When everything looks good, nail the pieces together, using one nail and a dab of glue at every intersection. Keep the nails 3/4 in. away from the ends of the boards to prevent splitting.

Add five more layers each consisting of two long and one short piece, with glue and a nail at every overlap. Check the sides with the square as you go to keep them straight. At the seventh layer, add two more platforms, with the 10-3/4-in. pieces running perpendicular to the pieces on the first platform. Add another five layers, with just two 10-3/4-in. pieces per layer, then fill in the top layer to create the final display platform (Photo 2). When you're done nailing, sand all the outside edges of your stand and apply an exterior stain or preservative. Wait a few days for the finish to dry completely, then start moving in the plants!

Tip

Always nail at least 3/4 in. in from the end, and if the wood still splits, predrill the nail holes using a bit the size of the nail or the nail itself with the head snipped off. Your boards may also differ in thickness from those shown, which were 13/16 in. thick. If so, simply adjust the spacing between the boards.

Figure A
Exploded view

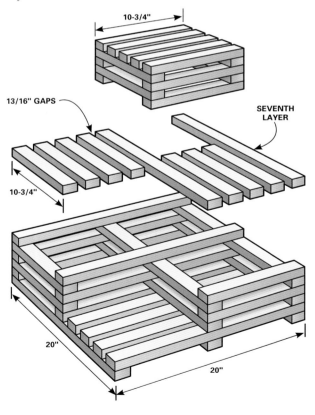

Patio planters

Build them any size and give your potted plants a simple, stylish home— outdoors or in

This planter is designed to make your patio or deck gardening much easier. Instead of filling it with dirt and planting each flower or plant individually, you simply set prepotted plants right into the planter. You can conveniently switch plants as the season changes or unload the planter and move it to a new location.

We designed this project to fit any pot with an 11-in. diameter or less and a maximum height of 10-1/2 in. To create the illusion of a fully planted box, you just fill in around the pots with wood chips, bark or other mulch covering. The base or bottom of the planter has 7/8-in. holes drilled every 6 in. to drain away any excess water. The side boards have a 1/4-in. space between them to ventilate the mulch and keep it from getting soggy.

Figure A
Leg template
(enlarge 400%)

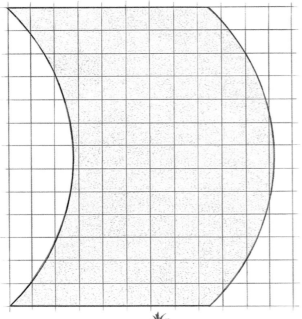

Cutting list for large planter

KEY	QTY.	SIZE & DESCRIPTION
A	4	1-1/2" x 11-1/4" x 13" treated pine legs
B	1	1-1/2" x 11-1/4" x 48" treated pine base
C	4	1-1/2" x 5-1/2" x 48" cedar side panels
D	4	1-1/2" x 5-1/2" x 14-1/4" cedar end panels*
E	2	1-1/16" x 4-1/2" x 57" cedar side aprons
F	2	1-1/16" x 4-1/2" x 20-1/4" cedar side aprons*

Cutting list for small planter

KEY	QTY.	SIZE & DESCRIPTION
A	4	1-1/2" x 11-1/4" x 13" treated pine legs
B	1	1-1/2" x 11-1/4" x 36" treated pine base
C	4	1-1/2" x 5-1/2" x 36" cedar side panels
D	4	1-1/2" x 5-1/2" x 14-1/4" cedar end panels*
E	2	1-1/16" x 4-1/2" x 45" cedar side aprons
F	2	1-1/16" x 4-1/2" x 20-1/4" cedar side aprons*

*Cut to fit

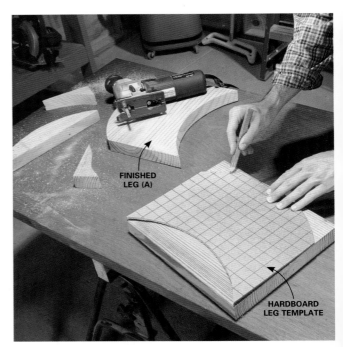

1 Using a full-size template made from Figure A, trace the outline of the planter legs onto pressure-treated 2x12 pine boards. Sand the edges with a finish or belt sander followed by 100-grit hand-sanding to gently ease the edges.

FINISHED LEG (A)

HARDBOARD LEG TEMPLATE

C

12" SPEED SQUARE

SUPPORT BLOCK

D

2 Make straight cuts using a 12-in. Speed square held firmly against the back of the 2x6.

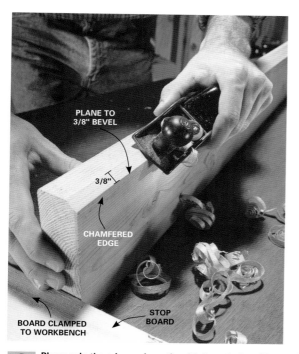

PLANE TO
3/8" BEVEL

3/8"

CHAMFERED
EDGE

STOP
BOARD

BOARD CLAMPED
TO WORKBENCH

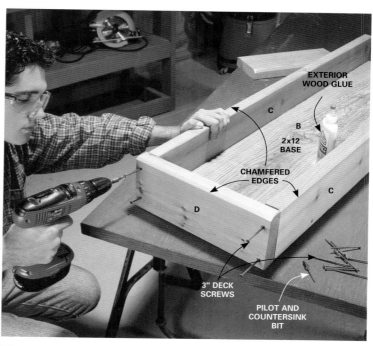

EXTERIOR
WOOD GLUE

C

B

2x12
BASE

CHAMFERED
EDGES

C

D

3" DECK
SCREWS

PILOT AND
COUNTERSINK
BIT

3 Plane only the edges where the side boards C and D meet. This chamfered edge should be about 3/8 in. wide when completed. Clamp a board to the edge of your workbench to stop the workpiece from drifting while you stroke the edge of the board with the plane.

4 Cut your 2x12 base to length, then screw the lower sides (C) to the base. Align the base and sides so they're flush on the bottom sides. Predrill for each screw using a pilot/countersink combination bit. Then screw the ends to the sides.

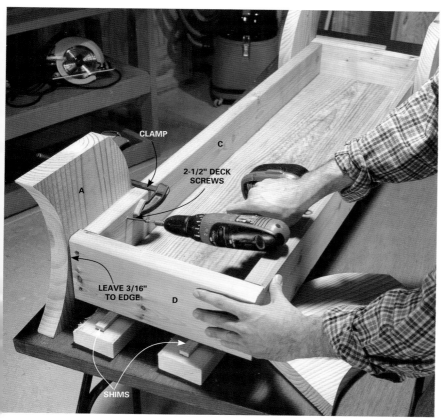

CLAMP

C

2-1/2" DECK
SCREWS

A

LEAVE 3/16"
TO EDGE

D

SHIMS

5 Shim the base up 1-3/4 in. on each side using scrap pieces of wood, then clamp the legs one at a time to the sides (C). Screw the sides to the legs with 2-1/2 in. deck screws. Use three screws per leg.

We've shown you two planters of different lengths, but you can adapt them to fit your unique space. You can even change the width by nailing a treated 2x2 to the side of the 2x12 base piece to accommodate a slightly wider pot. To build either the small or large planter shown, follow our clear step-by-step photos and refer to the Cutting List for lumber lengths.

Buying the right lumber

You'll notice the legs are treated pine and not cedar like the sides and top apron. Treated pine is less likely to split along the grain (a nasty problem with cedar). Pick treated 2x12 material for the legs with as few large knots as possible. You'll be able to cut around knots on a single board, so bring a tape measure when you select the lumber. Choose straight cedar for the sides and remember that some knots here can add to the overall beauty.

Feel free to use other species of wood such as redwood, cypress or even a plantation-grown tropical wood like ipe (available at some lumberyards).

DRILL 7/8"
DRAIN HOLES
EVERY 6"

5/4 x 6
CEDAR DECK
BOARD

6 Clamp the upper sides flush to the tops of the legs. Be sure to align the upper and lower side ends before drilling and screwing this piece in place. Again, use three 2-1/2 in. deck screws per leg. Next, screw the upper end panels (D) to the upper sides. Make sure the chamfers face each other on each side.

7 Rip the 5/4 x 6 deck boards to 4-1/2 in. to make the top apron frame. Use a rip guide on your circular saw or a table saw if you have one. Plane and sand the cut edge to match the factory-machined edge of the deck board.

Use paint, stain or a combination of both

We chose an exterior enamel paint for the legs and apron pieces to accent the deck oil stain/sealer on the base and sides. Stain is a better choice than paint for the base and sides because they'll be exposed to more moisture than the legs and top. The photo below shows the excellent results you can get by staining the entire project with an exterior oil deck stain.

6d GALVANIZED
CASING NAILS

8 Glue and nail the side apron pieces (E) flush with parts C below. Next, nail the apron end pieces to the end panels (D). You'll notice the inside edge of F will be about 1/4 in. out from the inside of the planter to adequately cover the tops of the legs.

Rot-proof window-planter

WHAT IT TAKES

TIME: 2 hours
SKILL LEVEL: Beginner

You can't beat the look of a real wood window box on a home. Wood takes paint well, so you can tailor the box's color scheme to complement your house. But ordinary wooden boxes rot out in just a few

years, and plastic window boxes won't rot but don't look as nice as the traditional wood box.

This window box design incorporates the best of both materials. Buy a plastic window box at a home or garden center, then construct a cedar frame around it. Size the frame so the lip of the plastic window box rests on the wood. There's no need for a bottom. Cut the front side of each end piece at a 5-degree angle, then screw together the frame with 2-in. deck screws. Attach the box to the house with a pair of L-brackets, and you're ready to get growing.

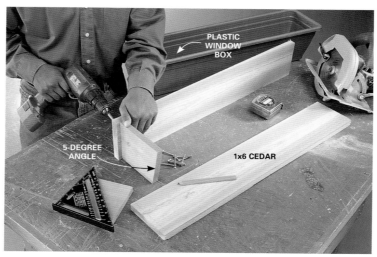

PLASTIC WINDOW BOX

5-DEGREE ANGLE

1x6 CEDAR

3-hour cedar bench 189
North woods bench...................................... 194
Simplest bench in the world......................... 198
Garden bench 200

13 BENCHES

3-hour cedar bench

WHAT IT TAKES

TIME: 3 hours

SKILL LEVEL: Beginner to intermediate

Materials list

QTY.	ITEM
2	1x3 x 8' cedar
1	2x10 x 8' cedar
5	2x4 x 8' cedar
1 lb.	3" deck screws
1/4 lb.	6d galv. casing nails
2	3/8" x 5" bolts with nuts and washers

Build it in an afternoon!

The beauty of this cedar bench isn't just that it's easy to assemble and inexpensive—it's that it's so doggone comfortable. You can comfortably sit on your custom-fit bench for hours, even without cushions. Here, you'll learn how to build the bench and how to adjust it for maximum comfort.

Sloping the back and the seat is the secret to pain-free perching on unpadded flat boards. But not all bodies are the same, and it's a rare piece of furniture that everyone agrees is seatworthy. This bench has a bolted pivot point where the back and the seat meet that lets you alter the backrest and seat slopes to fit your build during one of the final assembly steps (Photo 10). Cutting all the parts and assembling them will only take about three hours. Follow the step-by-step photo series for details on the simple construction.

Figure A
Bench parts

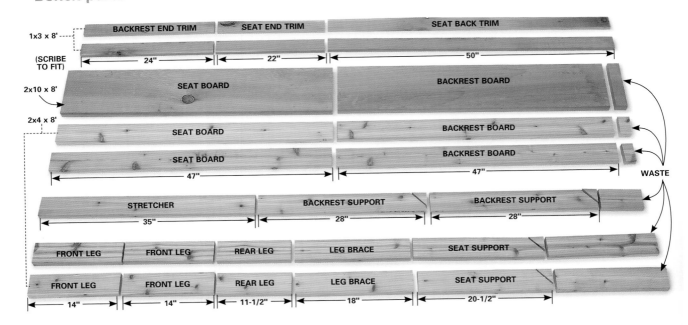

1x3 x 8'
(SCRIBE TO FIT)

BACKREST END TRIM | SEAT END TRIM | SEAT BACK TRIM
24" | 22" | 50"

2x10 x 8'

SEAT BOARD | BACKREST BOARD

2x4 x 8'

SEAT BOARD | BACKREST BOARD

SEAT BOARD | BACKREST BOARD
47" | 47"

WASTE

STRETCHER | BACKREST SUPPORT | BACKREST SUPPORT
35" | 28" | 28"

FRONT LEG | FRONT LEG | REAR LEG | LEG BRACE | SEAT SUPPORT

FRONT LEG | FRONT LEG | REAR LEG | LEG BRACE | SEAT SUPPORT
14" | 14" | 11-1/2" | 18" | 20-1/2"

Build it from eight 8-ft.-long boards and a handful of fasteners

A circular saw and a screw gun are the only power tools you really need for construction, although a power miter saw will speed things up and give you cleaner cuts. Begin by cutting the boards to length. Figure A shows you how to cut up the eight boards efficiently, leaving little waste. When you're picking out the wood at the lumberyard, choose boards that above all are flat, not twisted. That's especially important for the seat and back parts. Don't worry so much about the leg assembly 2x4s because you cut them into such short pieces that warps and twists aren't much of a concern.

After cutting the pieces to length, screw together the leg assemblies (Photos 2 – 6). It's important to use a square to keep the leg braces square to the legs (Photo 2). That way both leg assemblies will be identical and the bench won't wobble if it's put on a hard, flat surface. The leg brace is spaced 1/2 in. back from the front of the legs to create a more attractive shadow line. Then it's just a matter of connecting the leg assemblies with the stretcher (Photo 7), screwing down the seat and backrest boards, and adjusting the slopes to fit your body.

The easiest way to adjust the slope is to hold the four locking points in place with clamps and then back out the temporary screws (Photo 10). To customize the slopes, you just loosen the clamps, make the

GUIDE SQUARE

1 Cut out the bench parts following the measurements in Figure A. Use a square to guide the circular saw for accurate, square cuts. Cut 45-degree angles on the ends of the seat and back supports 1 in. down from the ends as shown (also see Photos 4 and 5).

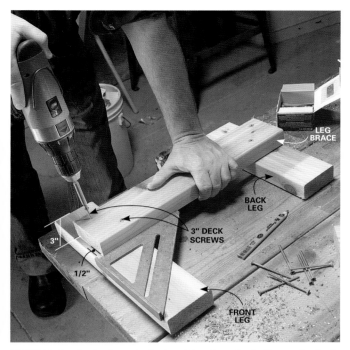

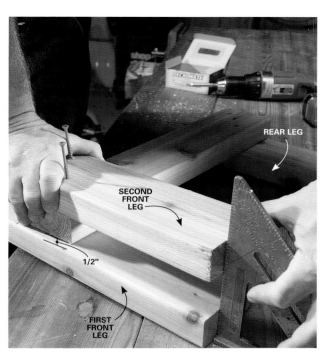

2 Fasten the leg brace to the legs 3 in. above the bottom ends. Angle the 3-in. screws slightly to prevent the screw tips from protruding through the other side. Hold the brace 1/2 in. back from the front edge of the front leg. Use a square to make sure the brace and legs are at exact right angles.

3 Align the second part of the front leg with the first one using a square and screw it to the leg brace as shown.

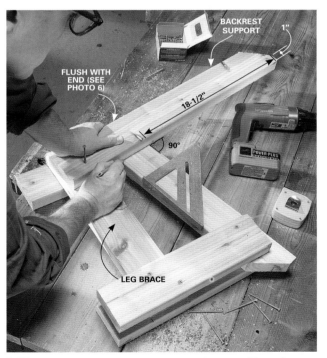

4 Slip the seat support between the two front legs, positioning it as shown. Drive a single 3-in. screw through the front leg into the seat support.

5 Position the backrest support on the leg assembly as shown, making sure it's at a right angle with the seat support, and mark the position on the seat support. Then drive a 3-in. screw through the middle of the backrest support into the leg brace.

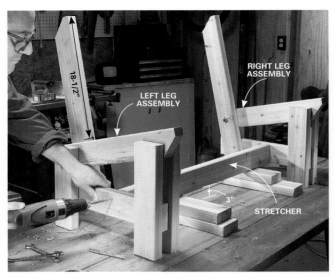

6 Clamp the backrest support, seat support and rear leg as shown using the line as a guide. Drill a 3/8-in. hole through the center of the assembly. Drive a 3/8-in. x 5-in. bolt fitted with a washer through the hole and slightly tighten the nut against a washer on the other side.

7 Assemble the other leg assembly to *mirror* the first as shown. (The back support and rear leg switch sides.) Prop the stretcher 3 in. above the workbench, center it between the front and rear bench legs and screw the leg braces into the ends with two 3-in. deck screws.

adjustments, retighten and test the fit. When you're satisfied, run a couple of permanent screws into each joint. If you don't have clamps, don't worry—you'll just have to back out the screws, adjust the slopes, reset the screws and test the bench. Clamps just speed up the process.

Round over the edges

We show an option of rounding over the sharp edge of the 1x3 trim, which is best done with a router and a 1/2-in. round-over bit (Photo 12). Rounding over the edges can protect shins and the backs of thighs and leave teetering toddlers with goose eggs on their melons instead of gashes. So the step is highly recommended. If you don't have a router, round over the edge either by hand-sanding or with an orbital or belt sander. In any event, keep the casing nails 1 in. away from the edge to prevent hitting the nailheads with the router bit or sandpaper (Photo 12).

Building a longer bench

We demonstrate how to build a 4-ft.-long bench, plenty of space for two. But you can use the same design and techniques for building 6- or 8-ft. long benches too. You'll just have to buy longer boards for the seat, back, stretcher and the trim boards. While you're at it, you can use the same design for matching end or coffee tables. Just match the double front leg design for the rear legs, and build flat-topped leg assemblies with an overall depth of 16-3/4 in.

Seal the legs to make it last

If you want to stain your bench, use a latex exterior stain on the parts after cutting them to length. After assembly, you won't be able to get good penetration at the cracks and crevices. Avoid clear exterior sealers, which will irritate bare skin. But

8 Center the first 2x4 seat board over the leg assemblies and flush with the front ends of the seat supports. Screw it to the seat supports with two 3-in. deck screws spaced about 1 in. away from the edges. Line up the 2x10 with the first 2x4, space it about 5/16 in. away (the thickness of a carpenter's pencil) and screw it to the seat supports with two 3-in. deck screws. Repeat with the rear 2x4.

Tip

If you want to save a few bucks—or if cedar is difficult to find in your area—you can build this bench from pressure-treated lumber. Just make sure the boards are relatively dry and don't contain too many large knots.

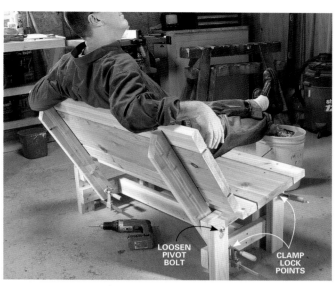

9 Rest the bottom backrest 2x4 on carpenter's pencils, holding the end flush with the seat boards and screw it to the seat back braces. Then space and screw on the center 2x10 and the top 2x4 backrest boards.

FLUSH EDGES

10 Sit on the bench and decide if you'd like to tilt the seat or the backrest or both to make the bench more comfortable. To make seat or back adjustments, loosen the bolts and clamp the bottoms of the seat back supports and the fronts of the seat supports. Then back out the four screws at those points. Loosen the clamps, make adjustments, then retighten and retest for comfort. When you're satisfied with the fit, drive in the four original screws plus another at each point. Retighten the pivot bolts.

LOOSEN PIVOT BOLT

CLAMP LOCK POINTS

FLUSH

BACKREST TRIM BOARD

SCRIBE BACK SIDE

FLUSH

SEAT TRIM BOARD

TURN ROUTER SIDEWAYS HERE

1"

1/2" ROUND-OVER BIT

11 Tack the seat trim boards to the seat with the ends flush with the front and top. Scribe and cut the trim boards to fit. Nail the boards to the seat and backrest boards with 6d galvanized casing nails, keeping the nails 1 in. back from the seat edges.

12 Ease the edges of the trim boards with a router and a 1/2-in. round-over bit. Hold the router sideways to get at the seat/back corner.

he bench will last outside for more than 20 years without any stain or special care even if you decide to let it weather to a natural gray. However, the legs won't last hat long because the end grain at the bottom will wick up moisture from the ground, making the legs rot long before the bench does. To make sure the legs last as long as the bench, seal the ends with epoxy, urethane or exterior woodworker's glue when you're through with the assembly.

Tip

You can use the same design and techniques for building a 4-, 6- or 8-foot-long bench.

North woods bench

An inexpensive, easy-to-build classic

WHAT IT TAKES

TIME: Half day
SKILL LEVEL: Beginner to intermediate

The cute red stool shown below was made by an anonymous carpenter, and it's simplicity itself: pine boards, nailed together. It also has an interesting and ingenious design detail: a cloverleaf, clearly made with three overlapping drill holes. It's just the kind of little bench that's perfect for the backyard, so we went into the shop and made this modern version. A little longer and a little stronger than the original, but the same folk art detail. And since it's made from lumberyard pine, the price can't be beat. Here's how to make one.

This bench is simple enough to build with a few hand tools, but to speed things up, we chose to take advantage of the power tools in our shop. We used a miter saw to cut the stretchers to length and to cut the 10-degree angles on the ends of the center stretcher, and a circular saw for all the other cuts. If you don't own a miter saw, you can use a circular saw or jigsaw for all the cuts.

To make the holes for the clover shapes, you'll need a 1-in. hole saw mounted in a corded drill, or a powerful cordless drill.

We used No. 2 knotty pine to build this bench. You'll need one 6-ft. 1x12 and one 10-ft. 1x4. Select boards that are straight and flat, with solid, not loose, knots. We assembled the bench with countersunk 2-in. trim screws and then filled the holes with wood filler. If the bench is going outdoors, be sure to use corrosion-resistant screws.

Cut out the parts

Using the Cutting List, p. 53 as a guide, cut the two legs and the top from the 1x12 (Photo 1). The legs require a 10-degree bevel on the top and bottom. Be careful to keep both bevels angled the same direction. Then cut the stretcher and aprons to length. The stretcher has a 10-degree angle on each end.

Next, mark the legs and aprons for drilling and cutting, using the dimensions in Figures B and C as a guide. Draw the grid layout as shown in Photo 2 to locate the holes. Use a nail or a punch to make starting holes for the hole saw at the correct intersections.

1 Cut the leg blanks. Set the saw to cut a 10-degree bevel. Mark the 1x12 and align the saw with the mark. Then use a large square to help guide the cut.

10-DEGREE BEVEL

1" HOLE SAW

1/2"

1/2"

2 Drill out the clover shape. Mark out a grid with lines spaced 1/2 in. apart. The centers of the holes are on four of the intersections. Drill all four holes halfway through the board. Then flip the board over and drill from the other side to complete the holes.

3 Cut the leg angles. Mark the "V" in the center and the two outside angles on the legs. Then cut along the lines with a circular saw. Accurate cutting is easier if you clamp the leg to the workbench.

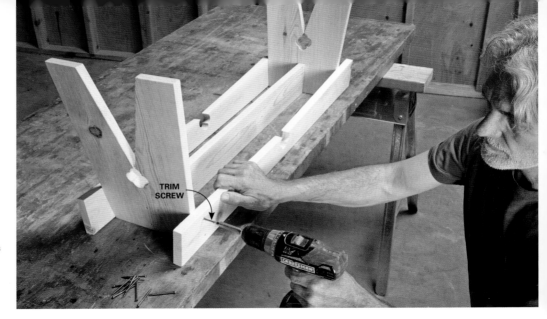

4 Screw the aprons to the legs. Drive trim screws through the legs into the stretcher. Then attach the outside aprons with trim screws.

TRIM SCREW

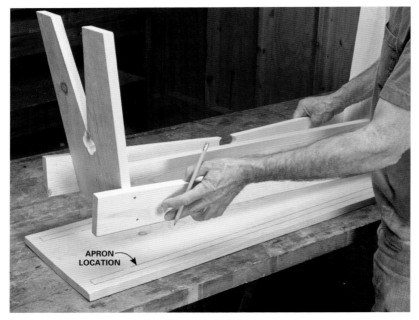

APRON LOCATION

5 Position the seat screws. Here's a goof-proof way to position the screws that fasten the seat to the bench frame. Center the frame on the seat and trace around the aprons. Then drill pilot holes through the seat to mark screw locations. Drive screws through the seat and into the aprons.

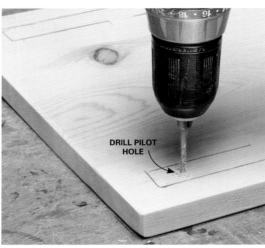

DRILL PILOT HOLE

Drill the 1-in. holes halfway through the boards (Photo 2). Make sure the pilot bit on the hole saw goes through the board so you can use the hole to guide the hole saw from the opposite side. Then flip the boards over to complete the holes.

Make the remaining cuts on the legs and aprons with a circular saw (Photo 3). Finish up by sanding the parts. We wrapped 80-grit sandpaper around a 1-in. dowel to sand the inside of the holes. Sand off the saw marks and round all the sharp edges slightly with sandpaper. If you plan to paint the bench, you can save time by painting the parts before assembly.

Build the bench

Start by marking the location of the stretcher on the legs. Arrange the legs so the bevels are oriented correctly, and screw through them into the stretcher. Next screw the two aprons to the legs (Photo 4).

The only thing left is to screw the top to the aprons. It'll be easier to place the screws accurately if you first mark the apron locations on the underside of the top and drill pilot holes for the screws (Photo 5). Stand the bench upright and align the top by looking underneath and lining up the apron marks. Then attach the top with six trim screws.

We finished this bench with old-fashioned milk paint. You can find milk paint online and at some paint stores. If the bench is going outdoors, rub some exterior glue on the bottom ends of the legs. That will prevent the end grain from soaking up moisture and rotting.

Figure A Exploded view

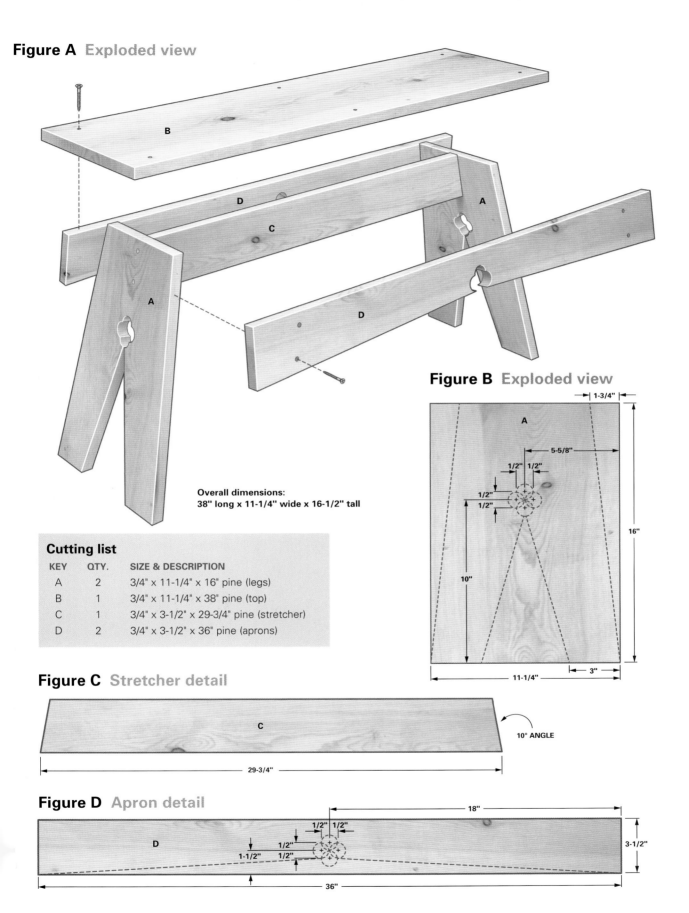

Overall dimensions:
38" long x 11-1/4" wide x 16-1/2" tall

Cutting list

KEY	QTY.	SIZE & DESCRIPTION
A	2	3/4" x 11-1/4" x 16" pine (legs)
B	1	3/4" x 11-1/4" x 38" pine (top)
C	1	3/4" x 3-1/2" x 29-3/4" pine (stretcher)
D	2	3/4" x 3-1/2" x 36" pine (aprons)

Figure B Exploded view

1-3/4"

5-5/8"

1/2" 1/2"

1/2"

1/2"

16"

10"

11-1/4"

3"

Figure C Stretcher detail

10° ANGLE

29-3/4"

Figure D Apron detail

18"

1/2" 1/2"

1/2"

1-1/2" 1/2"

3-1/2"

36"

Simplest bench in the world

WHAT IT TAKES

TIME: 2 hours
SKILL LEVEL: Beginner

Build it with a few 2x8s and a handful of screws

One of the easiest ways to make a good garden even better is to set a comfortable bench in a secluded corner. Just having a place to sit transforms an ordinary patch of flowers into a quiet contemplative refuge.

So if you're looking for a simple bench, take a look at this one, based on a design by Aldo Leopold, whom many consider the father of wildlife ecology.

Leopold's writings have led many to discover what it means to live in harmony with the land. If this bench was good enough for him, it's definitely good enough for the rest of us!

A little research led to this sturdy design which can be built quickly with a few 2x8s, glue and screws. Best of all, it's amazingly comfortable, perfect for bird-watching—even for two people.

1 Mark one end of the 2x8 x 10 at a 22-1/2-degree angle with a speed square or protractor, then cut with a circular saw. Make a mark 36 in. away and repeat the cut at the same angle. Cut the remaining front leg and two back legs from the same piece. Cut the seat and the backrest from the 2x8 x 8.

2 Fasten the legs together. Stack and clamp the seat and backrest to the edge of the worktable as guides, and then align the legs against them. Spread adhesive on the front leg, set the rear leg in place, and fasten the legs together with three 2-1/2-in. screws.

Building tips

To make a simple project even simpler, remember these tips:

- Be sure to assemble the legs (Step 2) so they're mirror images of each other, and not facing the same direction.

- Use clamps or a helper to hold the legs upright when securing the seat.

- Predrill all your screw holes to prevent splitting the wood.

Tools

Speed square or protractor

Drill with #8 countersink drill bit

Circular saw

Caulking gun

Materials list

1 2x8 x 8' cedar, redwood or treated lumber (seat and backrest)

1 2x8 x 10' cedar, redwood or treated lumber (front and rear legs)

Exterior construction adhesive

2-1/2" galvanized deck screws

3 Attach the seat and backrest. Stand the two ends up, 42 in. apart, spread glue on the tops of the rear legs, and screw the seat in place. Lay the bench on the worktable and attach the backrest with glue and screws.

SIMPLEST BENCH IN THE WORLD **199**

Garden bench

WHAT IT TAKES

TIME: 1–2 days
SKILL LEVEL: Beginner to intermediate

A curved seat makes it comfortable; biscuit joinery makes it simple, strong

The first thing people notice about this bench is the design—simple but handsome. Then, as soon they sit down, they're all surprised by how comfortable it is.

This bench is just plain easy to build. It uses only biscuits and screws—the simplest types of joinery. Still, the bench is surprisingly strong. This one has been hauled around, knocked around and used as a mini scaffold—and once it even fell out of a moving pickup. But it's still solid.

Round up the tools and materials

You may have to buy more lumber than what it says in the Materials List, p. 58, to get knot-free pieces. You'll find everything you need to build this bench at your local home center or lumberyard. Refer to the Materials List; then choose the lumber carefully to avoid large knots.

In addition to the lumber, screws and wood plugs, you'll need No. 20 wood biscuits and a special tool called a plate or biscuit joiner to cut the biscuit slots. You can buy a good-quality biscuit joiner at any home center or online. You'll also need some clamps, a table saw and a router fitted with a 1/4-in. round-over bit.

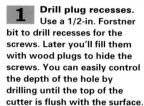

1 **Drill plug recesses.** Use a 1/2-in. Forstner bit to drill recesses for the screws. Later you'll fill them with wood plugs to hide the screws. You can easily control the depth of the hole by drilling until the top of the cutter is flush with the surface.

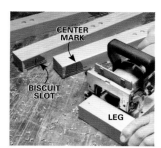

2 **Cut biscuit slots for the seat rails.** Mark the centers of the biscuit slots on masking tape. Then, with the plug recesses facing up, cut the slots in the narrow sides of the legs. Keep the plate joiner and leg tight to the bench top as you cut. Use tape to avoid marks on the wood and to keep track of the orientation of the pieces.

3 **Position slots for the long rails with a spacer.** Orient the leg so the previously cut slot is facing up, and cut a slot on the side opposite the plug holes. Use a spacer to position the slot so the long rail will be centered on the leg when it's installed.

Cut, drill and slot the parts

Start by inspecting your boards and planning the cuts to take advantage of the knot-free sections. Use a table saw to rip the boards to the right width. For crisp, clean edges, rip about 1/4 in. from the edge of the boards before you rip them to the final width. To work around knots, you may have to rough-cut some of the boards to approximate length before ripping them. When you're done ripping, cut the parts to length. We used a 1/4-in. round-over bit and router to ease the edges of the seat boards. It's a great task for a router table setup if you have one.

Next, measure and mark the center of all the screw holes and drill 3/8-in.-deep holes for the 1/2-in. wood plugs. We used a Forstner bit to create clean, flat-bottom holes. The final step in preparing the parts for assembly is cutting the biscuit slots. Rather than use the adjustable fence to position the slots, simply place your workpiece and the base of the biscuit joiner against the bench top and cut the slot.

4 **Cut slots in the rail ends.** Mark the centers of the curved seat rails and long rails on masking tape. The tape also helps you keep track of the orientation of the slots.

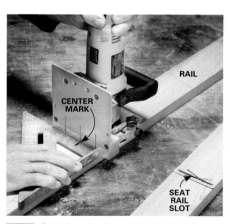

5 **Cut slots in the long rails.** Position the long rails with the masking tape facing down. Use a Speed Square as a guide for cutting biscuit slots for the intermediate rails. Align the square with the edge mark for the seat rail. Make a center mark on the square as a reference for lining up the plate joiner.

6 **Join the seat rails and legs with biscuits.** Put a biscuit in the slot and dry-fit the leg and seat rail to make sure the rail is oriented correctly. It should be centered on the leg. Then spread glue in the slots and on the biscuit and press the leg and the seat rail together.

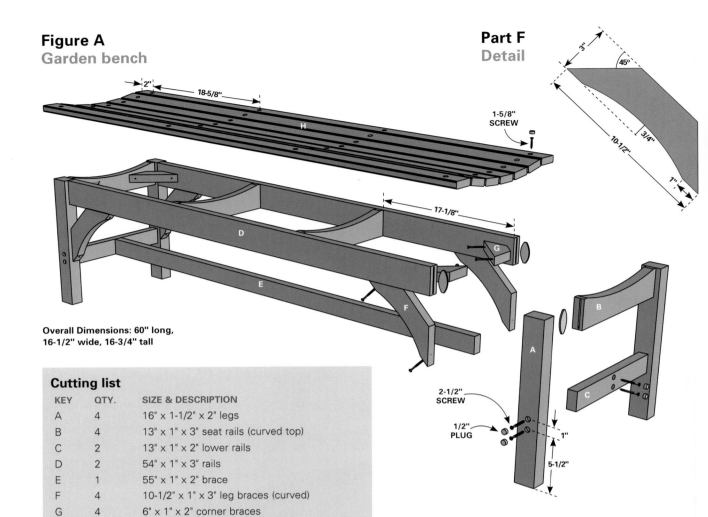

Overall Dimensions: 60" long,
16-1/2" wide, 16-3/4" tall

Part F
Detail

1-5/8"
SCREW

Cutting list

KEY	QTY.	SIZE & DESCRIPTION
A	4	16" x 1-1/2" x 2" legs
B	4	13" x 1" x 3" seat rails (curved top)
C	2	13" x 1" x 2" lower rails
D	2	54" x 1" x 3" rails
E	1	55" x 1" x 2" brace
F	4	10-1/2" x 1" x 3" leg braces (curved)
G	4	6" x 1" x 2" corner braces
H	7	60" x 3/4" x 2-1/8" seat slats

2-1/2"
SCREW

1/2"
PLUG

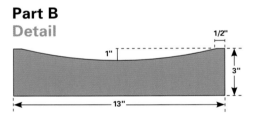

Part B
Detail

7 Complete the leg assembly. Use a spacer to support the lower
rail. Then drive screws through the legs into the rail.

Materials list

ITEM	QTY.
2x4 x 8' cedar*	1
5/4x6 x 10' cedar decking*	2
1x6 x 6' cedar*	4
No. 20 biscuits	12
1-lb. box of 2-1/2" deck screws	1
1-lb. box of 1-5/8" deck screws	1
8-oz. bottle of exterior wood glue	1
1/2" flat-top wood plugs	40
Quart of exterior wood finish	1

*You may need extra if you want all knot-free parts.

Pay close attention to orientation as you cut the slots and assemble the bench. Use masking tape to keep track of the orientation. Photos 2 – 5 show the plate-joining techniques we used to cut slots in the parts.

Assemble the bench with biscuits and screws

Photos 6 – 11 show the assembly steps. Biscuits connect the legs to the rails for extra strength. Spread exterior wood glue in the slots and on the biscuits. Then clamp the parts until the glue sets. Use 2-1/2-in. deck screws to attach the legs to the braces (Photos 7 and 9). If you aren't using self-drilling screws, drill pilot holes to avoid splitting the parts. Attach the top slats to the frame with 1-5/8-in. deck screws. Plug the screw holes with 1/2-in. flat-top birch plugs. If you own a drill press, you can make your own cedar plugs using a 1/2-in. plug cutter.

We finished the bench with an exterior oil. This penetrating oil finish leaves the wood looking natural, but it has to be reapplied every year or two. For a glossy, more permanent finish, you could use spar varnish.

8 **Connect the seat rails with biscuits.** Join the two long rails with the two intermediate seat rails with biscuits and glue. Clamp them and let the glue set about 30 minutes.

9 **Join the leg and seat assemblies.** Connect the leg assembies to the seat assembly with biscuits and clamp them together. Then attach the brace with screws.

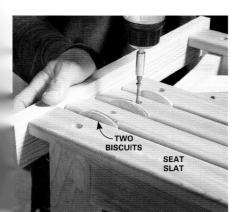

10 **Screw on the seat slats.** Start by attaching the two outside slats. Then center the middle slat and attach it with screws. Next, position the remaining slats so there's an even space (two biscuits wide) between them. Use a board to align the slat ends.

11 **Hide the screws with wood plugs.** Glue flat-top wood plugs into the plug recesses. Use a cutoff dowel or a small block of wood to pound them flush.

Patio chair 205
Yard & garden trio 209
Adirondack chair & love seat 215
Adirondack chair: version 2 221

14 GARDEN & DECK CHAIRS

Patio chair

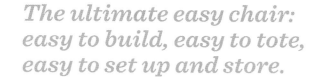

The ultimate easy chair: easy to build, easy to tote, easy to set up and store.

Whether you're staking out a curbside spot for watching a parade, heading to the woods for a weekend or simply trying to catch a few rays, you'll love the portability and comfort of this chair. Interlocking legs and gravity keep the two sections together when in use. And when it's time to pull up stakes, the seat section tucks neatly inside the back. A handle cutout in the top slat makes for easy carrying and storing too.

WHAT IT TAKES

TIME: 8 hours for 1; 10 hours for 2
SKILL LEVEL: Intermediate

Getting started

We made our chair from cedar because it's lightweight, but you could use cypress, fir, treated or other decay-resistant woods. We didn't want knots weakening the legs or seat, so we spent extra for knot-free "D-grade" cedar, but you can find suitable pieces if you pick hrough the lumber piles. You'll need basic tools: a jigsaw, drill, Phillips bit, file, combination square, carpenter's square and screwdriver, plus a table saw and belt sander. If you don't own these last two tools, borrow them (or use this project as an excuse to add a few more tools to your workshop).

Building one chair takes about eight hours. But once you're "jigged up" and have your patterns made, building additional ones only takes an hour or two more each.

Make the patterns (by connecting the dots or with a photocopier)

The backrest and seat support struts must be the exact length and shape for the chair to set up and "nest" for storage properly. You can ensure accuracy two ways: You can place the strut grid (below) on a photocopier, then enlarge it until the squares are exactly 1 in. On our office machine, that meant first enlarging the grid 2x, taking that copy and enlarging it 2x, then taking that copy and enlarging it 1.30x. We taped two pieces of 8-1/2 x 11 paper together lengthwise to create the 18-in.-long pattern. Every copier is slightly different, so make sure the final grid is 18 in., and 18 squares, long. Then cut it out to create your pattern.

Materials list

2 pieces of 2x6 x 8' D and better-grade cedar (or equivalent)
2 pieces of 1x6 x 8' D and better-grade cedar
1 piece of 1/8" x 24" x 48" hardboard (for templates)
Eighty 2" galvanized deck screws
1 pint of exterior finish
Glue

Cutting list

KEY	PCS.	SIZE & DESCRIPTION
A	2	1-1/2" x 5-1/2" x 36" cedar (backrest struts)
B	2	1-1/2" x 4-15/16" x 34" cedar (seat struts)
C	1	3/4" x 4" x 20" cedar (top slat)
D	2	3/4" x 2-1/2" x 20" cedar (seat supports)
E	11	3/4" x 2" x 20" cedar (slats)

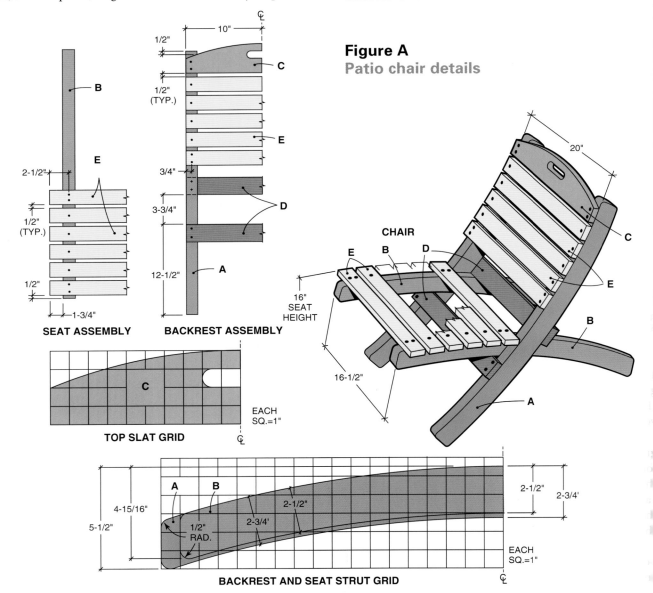

Figure A
Patio chair details

SEAT ASSEMBLY

BACKREST ASSEMBLY

TOP SLAT GRID

CHAIR

BACKREST AND SEAT STRUT GRID

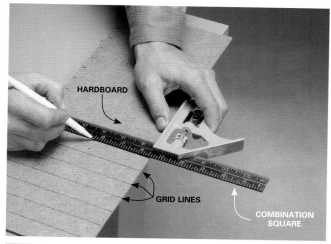

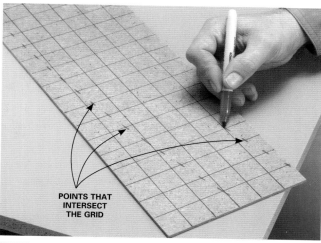

1 Measure and mark 1-in. increments on both ends and one side of the hardboard. Then draw grid lines using a combination square, straightedge and fine-point permanent marker. Or, if you like, you can use the photocopy method explained on p. 62.

HARDBOARD

GRID LINES

COMBINATION SQUARE

2 To develop the pattern, transfer the points to your hardboard grid where the shape intersects the grid lines in the drawing.

POINTS THAT INTERSECT THE GRID

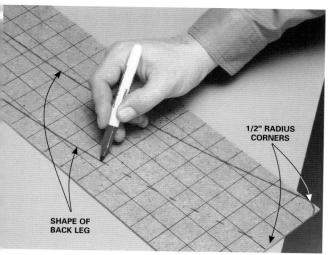

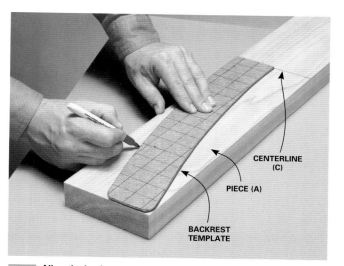

1/2" RADIUS CORNERS

SHAPE OF BACK LEG

3 Draw lines connecting the points made on the grid. Use a smooth, arcing arm movement to draw the gradual curve. Use a quarter to trace the 1/2-in. radiuses at the bottom of the leg. Use a jigsaw to cut out the pattern.

CENTERLINE (C)

PIECE (A)

BACKREST TEMPLATE

4 Align the backrest strut template to the centerline and bottom edge of the cedar piece and trace the shape. Flip the template along the centerline to draw the other half. Cut out the pieces with a jigsaw.

A second way is to use the transfer grid method (Photos 1 – 4). The shapes in Figure A are drawn on a scaled-down grid. Draw a full-size grid of 1-in. squares on hardboard (Photo 1) and transfer the shapes to it; you'll have a template you can use over and over.

We've drawn only half of the backrest and seat struts on our grids because the halves are symmetrical. Make one template for half of the shape, then flip it to draw the other half. Since the shapes of the seat and backrest struts are so similar, you can make only the backrest strut template, then use it to draw the seat strut pieces, making them 1/4 in. narrower and 1 in. shorter (2 in. shorter overall).

To use the template, align it to centerlines drawn on the boards (Photo 4), trace around it, then flip it over the centerline and trace the rest of the shape. Remember, the seat struts are 1/4 in. skinnier and 2 in. shorter than the backrest struts.

Putting it all together

Cut all the pieces to the dimensions given in the Cutting List, using the templates for the legs and the top slat. Cut out the shapes with a jigsaw, then sand the pieces with a belt sander (Photo 5). Lay out the hand grip hole in the top slat (C), then cut it out using a jigsaw and spade bit (Photo 6). You'll need to rip the back and seat slats 2 in. wide using a table saw.

Lay out, countersink and drill all the screw holes for the

Tip

Cedar is soft, so when screwing the pieces together, finish driving the screws by hand to avoid setting their heads too deep.

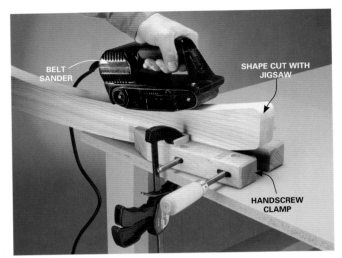

5 Sand the edges of the curved pieces with a belt sander. If you don't have a bench vise, you can support the legs with a handscrew clamp while you sand.

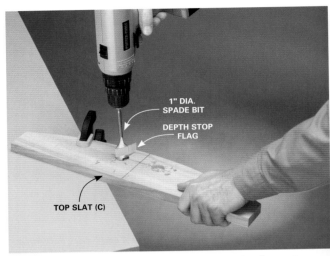

6 Drill the ends of the hand grip holes with a 1-in.-dia. spade bit. Drill partway in from both sides so you won't tear out the wood.

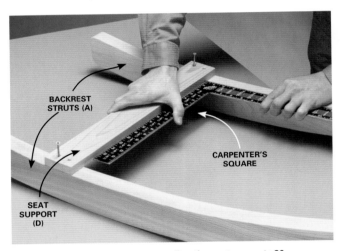

7 Use a carpenter's square to align the seat supports 90 degrees to the backrest struts, then glue and screw them in place. Use both glue and screws to attach the slats, too.

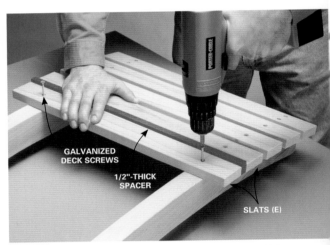

8 Attach the slats to the seat struts using a 1/2-in.-thick spacer to align them. Finish driving the screws by hand to avoid setting their heads too deep.

slats and supports. Finish-sand all the pieces with 120-grit, then 150-grit sandpaper. Round over the sharp edges with the sandpaper.

Screw the two seat supports (D) and curved top slat to the backrest struts (Photo 7) using the spacing given in Figure A. Then attach the five slats to the backrest struts and six slats to the seat struts (Photo 8).

Finishing touches

Before applying the finish, unscrew the two seat supports and apply weather-resistant glue to the joints, then rescrew the seat supports to the backrest struts. The glue will strengthen the joint. The chair relies primarily on these seat supports for strength.

Brush on two liberal coats of a penetrating exterior wood sealer. Let the first coat dry for 24 hours, then apply the second coat. After an hour, wipe off any excess finish. Let the finish dry for a couple of days before using the chair. After a year or two, you'll want to recoat the chairs to keep them looking good. If you decide to paint the chairs instead, use an oil-based primer followed by a semigloss paint. Don't use a clear varnish; the sun will eventually break it down and you'll be refinishing every summer instead of relaxing.

Set up the chair by sliding the seat struts through the backrest struts and seat supports as shown in the photos on p. 61. Push the seat in all the way so the rear seat slat is firmly against the backrest struts. Then kick back and relax!

Yard & garden trio

WHAT IT TAKES

TIME: 2 weekends
SKILL LEVEL: Intermediate

A chair, love seat and table for your outdoor living room

At first glance, this trio of handcrafted outdoor furniture looks as if it's been part of the family for generations. The structure is solid and traditional, and the wood is stained a rich, weathered gray.

The carefully fitted joints give this chair, love seat and table the true look of furniture and not a stapled-together crate. Despite the refined look, they're not difficult to build. The construction-grade cedar parts are joined with dowels, glue, and screws hidden by wood plugs.

The knots and imperfections characteristic of lower grade cedar add to the furniture's charm. When you select your wood, however, be sure the knots are tight, the boards are straight, and there are no cracks to weaken the furniture.

To achieve the aged appearance, we brushed on a liberal coat of thinned-down gray deck stain (one part stain to two

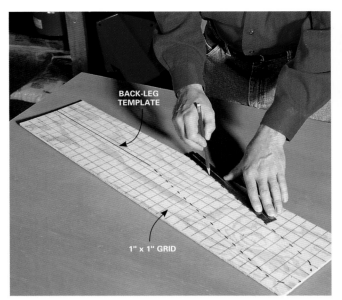

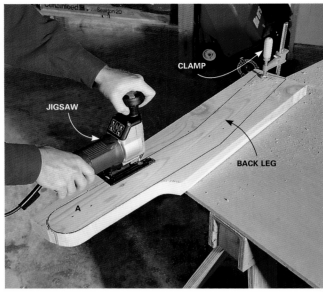

1 Make full-size templates for the shaped pieces. Transfer the intersecting points from our grid drawings to your full-size grids, then connect the points.

2 Cut out the shaped pieces using a jigsaw. Use a fine-tooth blade and carefully follow the drawn lines to reduce the amount of sanding needed to smooth the sawn edges.

parts mineral spirits). We continued brushing with the grain until the stain saturated the wood. To simulate wear, we brushed some areas even more to lighten the stain.

The three pieces should take you about two weekends to build. To simplify and speed up the cutting, we've provided templates for the shaped pieces that you can transfer to thin plywood.

Project background

The construction of all three pieces is very similar. We'll show you step-by-step how to build the chair; then you'll be able to build the love seat, which is essentially a longer version of the chair. One difference is the layout of the love seat's back top; see (B) in Figure A. Also, the love seat has an added center seat support (K) that's cut to fit between the back bottom and front seat supports (D). Glue and screw this extra piece in place just before attaching the seat slats (G). After making the chair and love seats, you'll find the table a snap (Figure B).

Make the chair templates

Gather all the tools plus your standard layout and carpentry tools. Using scrap

Cutting list

KEY	QTY.	SIZE	DESCRIPTION
Chair			
A	2	1-1/2" x 7-1/4" x 35" cedar	Back legs
B	1	1-1/2" x 5-1/2" x 22-1/4" cedar	Back top
C	2	1-1/2" x 3-1/2" x 25-1/4" cedar	Front legs
D	2	1-1/2" x 3-1/2" x 22-1/4" cedar	Back bottom and front seat support
E	2	3/4" x 3-1/2" x 23-1/2" cedar	Arms
F	2	3/4" x 3-1/2" x 14" cedar	Side seat supports
G	6	3/4" x 2-3/4" x 25-1/4" cedar	Seat slats
H	2	3/4" x 2" x 14" cedar	Side stretchers
J	9	3/4" x 1-1/2" x 13-1/2" cedar	Back slats
Love Seat			
A	2	1-1/2" x 7-1/4" x 34" cedar	Back legs
B	1	1-1/2" x 5-1/2" x 43-5/8" cedar	Back top
C	2	1-1/2" x 3-1/2" x 25-1/4" cedar	Front legs
D	2	1-1/2" x 3-1/2" x 43-5/8" cedar	Back bottom and front seat support
E	2	3/4" x 3-1/2" x 23-1/2" cedar	Arms
F	2	3/4" x 3-1/2" x 14" cedar	Side seat supports
G	6	3/4" x 2-3/4" x 46-5/8" cedar	Seat slats
H	2	3/4" x 2" x 14" cedar	Side stretchers
J	18	3/4" x 1-1/2" x 13-1/2" cedar	Back slats
K	1	1-1/2" x 3-1/2" x 16-1/4" cedar	Center seat support
Table			
A	4	1-1/2" x 2-1/2" x 19-1/4" cedar	Legs
B	4	3/4" x 4-1/2" x 13" cedar	Aprons
C	6	3/4" x 2-7/8" x 16-3/4" cedar	Top slats
D	2	3/4" x 2" x 13" cedar	Side stretchers

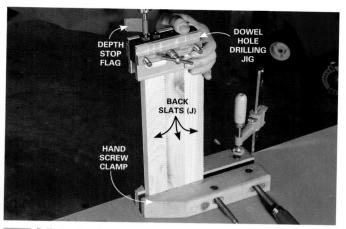

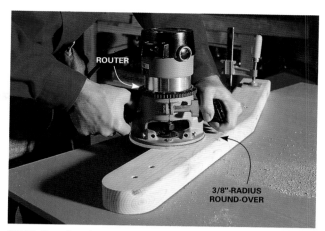

3 Drill the dowel holes in the ends of the back slats. Clamping the slats side by side like this gives the dowel-drilling jig more surface area to clamp onto.

4 Rout the edges of all the pieces (except the end cuts). Clamp the pieces to your work table, or use a router pad to hold the pieces as you rout them.

Materials list

ITEM	QTY.
Chair	
2x8 x 8' cedar	1 pc.
2x4 x 8' cedar	2 pcs.
1x4 x 8' cedar	4 pcs.
3/8"-dia. x 2" dowel pins	16
5/16"-dia. x 1-1/2" dowel pins	36
3" galvanized deck screws	12
1-5/8" galvanized deck screws	21
Love Seat	
2x8 x 8' cedar	1 pc.
2x6 x 8' cedar	1 pc.
2x4 x 8' cedar	2 pcs.
1x4 x 8' cedar	6 pcs.
3/8" dia. x 2" dowel pins	16
5/16" dia. x 1-1/2" dowel pins	72
3" galvanized deck screws	15
1-5/8" galvanized deck screws	28
Table	
2x4 x 8' cedar	1 pc.
1x6 x 8' cedar	1 pc.
1x4 x 8' cedar	2 pcs.
3/8" dia. x 2" dowel pins	16
3" galvanized deck screws	8
1-5/8" galvanized deck screws	12

Glue and finish for all three

Weatherproof or waterproof glue	16 ozs.
Exterior deck stain	1 qt.
Mineral spirits to thin stain	2 qts.

1/4-in.-thick plywood, make full-size templates of the shapes for the back legs (A), chair back top (B), arms (E), and side seat supports (F). Start by cutting your template stock to the rectangular sizes shown in the patterns in Figure A. Draw a 1 x 1-in. grid on your template pieces, then transfer and enlarge the shapes from our drawings to your templates (Photo 1). Mark the screw locations too. Cut out the template shapes and sand the sawn edges smooth.

Cutting the parts

Cut all the pieces A through J to the dimensions given in the Cutting List. Trace the shapes from your completed templates onto the back legs, chair back top, and side seat supports (A, B and F). Cut out the shapes using a jigsaw or band saw, then sand the sawn edges smooth (Photo 2). You'll shape the arms after you assemble the chair by cutting and fitting the notches at the rear of the arms around the back legs.

Drilling screw and dowel holes

Lay out and drill the screw plug holes and screw clearance holes in the legs (A and C). Lay out and drill the dowel holes on the edges of the back top and back bottom (B and D), and in the ends of the side seat supports, side stretchers and back slats (F, H and J); see Photo 3.

Laying out the back slat dowel holes in the back top (B) and back bottom (D) can be a little tricky, so be careful. Don't measure from one mark to the next. Instead, add the dowel hole spread distances together, and measure and mark from one end with your tape measure. When you're done marking, double-check everything. Remember, you'll be using 5/16-in.-dia. dowels for these holes. To correctly mark these back-slat dowel hole locations, assume a spread of 3/4 in. between the dowel hole centers. The first hole center for the first slat is 1-1/4 in. from the end of B and D. The next hole center is another 3/4 in. from the first. The first hole center for the second slat is an additional 1-5/8 in. plus 3/4 in. for the next hole. For the first hole center for the third slat, measure an additional 1-5/8 in., then another 3/4 in. Continue this method until the last slat.

Routing and sanding

Now's the time to round some sharp edges and do some sanding before assembly. Mount a 3/8-in.-radius round-over bit in a router to rout the edges on the pieces (Photo 4). See Figure A for which edges to round. Leave the router set up this way to do the edges of the arms after the shapes are cut.

Using a belt sander first, then an orbital sander, finish-sand all the pieces. You'll still have a bit more to do later after the chair's assembled.

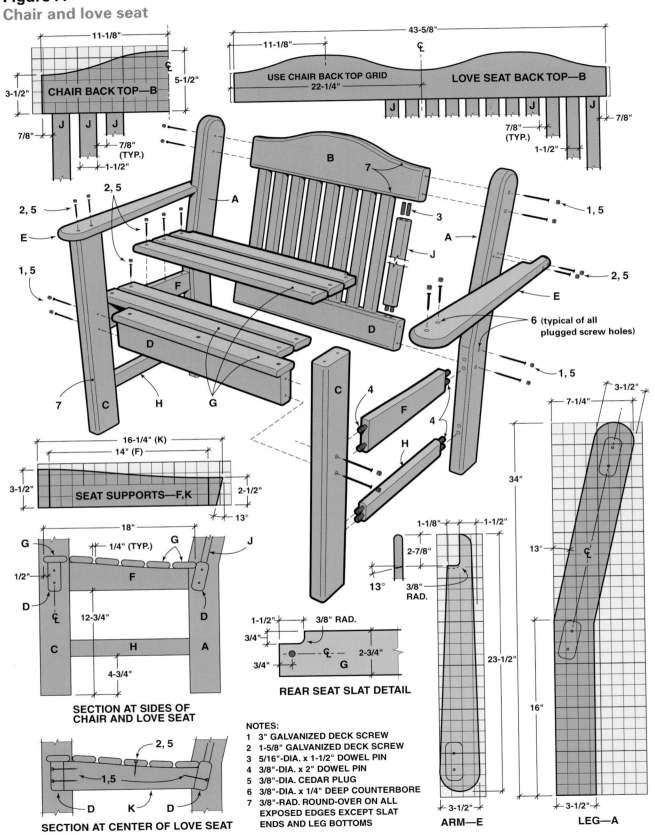

Figure A
Chair and love seat

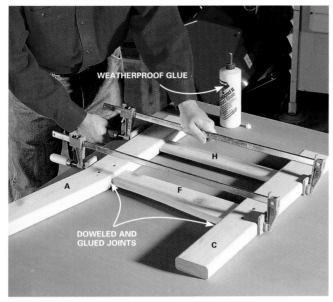

WEATHERPROOF GLUE

H

A

F

C

DOWELED AND
GLUED JOINTS

5 Glue, dowel and clamp the side pieces together. Be careful not to apply too much glue and create a mess.

FLUSH
TRIMMING
SAW

SCREW
COVER
PLUGS

6 Use a flush-trimming saw or sharp chisel to trim off the heads of the screw cover plugs. Finish-sand them with a sanding block, then an orbital sander.

ROUND FILE

ARM PRIOR
TO SHAPING

7 Using the partially finished chair as a convenient support, file the angled radiused corner of the arm notch so it fits around the back leg.

E

ARM
OVERHANGS
FRONT LEG 3/8"
ON
INSIDE

8 Align and clamp the arms to the front legs. Insert the screws that go into the back legs, remove the clamps and then screw the arms to the front legs.

Assemble the sides and back

Glue, dowel and clamp the side assemblies (A, C, F and H) together (Photo 5). Use a thin dowel or stick to spread the glue in the dowel holes. We found it was better to gently hammer the dowels in the ends of pieces F and H first. Putting dowels in the legs first may cause some of the ends of these pieces to split when all the pieces are assembled.

Glue, dowel and clamp the back pieces together (B, D and J). Start by inserting two dowels in one end of every back slat (J). Glue and clamp the back slats to the back top (B), one at a time. Insert the dowels in the other ends of the back slats. Then, with the help of a friend, align and attach the back bottom (D). Start at one end and work to the other end.

Align, glue and screw the sides to the assembled back and the front seat support (D). Once again, an extra set of hands is helpful here.

Figure B
Table

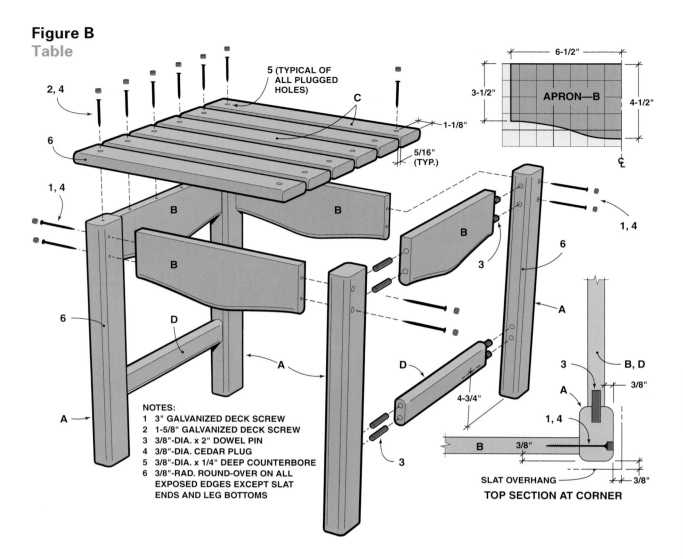

5 (TYPICAL OF ALL PLUGGED HOLES)

2, 4

6

1, 4

6

C

1-1/8"

5/16" (TYP.)

B

B

B

B

D

A

A

1, 4

6

3

A

6

1, 4

3

B, D

3/8"

A

D

4-3/4"

3

B

3/8"

SLAT OVERHANG

3/8"

TOP SECTION AT CORNER

6-1/2"

3-1/2"

APRON—B

4-1/2"

NOTES:
1   3" GALVANIZED DECK SCREW
2   1-5/8" GALVANIZED DECK SCREW
3   3/8"-DIA. x 2" DOWEL PIN
4   3/8"-DIA. CEDAR PLUG
5   3/8"-DIA. x 1/4" DEEP COUNTERBORE
6   3/8"-RAD. ROUND-OVER ON ALL
    EXPOSED EDGES EXCEPT SLAT
    ENDS AND LEG BOTTOMS

Attach the seat slats

Trim the length of the front seat slat (G) so it fits between the front legs. Cut the notched ends of the back seat slat as shown in Figure A and see that it fits between the back legs. Lay out and drill the screw plug and clearance holes (for the wood plugs) in the seat slats, then glue and screw the front and back seat slats in place. Attach the rest of the seat slats so the gaps between them are equal.

To make wood plugs to cover the recessed screws, use a 3/8-in.-dia. plug cutter. Glue and insert the plugs in the holes to cover the screws. Drill a shallow 3/4-in.-dia. hole in a piece of scrap wood. Fill the hole with glue and use it as a reservoir to dip the plugs in and apply the glue. When the glue is dry, trim off the tops of the plugs (Photo 6).

Attach the arms

Trace the back leg notches from your arm template to the arm pieces (E). Then cut out the notches using a jigsaw or band saw (see Figure A for the dimension and angle details). Make the final fit of the angled inside radiused corners using a round file (Photo 7). When that's done, trace and cut out the shapes of the arms and rout the rounded-over edges. Predrill the plug and screw holes, then finish-sand and attach the arms (Photo 8) with galvanized deck screws.

Apply the finish

You can protect your furniture with exterior deck stain as we described on p. 65. A clear exterior finish is another option, but it will slow down the aging process. It depends on the look you want. However, be sure you choose some type of waterproof finish to keep the pieces from drying out and splitting.

Adirondack chair & love seat

Finally, outdoor furniture that's easy to get in and out of

This chair and love seat combo is just perfect for outdoor lounging. The seat has a nice curved recess to conform to your body, and wide arms to hold your favorite snack and drink. And because the seat doesn't slope steeply downward like on a traditional Adirondack chair, even your grandfather will be able to get himself up without a boost.

You won't need an arsenal of power tools to build this furniture. In fact, you'll only need a circular saw, a drill and simple hand tools. We've designed this project for simplicity as well: With a bit of patience, even a novice can do a great job.

The wood is pressure-treated pine, chosen for its low cost, high strength and longevity. And don't worry about the drab green look of treated wood. You can brush on an exterior oil or latex stain and give it a beautiful warm glow that makes it look more like mahogany or teak than treated pine.

WHAT IT TAKES

TIME: 1 weekend
SKILL LEVEL: Beginner to intermediate

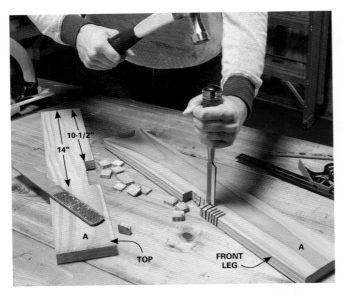

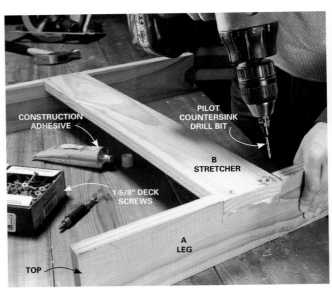

1 Clamp the two front legs together, measure for the 3/4-in. deep notch and make repeated cuts with your circular saw set to 3/4-in. depth of cut. Chisel the pieces between the cuts and then file smooth.

2 Spread a light bead of construction adhesive into each notch and align the front stretcher (B) with the edge of the legs. Drill and screw the stretcher to the legs.

3 Mark the angle on the back side of each arm and cut the arms (C) and arm supports (D) with your circular saw.

4 Align the arm supports with the top and front edges of the legs, then drill and screw each front leg to the arm support with two 1-5/8-in. deck screws.

Select straight, knot-free, pressure-treated pine

Most outdoor wood furniture is made from cedar or expensive teak, but regular treated boards from your home center or lumberyard are perfect for this project. The trick is to select boards that are as straight and free of knots as you can find.

A few tight knots are OK, and if you spot a board that looks great except for a huge loose knot, just cut it out and use the knot-free sections. It's a good idea to buy a couple of extra boards, just in case you end up cutting out more sections than you'd planned. Also avoid boards that are still wet from the treatment process (they'll feel cool and damp) because they might warp or crack as they dry.

Don't assume that the treated boards are dimensionally consistent. When we got our lumber, the boards varied by as much as 3/16 in. in width. These variations can screw up the assembly process, especially for the back slats, which require spacers to get an exact back width. Once you get the boards home and begin to cut the pieces, use a table saw or the rip guide on your circular saw

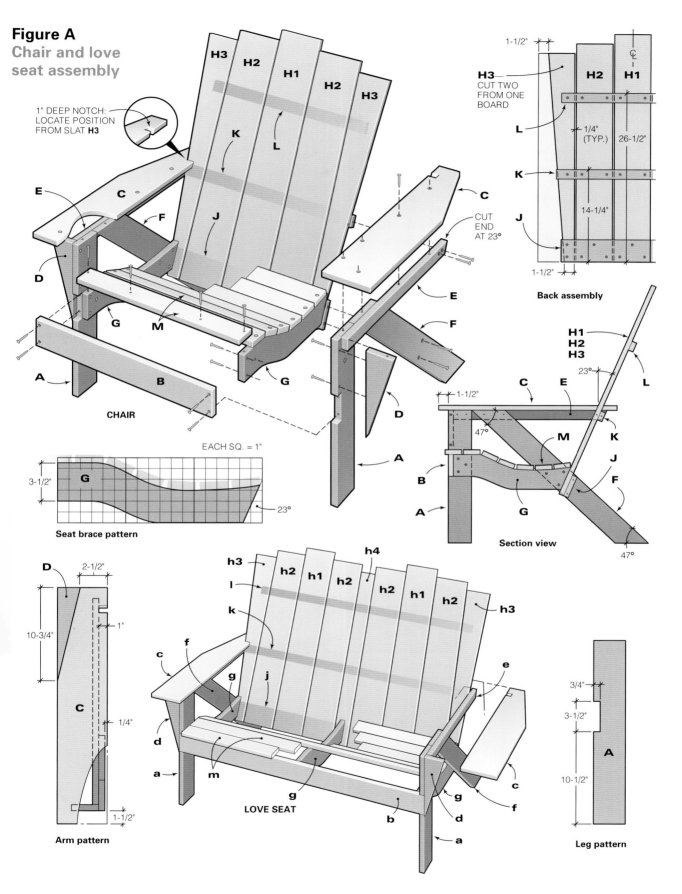

Figure A
Chair and love seat assembly

1" DEEP NOTCH:
LOCATE POSITION
FROM SLAT **H3**

E

C

F

D

K

L

J

G

M

A

B

CHAIR

C

E

F

G

D

CUT
END
AT 23°

A

1-1/2"

H3—
CUT TWO
FROM ONE
BOARD

H2

H1

L

1/4"
(TYP.)

26-1/2"

K

14-1/4"

J

1-1/2"

Back assembly

H1
H2
H3

23°

L

C

E

1-1/2"

47°

B

A

G

M

K

J

F

47°

Section view

EACH SQ. = 1"

3-1/2"

G

23°

Seat brace pattern

D

2-1/2"

10-3/4"

1"

C

1/4"

a

m

g

d

1-1/2"

Arm pattern

h3

h2

h1

h2

h4

h2

h1

h2

h3

l

k

f

c

g

j

d

a

m

g

b

e

c

f

g

d

a

LOVE SEAT

3/4"

3-1/2"

A

10-1/2"

Leg pattern

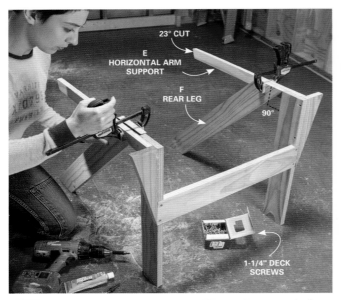

5 Fasten the horizontal arm supports (E) at 90 degrees to the front legs. Then glue, drill and screw the rear legs to the arm supports, making sure the arm supports are parallel to the floor.

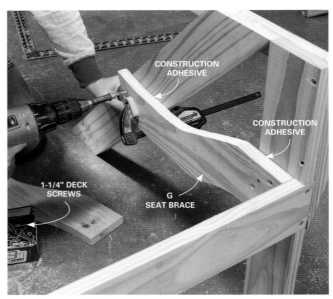

6 Cut the seat supports (G) from 1x6 boards. Align the square front edge of the seat brace with the back of the front stretcher (B) and glue and screw them to the front and back legs.

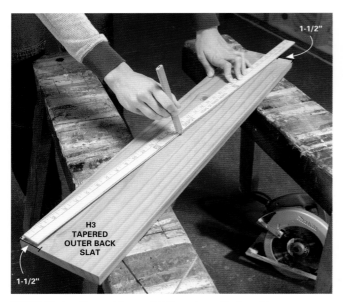

7 Mark a diagonal line on H3, then clamp the board to your sawhorses and cut along the line to make a pair of outer back slats.

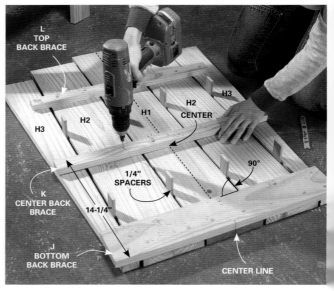

8 Set the back slats on a flat surface with 1/4-in.-wide spacers. Center the back braces on the slats. Glue, drill and screw them with 1-1/4-in. deck screws.

to trim them to the exact widths in the Cutting List. Or just let them dry out for a few weeks before assembly.

Assemble the main frame

Cut the notches in the front legs to accept the front stringer as shown in Photo 1. As you chisel out the waste wood in the notch, shave the bottom carefully and fine-tune it with a rasp to keep the notch from getting too deep.

As you assemble the basic frame (Photos 2 – 6), make sure your work surface is flat so each piece aligns with the adjoining pieces at the correct angle. Be sure to use a dab of construction adhesive in every joint and predrill a pilot and countersink hole for each screw. You can buy a bit at your local hardware store that drills a pilot and countersink in one operation for the No. 6 screws.

Spacers make the back assembly a snap

To achieve the gentle taper of the back assembly, you'll need to taper the outer seat slat and cut it as shown in Photo 7.

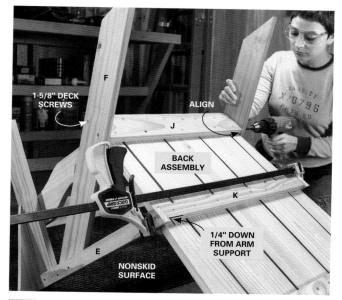

9 Align the bottom of the back assembly with the seat braces and the tops of the rear legs. Screw the legs to the back brace and screw the horizontal arm supports to the center back brace.

10 Space the seat slats (M), evenly starting at the back. Drill one pilot hole on each end of the slats and screw them to the seat brace. Screw the front seat slat to the seat brace as well as the front stretcher (B).

11 Set the arm flush with the edge of the arm support (E), overhanging the front leg 1-1/2 in. Mark the arm where it meets the back slat.

12 Notch the arm with a handsaw and fasten it to the horizontal support, the top edge of the back legs and to the front leg and arm support with 1-5/8-in. screws and glue.

First, place a mark 1-1/2 in. from the edge on opposite ends as shown. Connect the marks with a line and then saw right down the middle of the line with your circular saw. Sand or plane the cut edge to smooth away any saw marks.

Before you assemble the back of the chair or love seat, cut 1/4-in. thick spacers from scrap wood. The spacers (Photo 8) will ensure that the back

assembly is the right width. Lay each slat on the floor and make sure the best-looking side of each board is facing down. As you screw the three back braces to the back slats, use a framing square to make sure they're perpendicular. You'll find it easier to get the proper alignment if you match the center point of each brace with the center line drawn down the middle back slat. Drill

pilot holes and drive 1-1/4 in. deck screws through the braces into the slats as shown in Figure A and Photo 8.

Once you've assembled the back, it's time to fasten it to the chair frame. Flip the frame assembly upside down and insert the back assembly into it (Photo 9). This can be a bit challenging, so make it easier by laying two nonskid rugs or mats on the floor under the chair frame

Add a personal touch to your outdoor furniture

You can build our step-back version of the chair and love seat or experiment with other shapes to suit your sense of style. Feel free to try the gable or round back shown below or draw a different shape on paper, tape it to the chair and step back to see how you like it.

STEP BACK   **GABLE BACK**   **ROUND BACK**

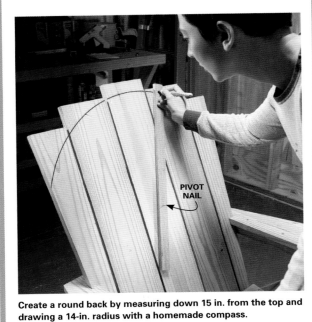

PIVOT NAIL

Create a round back by measuring down 15 in. from the top and drawing a 14-in. radius with a homemade compass.

Cutting list for chair

KEY	QTY.	SIZE & DESCRIPTION
A	2	3/4" x 3-1/2" x 21" front legs
B	1	3/4" x 3-1/2" x 23" front stretcher
C	2	3/4" x 5-1/2" x 27" arms
D	2	3/4" x 3" x 10-3/4" triangular arm supports
E	2	3/4" x 1-1/2" x 23-1/4" horizontal arm supports
F	2	3/4" x 3-1/2" x 34-1/2" rear legs
G	2	3/4" x 5-1/2" x 17-3/4" seat braces
H1	1	3/4" x 5-1/2" x 35-3/4" center back slat
H2	2	3/4" x 5-1/2" x 34-1/4" inner back slats
H3	1	3/4" x 5-1/2" x 32-3/4" outer back slats (taper cut into two pieces)
J	1	3/4" x 3-1/2" x 21-1/2" bottom back brace
K	1	3/4" x 1-1/2" x 23" center back brace
L	1	3/4" x 1-1/2" x 21-1/2" top back brace
M	7	3/4" x 2-1/2" x 21-1/2" seat slats

Cutting list for love seat

KEY	QTY.	SIZE & DESCRIPTION
a	2	3/4" x 3-1/2" x 21" front legs
b	1	3/4" x 3-1/2" x 43" front stretcher
c	2	3/4" x 5-1/2" x 27" arms
d	2	3/4" x 3" x 10-3/4" triangular arm supports
e	2	3/4" x 1-1/2" x 23-1/4" horizontal arm supports
f	2	3/4" x 3-1/2" x 34-1/2" rear legs
g	3	3/4" x 5-1/2" x 17-3/4" seat braces
h1	2	3/4" x 5-1/2" x 35-3/4" back slats
h2	4	3/4" x 5-1/2" x 34-1/4" back slats
h3	1	3/4" x 5-1/2" x 32-3/4" outer back slat (taper cut into two pieces)
h4	1	3/4" x 2-1/2" x 32-3/4" center back slat (trim to fit)
j	1	3/4" x 3-1/2" x 41-1/2" bottom back brace
k	1	3/4" x 1-1/2" x 43" center back brace
l	1	3/4" x 1-1/2" x 41-1/2" top back brace
m	7	3/4" x 2-1/2" x 41-1/2" seat slats

and the top of the back assembly. These will help keep everything in place. As you align these assemblies, it's critical to get the back of the seat braces flush with the outer back slats (H3) and then screw through the rear legs into the bottom back brace (J) as shown in Photo 9 and Figure A. Next, glue and screw the horizontal arm supports (E) into the center back brace (K) and then into the side of the outer back slat as well.

With the completion of this phase, you'll start to see a chair emerging. Flip the chair onto its legs and cut and predrill the seat slats. Glue and screw

them to the seat braces with 1-5/8-in. deck screws (Photo 10). Don't overdrive the screws—the heads should be just flush with the seat slats. The last step of the assembly is to fasten the arms to the arm supports and the legs as shown in Photos 11 and 12. The notches you cut near the back of the arms hold the back assembly firmly in place and reduce the stress on the screws at other joints. These compound notches slice through the arm at an angle. Cut the depth carefully with a handsaw and then chisel out the notch. Brush on an exterior stain

Once the chair is assembled, ease

all the edges with 100-grit sandpaper, paying particular attention to the seat and arms. If the wood feels damp or cold to the touch, you may need to let the chair dry in a shaded area for a few days before you sand or stain it.

We used an oil-based cedar natural tone stain that lets the grain show through. Several options are available, including custom semi-transparent stains that a paint supplier can mix for you. A quart will easily do a pair of chairs or a chair and love seat. This finish will last at least several years and can be cleaned and recoated as it shows signs of wear.

Adirondack chair: version 2

WHAT IT TAKES

TIME: 1 weekend
SKILL LEVEL: Beginner to intermediate

Plop down in one of these solid wood chairs and you'll appreciate the comfort of this traditional design. You don't have to be an expert to build it either. All the parts can be cut with a circular saw and jigsaw, then assembled with a drill with a Phillips-tip bit, a few clamps and glue. Even if you're a novice, you'll be able to follow our plan drawing and clear step-by-step photos. And the Materials List and Cutting List will help you spend less time head-scratching and more time building.

We made our chair from yellow poplar. Poplar is lightweight,

strong, inexpensive and easy to work with, plus it takes paint beautifully. If you have trouble finding it, almost any other wood will do: Alder, aspen, maple and white oak are excellent hardwood choices, and cedar, cypress, fir and pine are good softwood choices. Keep in mind that hardwood will be more durable, but softwood is certainly strong enough for this project.

Traditional Adirondack chairs are painted, but you can choose a clear outdoor deck finish if you prefer. If you do opt for paint, check out the painting tips on p. 81 to help achieve a tough, long-lasting and good-looking painted finish.

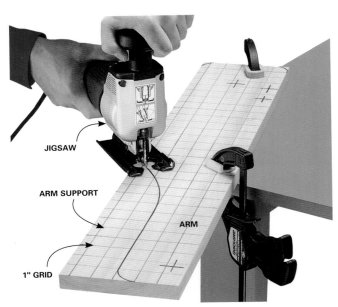

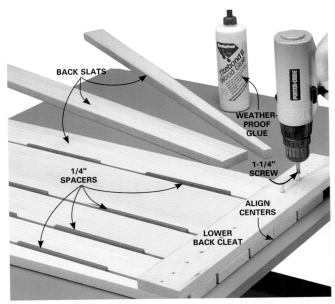

1 Draw full-size grids onto the arm and back leg pieces and follow the curves with a jigsaw.

2 Slip 1/4-in. spacers between the back slats as you screw the horizontal back supports (G, L and N) to the slats. Predrill and countersink each hole and apply weatherproof glue to each joint.

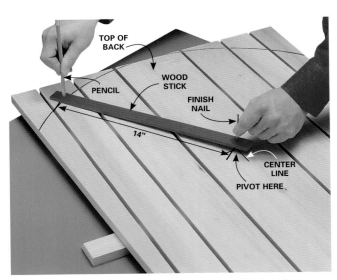

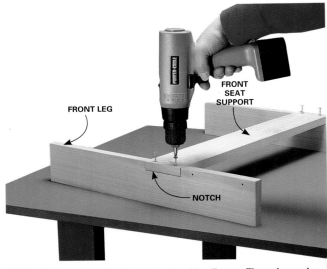

3 Make a compass from a scrap of wood by drilling a hole near each end. Put a nail in one end and use a pencil in the other hole to draw the 14-in. radius to form the curved top.

4 Cut and notch the front legs (E) with a jigsaw. Then glue and screw the front seat support into the notches.

Transfer the grid patterns

Enlarge the grids directly onto the board, or make a full-size pattern and transfer the shape to the board.

Once the shape is drawn, follow the lines with a jigsaw (Photo 1). Write "pattern" on the first leg and arm pieces and use them to make the others. If you're making more than one chair, now's the time to trace all the arm and leg pieces for each chair. The left arms and legs are mirror images of the right. Also, trim the small cutout piece of each arm (C) to make the arm support (K) for each side.

Cut the tapered back pieces

The two tapered back pieces are tricky to cut, and the safest way to do it is to cut them from a wider board. Draw the tapers shown in Figure A onto a 1x6 cut to length. Nail each end of the board to the tops of a sawhorse, placing the nails where they'll be out of the saw's path. Use a No. 4 finish nail on each end and hammer it in flush with the surface. Set the depth of your circular saw 1/8 in. deeper than the thickness of the board, and cut the taper from the wide end to the narrow end. Next, draw a straight line on the remaining part to define the second piece and cut it. Note: Before you begin assembly,

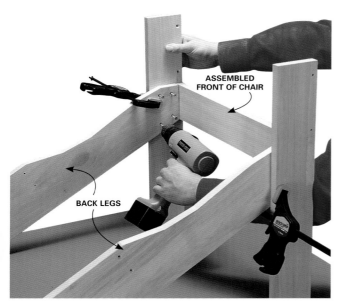

ASSEMBLED FRONT OF CHAIR

BACK LEGS

5 Clamp the back legs (B) to the front assembly to accurately position them. Work on a flat workbench surface so the chair won't wobble. Apply glue, drill pilot holes and drive 1-1/4-in. deck screws.

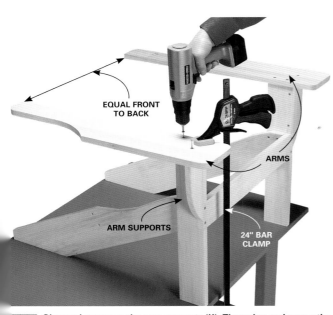

EQUAL FRONT TO BACK

ARMS

ARM SUPPORTS

24" BAR CLAMP

6 Glue and screw on the arm supports (K). Then glue and screw the arms to the front legs and arm supports. Use clamps to position the arms so they overhang the insides of the front legs by 1/4 in.

sand all the pieces and ease the edges with 100-grit sandpaper, followed by 150-grit.

Assemble the back first

Lay the back pieces face down on your workbench (Photo 2). Line up the bottoms and insert 1/4-in. spacers between the slats. Cut your 1/4-in. spacers from scrap boards or scrap 1/4-in. plywood. Screw each of the horizontal back supports G, L and N to the slats with 1-1/4- in. exterior deck screws. Predrill and

Materials list

ITEM	QTY.
1x6 x 10' poplar	1 piece
1x6 x 8' poplar	1 piece
1x6 x 12' poplar	1 piece
1x4 x 12' poplar	1 piece
1-5/8" galvanized deck screws	24
1-1/4" galvanized deck screws	68
Exterior oil primer	1 qt.*
White exterior gloss enamel	1 qt.*
*Enough paint to finish two chairs	

Cutting list

KEY	PCS.	SIZE & DESCRIPTION
A	1	3/4" x 5-1/2" x 35" poplar (center back slat)
B	2	3/4" x 5-1/2" x 33" poplar (back legs)
C	2	3/4" x 5-1/2" x 29" poplar (arms)
D	1	3/4" x 3-1/2" x 23" poplar (front seat support)
E	2	3/4" x 3-1/2" x 21" poplar (front legs)
F	2	3/4" x 3-1/4" x 35" poplar (back slats)
G	1	3/4" x 3" x 20" poplar (lower back cleat)
H	4	3/4" x 2-1/2" x 35" poplar (back slats)
J	6	3/4" x 2-1/2" x 21-1/2" poplar (seat slats)
K	2	3/4" x 2-1/2" x 9" poplar (arm supports)‡
L	1	3/4" x 2" x 25-1/2" poplar (center back support)
M	1	3/4" x 2" x 21-1/2" poplar (back leg support)
N	1	3/4" x 2" x 21" poplar (upper back support)
‡Cut from pieces C		

countersink each screw hole.

You'll need to cut a bevel on the top side of the center horizontal back support (L). A table saw works best, but you could use the same circular saw method you used earlier to cut the tapered side back slats (H). Just set the bevel on your circular saw to 33 degrees, nail the 1x6 board to the sawhorses, mark the width and make the cut.

With a framing square, check that the back slats and horizontal supports are positioned 90 degrees to each other as you glue and screw the assembly (Photo 2). Once the back is fastened, turn the back assembly over, mark the top radius and trim it with a jigsaw (Photo 3). Screw the chair frame together Using your jigsaw, cut the notches on parts E as shown in Figure A. Glue and screw the front seat support (D) to the front legs (Photo 4). Next set the front assembly vertically on your workbench and glue and screw the back legs B to the front legs (Photo 5). Again, drill pilot and countersink holes for each screw. Then glue and screw the arm supports to the outer sides

> ## Work smart
>
> When you're building more than one chair, set up an assembly line and cut the building time per chair by 40 percent.

Figure A
Adirondack chair, version 2

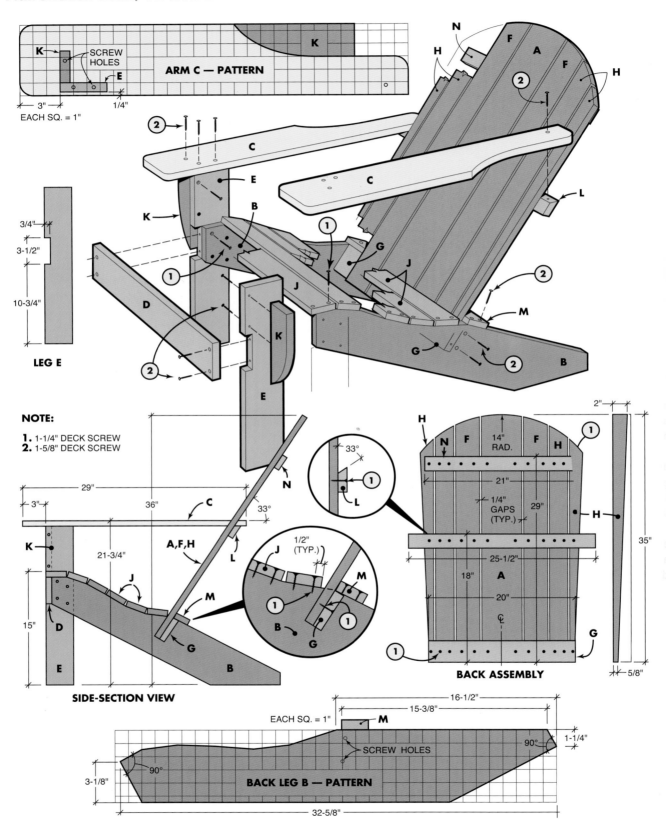

ARM C — PATTERN

K ← SCREW HOLES

3" 1/4"
EACH SQ. = 1"

3/4"
3-1/2"
10-3/4"

LEG E

N
H
F
A
F
H
2
L

C
2
E
B
1
G
J
J
2
M
G
B
D
2
E
K
E
N

NOTE:

1. 1-1/4" DECK SCREW
2. 1-5/8" DECK SCREW

29"
3"
36"
C
33°
K
21-3/4"
A,F,H
L
J
M
D
15"
G
E
B

SIDE-SECTION VIEW

33°
1
L

1/2"
(TYP.)
J
M
1
B
G
1

2"
H
N
F
14" RAD.
F
H
1
21"
1/4" GAPS (TYP.)
29"
H
25-1/2"
18"
A
20"
35"
G
1
G
5/8"

BACK ASSEMBLY

16-1/2"
15-3/8"
EACH SQ. = 1"
M
SCREW HOLES
90°
1-1/4"
90°
3-1/8"
BACK LEG B — PATTERN
32-5/8"

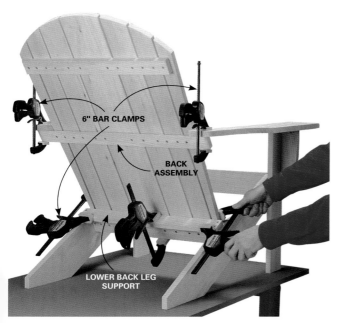

6" BAR CLAMPS

BACK ASSEMBLY

LOWER BACK LEG SUPPORT

7 Glue, clamp and screw the lower back leg support (M) to the back legs first. Then glue and clamp the back assembly, first to the back legs, then to the arm supports. Drill pilot and countersink holes for the screws.

1/4" GAPS

SEAT SLATS

8 Predrill all the pilot and countersink holes in the seat slats before you position them. Screw the seat slats (J) to the back legs with 1-1/4-in. deck screws (use 1-5/8-in. screws in softwood), spacing them 1/4 in. apart.

of the front legs (E).

Position the arms on the tops of the front legs and the arm supports (K). Make sure the arms hang 3 in. over the front leg and 1/4 in. over the inside edge of each leg. Before fastening the arms, make sure they're parallel (Photo 6).

Screw the back leg support (M) to each leg (see Figure A) and then set the back assembly into the frame and clamp it in place (Photo 7). Make sure the back of each arm projects 3/4 in. past the center back support (L). Glue and predrill each joint, screw the assembly together and then remove the clamps.

To finish the assembly, predrill and countersink holes in the ends of the seat slats. Position them approximately 1/4 in. apart and screw them to the back legs as shown. Use a power screwdriver where possible, and a hand screwdriver in tight places.

Painting tips

You can use either a water-based or oil-based exterior primer and enamel topcoat.

Start applying the primer with the chair upside down. Use a 1-in.-wide sash brush for coating the edges of the seat slats, and then use a 3-in.-wide roller to apply primer to the flat surfaces and a 2-in. brush to smooth out the primer. Prime the back, then turn the chair over and prime the other surfaces in the same manner.

Let the primer dry overnight, then use a paint scraper to remove any runs and 120-grit sandpaper to lightly sand the entire surface. Apply the topcoat in the same order you applied the primer, then let the paint dry for at least three days before use.

Simple retaining wall.......................................227
Simple deck...231
1-day patio pond...235

15 YARD PROJECTS

Simple retaining wall

WHAT IT TAKES

TIME: 1 weekend
SKILL LEVEL: Beginner

This 32-in.-high, 32-ft.-long wall was built in one fairly laid-back day, by two fairly laid-back DIYers and a skid steer loader (Photo 7). They hired a skid steer loader operator and his machine. Having the loader meant there was very little shovel work.

The skeleton of the wall is a treated wood, 2x4 stud wall clad on both sides with 1/2-in. treated plywood. It's held in place with 2x4 "dead men" assemblies buried in the backfill. The dead men are 2x4 struts bolted to the wall studs and anchored to a perpendicular 2x4 sleeper (see Figure A). The weight of the soil on the dead men anchors the wall against the backfill pressure. It's important to locate the bottom of the wall below grade a few inches so the earth in front of the wall will anchor the base in place.

Get the right stuff

Ordinary treated wood will last a good long time depending on soil conditions, although wet sites with clay will shorten the wall's life somewhat. If you use ordinary treated wood from the home center, figure the wall will last at least 20 years. To build a wall that'll last forever, use foundation-grade treated wood, the material used for basements. It's usually Southern yellow pine, a very strong softwood that accepts treatment better than most, and contains a higher concentration of preservatives. You may find it at lumberyards where

contractors shop. Or you can special-order it from any home center or lumberyard, although you'll pay a premium.

Choose nails rated for treated wood: 16d for the framing and 8d for the sheathing. Use 3-in. construction screws for standoffs and dead men connections—again, ones that are rated for treated wood. You'll also need a box each of 2- and 3-in. deck screws for the trim boards. See the Materials List on p. 86.

Prepping the site

This site had a gentle slope to retain, not a huge hill. This 32-in.-high wall is designed to hold back a gentle slope and is good for walls up to 40 in. For walls 40 to 48 in. place the studs on 12-in. centers and keep the rest of the wall the same. Don't build the wall more than 48 in. high—a taller wall requires special engineering.

Do the digging with a shovel if you wish. The trick is to dig halfway into the hill and throw the soil on top of the hill. That way you'll have enough fill left for behind the wall. The downside is that if you hand-dig, you'll also need to dig channels for the 2x4 struts and sleepers (see Photo 5).

It's much easier to hire a skid steer loader and an operator to dig into the hill and then cut down a foot or so behind the wall to create a shelf for resting the dead men. The operator can also scoop out the 12-in.-wide by 10-in.-deep trench for the gravel footing, and deliver and dump a 6-in. layer of gravel into the footing. Then you'll only need to do a bit of raking to level off the trench. A yard of gravel will take care of 50 linear feet of wall. If you have extra gravel, use it for backfill against the back of the wall for drainage. Have the skid steer and operator return to fill against the back side of the wall and do some final grading.

Get the footings ready

Fill the trench with gravel. Any type will do, but pea gravel is the easiest to work with. Roughly rake it level, then tip one of the footing plates on edge and rest a level on top to grade the footing (Photo 1). Use the plate as a screed, as if you're leveling in concrete, and you'll get it really close, really fast. Try to get it within 1/4 in. or so of level. Offset any footing plate joints at least 2 ft. to either side of wall joints. To drive down the plate until it's level, stand on it as you pound it into the gravel with another board, occasionally checking it with a level. If you can't drive the board down to achieve level, scoop out shallow trenches on either side of the footing plate with your hand. Then there will be a place for gravel to flow as you drive down the plate.

Frame and set the walls

Frame the walls in your driveway or on the garage floor. The walls are very light, so you can carry them a long way if you need to. Build them in sections, whatever length you like, and screw the end studs together at the site. Leave off the sheathing for now. Snap a chalk line 1 in. in from the outside of the footing plate to align the walls (Photo 2). Place them, screw the joining studs together with four 3-in. construction screws and screw the wall plates to the footing plates in every other stud space with 3-in. construction screws.

Plumb, straighten and brace the walls from the front side and then add the tie plate. Make sure to seam the tie plate joints at least 4 ft. away from the wall joints.Sheathe and waterproof the walls

Set the plywood panels in place one at a time. Draw and cut 1-5/8-in. x 3-5/8-in.

Figure A
Wall anatomy

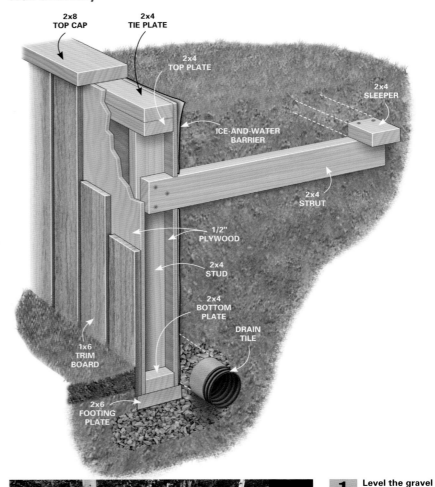

1 Level the gravel base. Lay the 2x6 footing plates on edge and use a 4-ft. level to level the gravel. Pack the gravel with the footing plate to drive it down until it's flat and level.

2 Frame and set the walls. Frame the walls and stand them on top of the footing plates. Snap a chalk line on the footing plate 1 in. from the edge and then screw the bottom plates to the footing plate even with the line.

3" CONSTRUCTION SCREWS

CHALK LINE

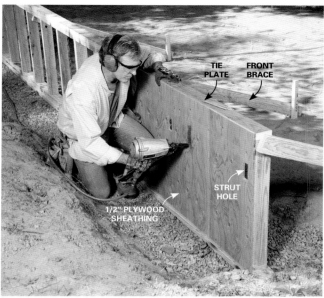

3 Brace and sheathe the wall. Plumb and brace the wall, then screw down the tie plate. Dry-fit the plywood to the back of the framing, mark the strut holes and cut out the holes. Then nail the plywood to the studs.

TIE PLATE   FRONT BRACE

STRUT HOLE

1/2" PLYWOOD SHEATHING

4 Waterproof the walls. Clad the back of the wall with ice-and-water barrier and cut out the strut holes with a utility knife.

ICE-AND-WATER BARRIER

CUT OFF EXCESS

5 Assemble the dead men. Poke the struts through the holes and screw them to each stud. Roughly prop up the struts and secure a continuous 2x4 sleeper to the end of each one with two 3-in. screws.

SLEEPER

STRUT

openings spaced 6 in. down from the underside of the top plate and directly next to every other stud. Nail each panel into place with 8d nails spaced every 8 in. before moving on to the next one. Cover the outside with ice-and-water barrier (Photo 4). The adhesive won't hold the barrier in place, so staple it as needed. Cut off the excess at the top and cut out the strut openings with a utility knife.

Add the struts and sleepers

Slip the struts through each hole. Prop them up so they're close to level, either by piling up dirt or supporting them on chunks of scrap wood. Screw each one to a stud with three 3-in. construction screws. (Predrill the holes to prevent splitting since it's so near the end.) Screw the sleeper to the other end of each strut with two more screws.

6 Add the trim. Nail vertically oriented plywood to the top and bottom plates and to the front of the wall. Make sure to seam plywood over studs. Screw a 2x8 top cap to the top plate, hanging it over the front of the wall 1-1/2 in. Fasten vertical 1x6s to the sheathing with 1-1/2-in. spaces between boards.

7 Time to backfill. Plumb and brace the wall from the back. Backfill, starting at the sleeper, to anchor the wall into place as you continue filling the space behind the wall.

Skin and finish the front

Before you can finish the front of the wall and backfill behind it, you'll have to remove the front braces. So prop up the dead men to keep the wall near plumb while you finish the front. Cut the plywood and nail it on, orienting it vertically to the front so the exposed grain will match the 1x6 boards applied over them. Add the 2x8 cap, keeping a 1-1/2-in. overhang at the front. Screw it to the tie plate with 3-in. deck screws. Screw the 1x6 treated boards to the sheathing with 2-in. deck screws. These boards are spaced every 1-1/2 in. using a scrap 2x4 as a spacer. Don't trust the spacer for more than a few boards at a time. Occasionally check a board with a level and make any necessary adjustments.

Backfill and finish

Plumb and brace the wall from the back by nailing braces to the top cap and stake them on the hill. Prop up every other strut and the sleepers with scraps of wood or the fill falling on the struts and sleepers will force the wall out of plumb. Backfill first against the front of the wall over the footing to lock the wall base into place, then fill behind it. Then fill over the sleeper, working your way toward the wall itself. The object is to lock in the sleeper before the fill pushes against the wall. Once the backfill is in place, it's a good idea to run a sprinkler over the fill for several hours to make it settle before you remove the braces.

If you like the look of your wall, you're good to go—no finish required. The treated wood will weather from green to gray in a year or two. Here, two coats of exterior stain was applied.

Materials list

This 32-ft.-long wall required the materials listed below. If you're building a shorter or longer wall, just figure a percentage of these quantities and you'll get close.

ITEM	QTY.
Roll of ice-and-water barrier	1
50' roll of 4" drain tile	1
Sheets of 1/2" plywood (sheathing)	8
2x6 x 16' (footing plates)	2
2x4 x 8' (studs and struts)	20
2x4 x 16' (sleeper and wall plates)	8
2x8 x 16' (top cap)	2
1x6 x 8' (trim boards)	20

Simple deck

Just follow these step-by-step photos

We can't promise you a beachfront view, but we know you'll enjoy relaxing on this simple deck wherever you choose to build it. Since it's at ground level and is freestanding, you don't have to fuss with challenging railings or footings. All you need are basic carpentry tools and a relatively flat area in your yard or garden. The foundation is nothing more than 4x6 treated timbers buried in the soil, with decorative treated joists and construction-grade cedar decking and a bench. Follow the instructions along with the photos for detailed measurements and building techniques.

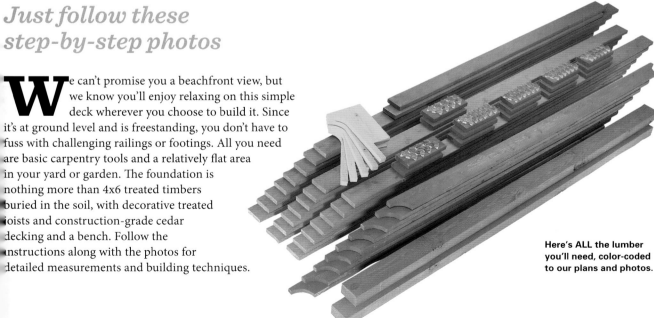

Here's ALL the lumber you'll need, color-coded to our plans and photos.

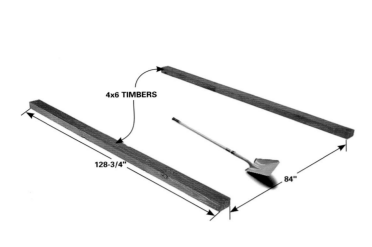

4x6 TIMBERS

128-3/4"

84"

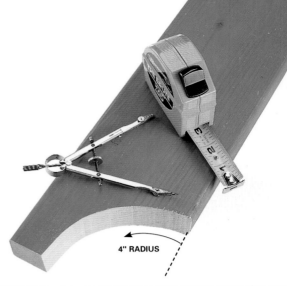

4" RADIUS

1 Dig the 4x6 timbers into the soil, leaving about 1-1/2 in. of the top exposed. The timbers must be parallel and level and the diagonal measurements must be equal.

2 Cut each treated 2x6 joist to 10 ft. Cut the decorative curve on each end, as shown, before installing them onto the 4x6 treated timbers.

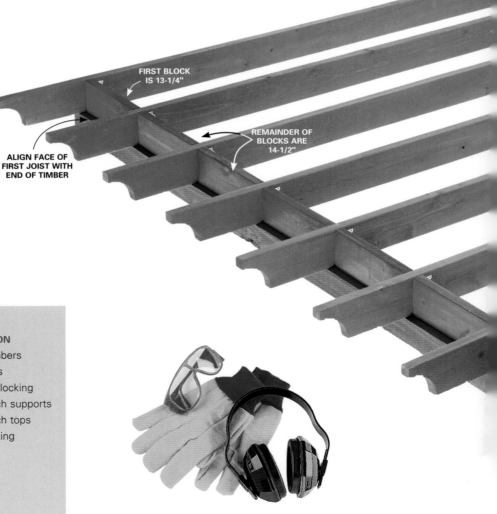

FIRST BLOCK IS 13-1/4"

REMAINDER OF BLOCKS ARE 14-1/2"

ALIGN FACE OF FIRST JOIST WITH END OF TIMBER

Tool list

Shovel
Square
Tape measure
Level
Compass
Chalk line
Jigsaw
Hammer
Circular saw
Hearing and eye protection
Gloves

Materials list

QTY.	SIZE	DESCRIPTION
2	4x6 x 12'	treated timbers
9	2x6 x 10'	cedar joists
2	2x6 x 10'	cedar for blocking
1	2x12 x10'	cedar bench supports
2	2x6 x 10'	cedar bench tops
22	2x6 x 12'	cedar decking
32	metal corner brackets	
3 lbs.	galv. joist hanger nails	
2 lbs.	No. 8 galv. box nails	
10 lbs.	16d galv. casing nails	
1 lb.	3-in. galv. deck screws	

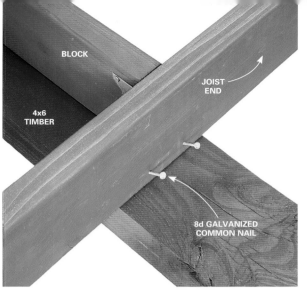

BLOCK

JOIST END

4x6 TIMBER

8d GALVANIZED COMMON NAIL

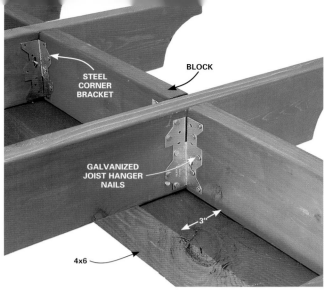

STEEL CORNER BRACKET

BLOCK

GALVANIZED JOIST HANGER NAILS

3"

4x6

3 Lay out the joist spacing so the joists are on 16-in. centers. Cut the blocks to fit between the joists. The first set of blocks (one on each side) will be 13-1/4 in., while the remainder will be 14-1/2 in. long. Toenail each joist to the timber as shown. Be sure the ends of all the joists align with each other as you toenail them in place.

4 Nail your steel corner brackets to the joists and each block between with 1-1/4-in. galvanized joist hanger nails. The blocks add stability and give the deck a finished look.

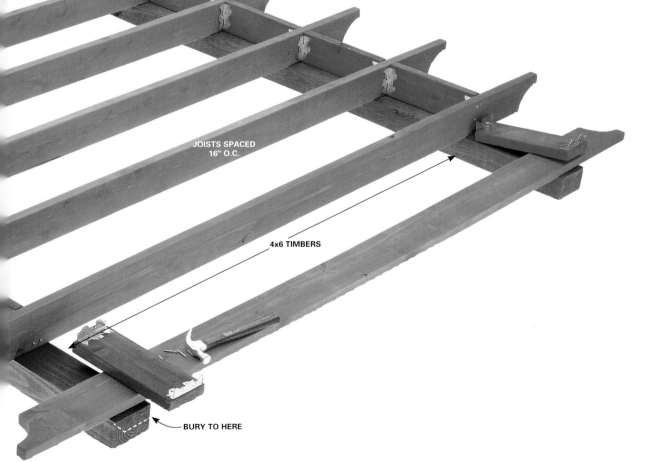

JOISTS SPACED 16" O.C.

4x6 TIMBERS

BURY TO HERE

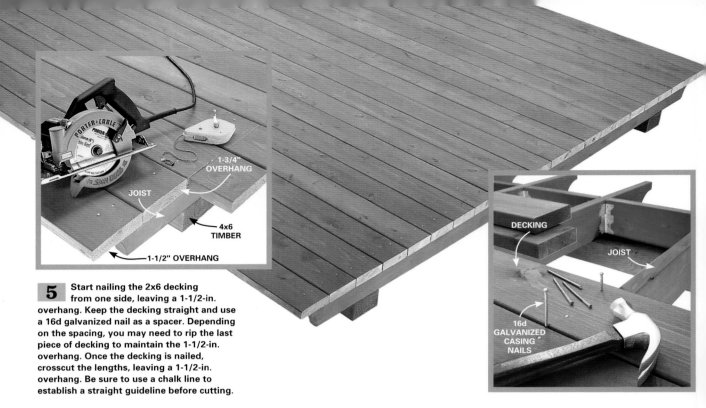

5 Start nailing the 2x6 decking from one side, leaving a 1-1/2-in. overhang. Keep the decking straight and use a 16d galvanized nail as a spacer. Depending on the spacing, you may need to rip the last piece of decking to maintain the 1-1/2-in. overhang. Once the decking is nailed, crosscut the lengths, leaving a 1-1/2-in. overhang. Be sure to use a chalk line to establish a straight guideline before cutting.

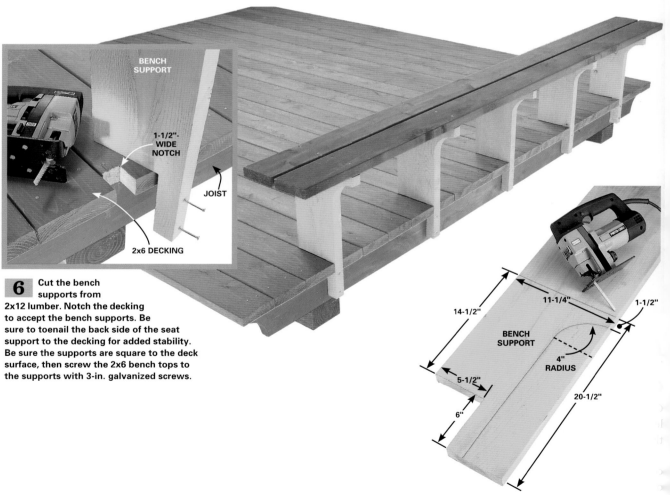

6 Cut the bench supports from 2x12 lumber. Notch the decking to accept the bench supports. Be sure to toenail the back side of the seat support to the decking for added stability. Be sure the supports are square to the deck surface, then screw the 2x6 bench tops to the supports with 3-in. galvanized screws.

1-day patio pond

If you can build a box, you can do it!

Getting started

Cut the two bottom boards (A and E; see Figure A, p. 95) to length. Cuts made at the lumber mill are usually rough, so trim the ends of all the boards before measuring.

Join all the components with both trim-head screws and construction adhesive. Adhesive works better than wood glue on rough-sawn lumber and is more forgiving on joints that

aren't super tight. Apply a bead of adhesive and clamp the two bottom boards together. Scrape off the excess adhesive with a putty knife, and clean the rest with mineral spirits.

Install temporary cleats on the smooth side of the boards, which will be the inside of the container (Photo 1). Hold them in place with 1-1/4-in. screws. We used cabinet screws, but other types of screws would work just fine. Don't worry about

A simple box with a rubber lining

We wanted a super-easy-to-build water feature, so we designed this wooden box that just about anyone can build with basic tools. What makes it work as a pond is a paint-on rubber lining. There are a few different brands of liquid rubber; check online. It's ultra-stretchy and UV-stable, and it can be used on lots of materials, including wood, metal and concrete. It's amazing stuff, though expensive.

You can use liquid rubber to fix leaky gutters and metal roofs, seal RVs and trailers, and for many other applications. Ranchers love it for sealing leaks in metal water tanks. And we love it because it can turn just about anything, even a simple wooden box, into a water feature.

the screw holes left behind when you remove the cleats; the liquid rubber will fill them in.

Cut the boards to size

The width of 1x12s can vary slightly, so double-check the width of the bottom before you cut the ends and dividers (B and C) to length. The rough-sawn cedar we used was 7/8 in. thick. If you're working with material that's only 3/4 in. thick, you'll have to adjust the length of the sides.

All the trim parts are made from 1x6s ripped in half. Some home centers sell 1x3 boards, so you wouldn't have to bother with ripping at all.

Assemble the container

Mark guidelines for the dividers with a framing square 14 in. in from the ends of the bottom. Transfer that line to the inside of the sides (D). Face the smooth sides of the dividers toward the center compartment. That will ensure more even coverage of the liquid rubber in the compartment where it matters most.

Attach the ends and dividers to the bottom with adhesive and three 1-1/2-in. exterior-grade trim-head screws (Photo 2). Join the sides with adhesive and screws, three in each side of each end and divider. Space the screws about 10 in. apart along the bottom. The end caps hide the end grain and strengthen the corners. Secure them with four screws and adhesive. Cedar isn't as prone to splitting as harder woods, so predrill holes for screws only in areas where a knot is in your way.

Install four aluminum angle brackets (Photo 3). Cut them to size with a hacksaw or a jigsaw fitted with a bimetal blade. Drill two holes in each side, and secure them with adhesive and 3/4-in. screws.

Assemble the base with two 3-in. screws into each joint. It's easier to center the base when the container is upside down. Hold it in place by driving in four screws at an angle. Flip the whole thing over and secure the base to the container with 3-in. screws driven down through the bottom of the container.

After removing the temporary cleats, drill four 1/2-in. drainage holes in the corners of the outside compartments and one in the middle. If you plan to install a water pump, drill a 1-1/2-in. hole for the cord with a hole saw. Figure out which side of the container has the best-looking wood grain and drill the hole on the opposite side about 3/8 in. down from the top edge.

Poor man's pocket hole

If you're a regular weekend woodworker, you really ought to get yourself a pocket hole jig. But if you don't have one, here's a quick and easy trick that works well on soft woods like cedar: Start by laying out the face frame, rough side down, and marking two guidelines at each joint. Then drill 1/8-in. holes through the end grain at an angle so the drill bit pops out about 3/4 in. to 7/8 in. down from the end of the board (Photo 4). At that length, a 1-1/2-in. trim-head screw will travel about 3/4 in. into the adjoining frame section. If you mess up and drill at a funky angle, you can always drill another hole a little bit over, and no one will be the wiser because it's on the underside of the face frame.

Build the face frame

Assemble the sides and the ends of the face frame with two 1-1/2-in. trim-head screws and adhesive (Photo 4). Keep downward pressure on both trim boards while driving in the first screw. A wood clamp on the seam works well as a third hand. Before installing the face frame dividers, measure diagonally from one corner to the other both ways to make sure the frame is square. If the frame is a little out of whack, adjust the frame until it's square, and clamp it to your workbench to hold it square.

Apply the liquid rubber and wood finish

Tape off the top edge of the container, the power cord hole and the drainage holes on the bottom. Brush the rubber

1 **Build the bottom.** Glue the bottom boards together with construction adhesive, and install three temporary cleats to hold them together until the project has been assembled.

2 **Install the dividers.** Fasten the dividers to the bottom, and then add the sides. Join all the parts with both adhesive and trim-head screws. Scrape any excess adhesive with a putty knife.

3 **Add corner brackets.** Cut aluminum angle stock to create corner brackets. Drill four holes in each bracket, and secure them with adhesive and screws.

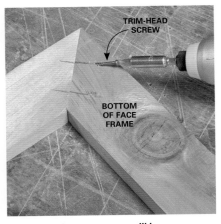

TRIM-HEAD SCREW

BOTTOM OF FACE FRAME

4 Build the face frame. Join the face-frame parts so that the new screws will be invisible. First, drill pilot holes through the end of one part (left photo). Then just hold the parts together and drive in screws (right photo).

5 Apply the liquid rubber. Glob a thick coat of the liquid rubber into all the seams, corners and defects in the wood. Apply one coat on the outside compartments and three on the middle.

6 Secure the face frame. Clamp the face frame into place and hold it down with adhesive and trim-head screws. Leave the screw heads flush with the surface to avoid pockets where water can pool and penetrate the wood.

on thick into the corners, seams, screw holes and defects in the wood (Photo 5). It takes three heavy coats to make a watertight seal and at least three hours between coats. Apply only one coat in the two outside compartments because they'll be filled with soil rather than water. Also apply just one coat on the very top edge of the container. Avoid blocking the drainage and cord holes with rubber by mopping the excess out with a cotton swab or rolled-up paper towel. The rubber needs to dry for a few days before it's ready for water.

Rough-sawn cedar isn't supposed to be smooth; hence the name. So resist the urge to sand, and embrace the imperfections. We applied a cedar-tinted wood finish, but any exterior stain or clear finish would work.

Finish up and add water

Once the finishes are dry, clamp the face to the container and fasten it with adhesive and 1-1/2-in. trim-head screws spaced every 10 in. or so (Photo 6). Set the screws flush with the surface of the wood to keep water from pooling.

A water pump isn't necessary but does help the water stay fresh. Some pumps have suction cups to hold them to the bottom, but the rubber-coated wood may not be smooth enough for them to stick. You can lay down a small chunk of Plexiglas at the bottom and stick the pump's suction cups to that. Floating water plants with exposed roots will clog the pump filter, so only use potted plants, or plan to build some sort of additional screen or filtration system. A pump that moves 120 gallons per hour is plenty big enough for this situation.

Now it's time to fill up your new creation with water and plants. If the local nursery doesn't carry water plants, you can order them online.

Figure A Patio pond

Overall dimensions: 66-3/4" x 21" x 15-1/2"

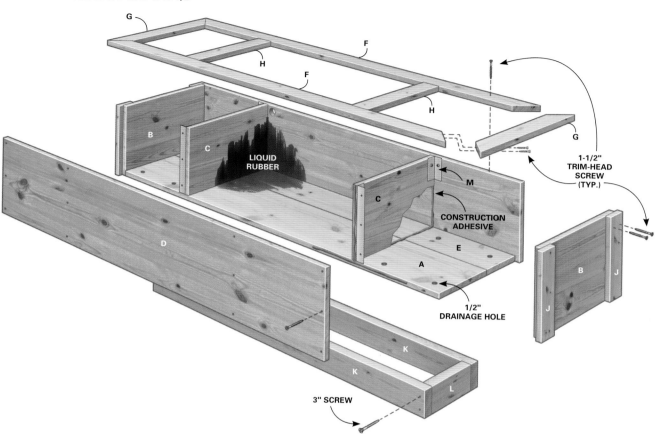

LIQUID RUBBER

1-1/2" TRIM-HEAD SCREW (TYP.)

CONSTRUCTION ADHESIVE

M

1/2" DRAINAGE HOLE

3" SCREW

Cutting list

KEY	DIMENSIONS	QTY.	NAME
Cut from rough-sawn 1x12 cedar*			
A	62-1/4" x 11-1/4" x 7/8"	1	Bottom
B	16-3/4" x 11-1/4" x 7/8"	2	Ends
C	16-3/4" x 10-3/8" x 7/8"	2	Dividers
D	64" x 11-1/4" x 7/8"	2	Sides

*Widths may vary

KEY	DIMENSIONS	QTY.	NAME
Cut from 1x6 rough-sawn cedar			
E	62-1/4" x 5-1/2" x 7/8"	1	Bottom
F	2-11/16" x 66-3/4" x 7/8"	2	Face frame sides
G	2-11/16" x 21" x 7/8"	2	Face frame ends
H	2-11/16" x 15-9/16"	2	Face frame dividers
J	2-11/16" x 11-1/4"	4	End caps

KEY	DIMENSIONS	QTY.	NAME
Cedar-tone pressure-treated 2x4			
K	54" x 3-1/2" x 1-1/2"	2	Base sides
L	8-1/2" x 3-1/2" x 1-1/2"	2	Base ends

KEY	DIMENSIONS	QTY.	NAME
Aluminum angle stock			
M	10-1/4" x 1-1/4" x 1/16"	4	Corner bracket

Materials list

ITEM	QTY.
1x12 x 12' rough-sawn cedar	2
1x6 x 8' rough-sawn cedar	3
2x4 x 12' cedar-tone pressure-treated lumber	1
1-1/4" x 1/16" x 4' aluminum angle stock	1
Small box of 1-1/2" exterior trim-head screws	1
Small box of 1-1/4" drywall or cabinet screws	1
Small box of 3" screws compatible with pressure-treated lumber	1
Small box of 3/4" screws	1
Tube of construction adhesive	1
Gallon of liquid rubber	

Easy garden arch 241
Pyramid trellis 244
Copper wire trellis 246
Entry arbors & trellis 250

16 GARDEN FEATURES

Easy garden arch

A small project that makes a big impression in your backyard

Building an arch is one of the easiest ways to give your landscape a striking centerpiece. And this arch is easier than most. Made from just six parts, it can be built in less than a day—even if you're a rookie carpenter. The design is versatile, too: The arch can become a gateway in a fence, frame a walkway through a hedge or stand alone in your yard or garden. You can stain it for a rustic look or paint it for a more formal look.

Money and materials

The total materials bill for the cedar arch shown here was a couple hundred dollars. Built from pressure-treated lumber, it would cost about half that. Depending on where you live, you may have other choices of rot-resistant lumber available, such as cypress or redwood. If you choose treated lumber, you'll find everything you need for this project at home

WHAT IT TAKES

TIME: 1 day
SKILL LEVEL: Beginner to intermediate

centers. If you choose another wood species, you may have to special-order lumber or visit a traditional lumberyard.

You'll need only standard tools like a drill, a circular saw and a jigsaw. Make sure your framing square is a standard model (16 x 24 in., with a longer leg that's 2 in. wide). If yours is an oddball, buy a standard version so you can easily mark out the brackets (see Photo 2). A few days before you dig the postholes, call 811 to have underground utility lines marked.

Cut the parts

To get started, cut notches in the tops of the posts (Photo 1). If you're using "rough-sawn" lumber as we did, you may have to change the length and depth of these notches to suit your 2x8 headers. (The dimensions of rough-sawn lumber vary.) Set the cutting depth of your circular saw to 1-1/2 in. to make the crosscuts for the notches. Then set your saw to full depth to make the other cuts.

Next cut the 2x8 headers to length and mark arcs at the ends as shown in Figure A. To mark the curves, use the bottom of a 5-gallon bucket or any circle that's 10 to 11 in. in diameter. Cut the curves with a jigsaw.

The curved brackets may look complicated, but they're easy to mark since they're based on a standard framing square. After marking with the square (Photo 2), set a nail in your sawhorse 20 in. from the edge of the board. Carefully adjust the position of the board until both corner marks of the bracket are 24 in. from the nail. Then, holding your pencil at the 24-in. mark on the tape, draw an arc. To draw the second arc, move your pencil to the 29-in. mark on the tape (Photo 3). Cut the straight edges of the brackets with a circular saw and the arcs with a jigsaw. If the curves turn out a bit wavy, smooth them with an orbital or belt sander. Don't be too fussy, though. Nobody will notice small imperfections.

Put it all together

Mark one header 12 in. from both ends and lay out the posts, aligned with the marks. Take measurements at the other end to make sure the posts are perfectly parallel. Drive 3-1/2-in. screws through the posts and into the header. At the tops of the brackets, drive 3-in. screws at a slight angle so they won't poke through the face of the header (Photo 4). Set 1-1/2-in.-thick blocks under the other ends of the brackets. Then drive screws at an angle through the sides of the brackets and into the posts. Be sure to drill 1/8-in. pilot holes so you don't split the brackets. Set the second header in place and screw it to the posts. Note: The brackets are not centered on the posts, so there's a 1-in. gap between the second header and the brackets.

Set it up

You'll set the arch posts into 10-in.-diameter holes 30 in. deep. But before you move the arch into place, screw on a temporary 2x4 "stretcher" 30 in. from the post bottoms. Then round up a helper or two and set the posts into the holes. Patiently level and plumb the arch, using stakes and 2x4s to brace it (Photo 5). Be careful not to nudge the posts out of position as you fill the holes with concrete. Let the concrete harden for at least four hours before you finish the wood. Brush on two coats of clear penetrating wood finish to deepen the color of the wood and repel moisture.

Figure A
Garden arch

Overall dimensions: 90" tall, 78" wide

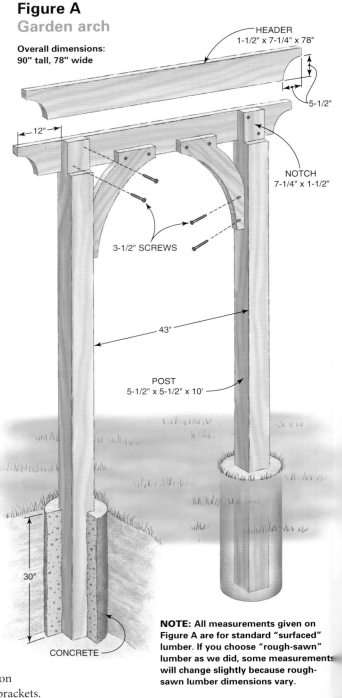

HEADER 1-1/2" x 7-1/4" x 78"

5-1/2"

12"

NOTCH 7-1/4" x 1-1/2"

3-1/2" SCREWS

43"

POST 5-1/2" x 5-1/2" x 10'

30"

CONCRETE

NOTE: All measurements given on Figure A are for standard "surfaced" lumber. If you choose "rough-sawn" lumber as we did, some measurements will change slightly because rough-sawn lumber dimensions vary.

Materials list

ITEM	QTY.
6x6 x 10' (posts)	2
2x8 x 8' (headers)	2
2x10 x 8' (brackets)	1
2x4 x 8' (stretcher, stakes, braces)	3
Concrete mix (60-lb. bags)	3
3" and 3-1/2" screws	

1 Notch the tops of the posts. Cut as deep as you can from both sides with a circular saw, then finish the cuts with a handsaw.

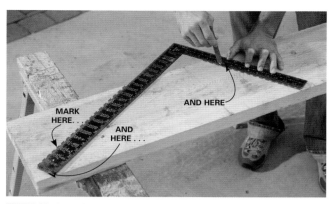

MARK HERE...

AND HERE...

AND HERE

2 Mark the brackets without fussy measurements or geometry—just align a framing square with the edges of a 2x10 and make three marks.

3 Draw perfect curves fast using a tape measure to guide your pencil. Cut out the bracket and use it as a pattern for the other bracket.

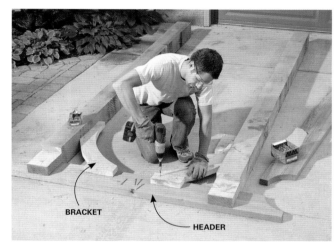

BRACKET

HEADER

4 Screw through the posts and brackets into the header. That way, one header will have no visible screws. Screw through the second header into the posts.

STRETCHER

SHIMS

5 Set the arch level and plumb before you pour concrete into the postholes. Wedge shims under the stretcher until the header is level, then plumb and brace the posts.

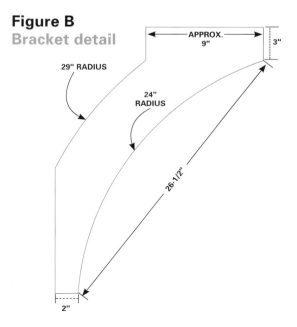

Figure B
Bracket detail

APPROX. 9"

3"

29" RADIUS

24" RADIUS

26-1/2"

2"

Pyramid trellis

A 7-foot trellis that's a cinch to build

Y ou would pay a bundle for a trellis like this at a garden center—or you can build it in an afternoon for less than half the retail price. If you use pressure-treated wood, the trellis will last a long time and never need a coat of stain.

How to build it

1. From four 2x2s, cut four 84-in.-long legs. Cut at 90 degrees.
2. Cut horizontal spacers from the remaining 2x2s. All of these pieces should be cut at 6 degrees, with the angles opposing. Cut four pieces each to these lengths (length given is for the widest side of the piece): 18-1/2 in.; 13-1/8 in.; 8-3/8 in.; and 4-1/8 in.
3. Rip just enough wood from the two 6-ft. 5/4-in. x 6-in. deck boards to eliminate both rounded edges. Then rip the boards 1-1/8 in. wide—you'll get four pieces from each board. From these, cut four pieces 60 in. long and eight pieces 36 in. long. Cut two 45-degree angles on one end of each to make a decorative peak.
4. Measure and mark positions of the four spacers on the legs. To do this, lay all four legs together, with sides touching and tops and bottoms aligned. Measure and mark as shown in Figure B. Work from the bottom up. Set aside two of the legs.
5. Lay the other two legs on your workbench, with their sides touching. Keep the legs together at the tops (a heavy-duty rubber band around the tops will help) while spreading them apart at the bottom. Center the longest spacer at the lowest mark on the legs, the second-longest spacer at the second mark, and so on.

   Fasten the spacers using 2-1/2-in. screws (drill pilot holes first). Start at the bottom and work your way up. As you screw the spacer to one leg, clamp the other down or nail a board behind it on your bench so you have something to push against. When positioning these screws, leave room for the screws you'll use to attach adjacent spacers (see Detail illustration). Assemble the other set of legs the same way.
6. Stand the two sets of legs upright on a level floor, with the tops touching. Spread the bottom legs to make room for the spacers that hold the two sets together. Hold the tops together temporarily by wrapping with duct tape.

   Drill a pilot hole and fasten the longest spacer between the sets with a 2-1/2-in. screw to one side. (Take care not to hit the screw on the adjacent side.) Next, attach the shortest spacer on the same side. Fasten the second and third spacers last. Attach spacers on the opposite side in the same order.
7. Make a 4-1/2-in.-square finial platform from a 2-in. x 6-in. scrap of pressure-treated lumber. (You can find these pieces in the scrap bin at most building centers for a small fee.) Rip the piece to 4-1/2 in. first, then cut a piece 4-1/2 in. long from the board.
8. Find the center point of the platform by drawing lines that connect the opposite corners with a straight edge. Mark the center where the lines

WHAT IT TAKES

TIME: 4 hours
SKILL LEVEL: Beginner to intermediate

Materials list

Note: Use pressure-treated lumber.

6   2" x 2" x 8'
2   5/4 x 6" x 6' deck boards
1   2" x 6" x 6" board
1   3/16" x 2-1/2" dowel screw
    3-1/2", 2-1/2", 2" and 1-5/8" galvanized deck screws
1   decorative finial

Tools
■ Table saw
■ Power drill
■ Duct tape

Figure A
Pyramid trellis

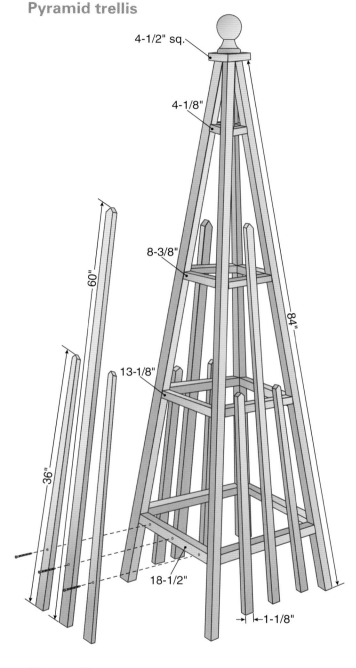

4-1/2" sq.

4-1/8"

8-3/8"

60"

13-1/8"

36"

84"

18-1/2"

1-1/8"

intersect with an awl. Predrill a hole for the 3/16-in. dowel screw (also called a double-ended wood screw) in the spot you've marked. Sand the platform for a rounded appearance.

9. Attach the platform to the legs. Predrill holes on the platform for 3-1/2-in. screws. Angle the holes so they run parallel to the legs. Screw the platform into the top ends of the legs.

   Attach a dowel screw for the finial in the center of the platform, then thread a decorative finial onto the screw.

10. Center the longest vertical "spear" on each side, drill pilot holes and attach to the spacers with 1-5/8-in. deck screws. Center short spears between the legs and the long spears, then fasten to the spacers with deck screws. The bottom of each spear should be about 1 in. off the ground. This will ensure that the trellis rests on the legs instead of the spears.

   If you plan to use the trellis in a windy spot, you may want to anchor it. Drive two pipes into the ground, then attach the trellis to them with cable ties or hose clamps.

   Remove the duct tape and plant some vining flowers.

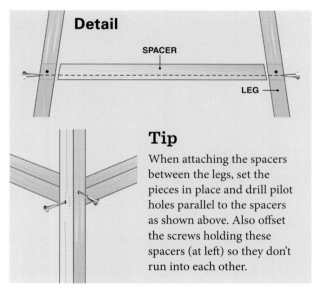

Detail

SPACER

LEG

Tip
When attaching the spacers between the legs, set the pieces in place and drill pilot holes parallel to the spacers as shown above. Also offset the screws holding these spacers (at left) so they don't run into each other.

Figure B
Spacer locations

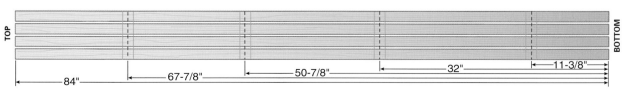

TOP

BOTTOM

84"

67-7/8"

50-7/8"

32"

11-3/8"

Lay legs together and mark. These are the centers where the spacers will attach.

Copper wire trellis

A garden project with a twist

The first reaction of most people when they see this trellis is, "Wow! I love it!" The second reaction is, "How in the world did you make it?"

Well, there's a trick to bending the wire, that's for sure, but once you understand it, this trellis goes together pretty easily. When you're done, you've got an elegant garden ornament that looks great even when the plants that climb on it have died back.

Give it a year or two outdoors and the wood will turn gray and the copper will turn a beautiful dark brown, and then eventually green. It wouldn't be hard to customize this trellis, forming the copper wire into initials or even more fanciful shapes.

Materials and tools

The copper scrollwork is made from No. 6 solid-copper wire, which is used for grounding electrical panels and is available at most home centers. This wire is stiff enough to hold its shape on the trellis, but soft enough to bend easily. The rest of the trellis is made from 2x2s and 1/2-in. copper pipe.

In the tool department, you'll need a drill and a 5/8-in. spade bit, a pair of medium to large wire-cutting pliers (test them out on the copper wire to see if they can cut it), a miter box or electric miter saw and an electric sander.

Make the trellis from treated lumber, or spend a bit more and use clear cedar, shown here.

Begin with the legs and rungs

Begin with the four legs, the wooden center posts and the copper pipe rungs that connect them.

1. Place your four 2x2 legs on sawhorses, get the top ends even and clamp them all together.
2. Mark one end as the top, and measure from that end at 28 in., 41-1/2 in. and 59 in. to mark where you will drill the holes. Use a square to transfer the marks to all four legs and to the adjacent side of one leg.
3. Make an angle guide by cutting a piece of scrap wood at an 80-degree angle (Photo 1). An inexpensive protractor works fine to set the angle.
4. Drill angled holes at each mark, using your guide, so you're drilling three holes in each leg (Photo 1). Mark your drill bit to indicate the 1-in. depth for the holes, and be sure the drill is always leaning toward the top of the legs.
5. Flip each leg 90 degrees, clamp them together and repeat the whole process. The marks you made on the second side of one leg will allow you to transfer your hole locations. Be careful—the drill may be a bit jumpy as the second hole meets the first.
6. Cut six pieces of pipe (C, D and E) as shown in Photo 2, inset. Note in the Cutting List (on p. 104) that there are two sets of

Choosing lumber

When you're shopping for the 2x2s, the best choice is clear D-grade cedar, typically stocked for deck railings. You can use pressure-treated lumber, which will be more economical, but you may have to sort through a lot of 2x2s to find straight, relatively knot-free ones. If you have a table saw, you can often cut fairly knot-free 2x2s from the edges of a wider board.

pipe rungs; one set is slightly longer. Cut the longer set now.
7. Temporarily assemble one side of the trellis—two legs and three pieces of pipe. Tap the legs to get the pipe seated. The tops of the legs should be within 1/4 in. of each other.
8. Cut the center posts (B) to length, and use a miter box or miter saw to cut points on the ends. A line marked around all four sides will help guide you.
9. Lay the center post on top of the assembled side. Be sure the post is centered and equidistant from the legs. Mark the post

1 Drill holes in the legs using a wood scrap cut at 80 degrees to guide you. With all four legs clamped together, it's easy to get the holes to line up.

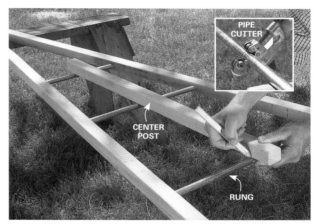

2 Lay a center post on the rungs, which are cut from copper pipe, and mark the rung holes directly on the post. Be sure the post is centered top-to-bottom and side-to-side.

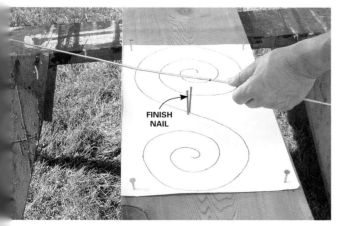

3 Your bending jig for the wire scrolls is a piece of scrap wood with a copy of the scroll pattern (p. 104) tacked to it. Two finish nails in the middle hold the pieces of copper wire.

4 Bend the scrolls with your hands, following the pattern. The copper wire is soft enough to bend easily. When you've bent one side, weight it down and bend the other.

Figure A
Copper wire trellis

For clarity, only one
of four sides is shown.

UPPER CAP (P)

GLUE

10d FINISH
NAIL

LOWER CAP (M)

PREDRILL
FOR NAIL

SAND FLUSH

LEG (A)

3/8" GALV.
FENCE
STAPLE

45°

28"

UPPER PIPE RUNG (C)

41-1/2"

MIDDLE
PIPE RUNG
(D)

SCROLL

59"

5/8" DIA.
1" DEEP
10°

CENTER
POST (B)

LOWER
PIPE RUNG
(E)

BURY A
FEW INCHES
IN THE GROUND

Figure B
Lower scroll

Enlarge to an overall
length of 16-3/4"

NAILS

USE 54" OF
#6 WIRE.
23" ABOVE NAILS
31" BELOW NAILS

Figure C
Middle scroll

Enlarge to an overall
length of 12-3/4"

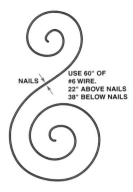

NAILS

USE 60" OF
#6 WIRE.
22" ABOVE NAILS
38" BELOW NAILS

Figure D
Upper scroll

Enlarge to an overall
length of 13-3/4"

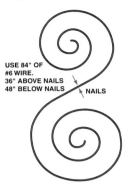

USE 84" OF
#6 WIRE.
36" ABOVE NAILS
48" BELOW NAILS

NAILS

Materials list

6   2x2 x 8'
1   4x4 x 1'
1   1x6 x 1'
115' of #6 solid-copper wire
16' of 1/2" copper pipe
One box fence staples
Six 10d finish nails
One tube construction adhesive

Cutting list
Overall Dimensions: 69"H x 26"W x 26"D

KEY	NAME	QTY.	DIMENSIONS
A	leg	4	1-1/2" x 1-1/2" x 72"
B	center post	4	1-1/2" x 1-1/2" x 35-1/2"
C	upper pipe	2	1/2" dia. x 11-1/4"
D	middle pipe	2	1/2" dia. x 15-3/4"
E	lower pipe	2	1/2" dia. x 21-3/4"
F	upper pipe	2	1/2" dia. x 10-3/4"
G	middle pipe	2	1/2" dia. x 15-1/4"
H	lower pipe	2	1/2" dia. x 21-1/4"
J	upper scroll	4	#6 wire x 60"
K	middle scroll	8	#6 wire x 54"
L	lower scroll	8	#6 wire x 84"
M	lower cap	1	3/4" x 4" x 4"
P	upper cap	1	3-1/2" x 3-1/2" x 2-1/4"

5 Attach the scrolls with small fence staples. You can bend the scroll out of the way temporarily to make room for the hammer.

6 Sand the top where all four legs come together, using coarse sandpaper, so they form a flat surface for nailing on the cap.

for the pipe holes, then transfer the marks to the other three center posts and drill the holes at 90 degrees. Drill from one side until the point of the spade bit pokes through, then drill the other side. This gives you cleaner holes.

Be careful inserting the pipe

10. Assemble two sides. Put the pipes through the center posts, get them centered, then place the ends of the pipes in the legs. Be careful as you insert the pipe in the center post. It's possible to split out a chunk of the wood as the pipe exits the post. When you're done, the tops of the legs should be within 1/4 in. of each other.

11. Lay an assembled side upside down on sawhorses so the remaining holes in the legs are pointing up and supported. Using a bolt, an old screwdriver or similar tool, mash the end of the pipe where you can see it at the bottom of each hole. This will lock the pipe in place and make room at the bottom of the hole for the other pipes.

12. Cut the remaining pipe rungs (F, G and H) and then fit the rungs and remaining center posts between the two assembled sides to form the complete trellis structure. If any of the joints are loose, put a bit of epoxy in the hole.

Bend the scrolls

Now the fun part: making the wire scrollwork.

13. Make your bending jig out of a 2x12 or a scrap piece of plywood at least 11 in. x 18 in. Enlarge the patterns in Figures B, C and D until the dimensions are correct, and tack a pattern to the jig (Photo 3). Nail two 10d finish nails on either side of the scroll shape to hold the wire (see Figures B, C and D).

14. Cut one piece of wire to the appropriate length for the scroll you're working on. Measure from one end to find the point that goes between the two finish nails (see pattern drawing), mark that spot and lay the wire on the jig so your mark is between the two nails. Using your hand only,

bend the wire to the shape on the pattern (Photo 4). There should be a few inches of extra wire on each end to give you something to hold. When you've got the first half bent to shape, snip the end. Put a weight or a clamp on the part you've done, then bend the other side. You don't have to be fussy about matching the pattern; close is good enough.

15. If your first scroll was a success, cut the remaining pieces of wire and bend the rest of the scrolls. For each of the three different shapes, do one for practice before cutting the remaining wire. If you have trouble, cut the wire a little long and you'll have more to work with.

Final assembly

16. Lay the trellis on its side and use fence staples to attach the scrolls to the 2x2s (Photo 5). Be sure to get the pairs of scrolls on each side of the trellis to be symmetrical (a right and a left), and to reverse the direction between the lower and middle scrolls (see Figure A).

17. When all the scrolls are attached, stand the trellis up, find yourself something to stand on, and sand the tops of the legs flat and even (Photo 6). If the pieces vibrate too much, tape them all together with duct tape or packing tape.

18. Cut the cap pieces (M and P). For the facets on the topmost cap piece (P), start with a 1-ft.-long piece of 4x4 so you have enough wood to hold on to while you cut the facets. Then trim off the finished cap piece. You can also buy deck caps at a home center to avoid the cutting completely. When both cap pieces are cut, drill pilot holes in M, nail it on, then glue on part P with construction adhesive or epoxy.

19. Install the trellis in your garden. Dig the bottoms of the legs into the earth and get the trellis plumb. You'll have to do it pretty much by eye. If your location is windy, anchor the bottoms of the legs into the ground. One way is to bend a couple of 3-ft. pieces of 1/8-in. rod into a U-shape, so they can be driven in around the legs. Then fasten them to the legs with fence staples and cover with dirt or mulch.

Entry arbors & trellis

Use this simple, versatile design to frame your walk, screen bland walls and decorate with ivy

You don't have to hire an architect to redesign your front entry to make it attractive and inviting. Sometimes a simple, inexpensive arbor or trellis will do the trick. This home featured a pretty brick facing . . . flanked by a big blank vinyl-sided wall that begged for screening. Our solution was to hide it behind a simple trellis. An even simpler version of the same design is used to frame an arbor that borders the sidewalk on both sides. This feature not only beautifies the entry but also guides guests to the front door.

Here, we'll show you a simple technique that'll allow you to build both projects. Photos 1 – 7 demonstrate the building of the open-sided arbors. Photos 8 – 10 show how to assemble the trellis. This truly is a relaxed weekend project. You just need to be able to dig a few holes and operate a circular saw and a screw gun. You cut and assemble everything in place, so it's easy to measure and cut the pieces to fit as you go.

1 Stake the post positions using a rectangular 2x4 template. Remove the template and dig the postholes.

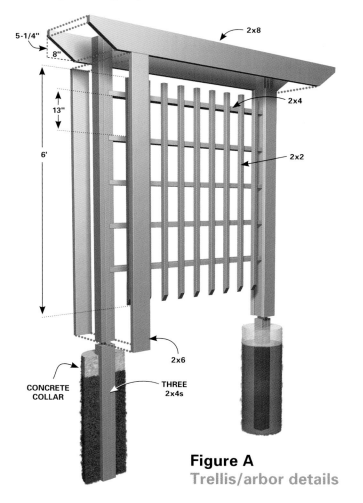

Figure A
Trellis/arbor details

Labels on figure:
5-1/4"
8"
2x8
13"
6'
2x4
2x2
2x6
CONCRETE COLLAR
THREE 2x4s

4'
3" DECK SCREWS
2x4 x 12' POST CENTER

2 Screw the lower post assemblies together with four pairs of screws on each side (Figure A).

3 Drop the posts into their postholes, then plumb them both ways and toe-screw them to the template. Tamp soil around it to brace it.

2x4 and 2x6 "sandwich" posts simplify assembly

The bottom portions of the posts are made from three treated 2x4s to keep the dirt-bound parts from rotting. The center 2x4 is continuous to keep the posts strong, but we cut the outside 2x4s off just above grade so we could transition to better-looking cedar. We chose cedar for its natural rot resistance, its ability to hold paint and its stability. If cedar isn't available in your area, use any naturally rot-resistant wood that's available for the above-grade wood. Redwood and cypress are excellent substitutes. If you want to save, you could even use common construction-grade lumber. If you paint all sides and the cut ends before assembly, the project will last for years. Or build it entirely with treated wood. But keep in mind that treated wood is often of low quality and has a tendency to warp, twist and crack. It may not be as handsome down the road as other choices. And you also may have to wait weeks for the treated wood to dry well enough to hold paint.

4 Mark the short side posts a few inches above grade and cut them off with a circular saw. Take care not to cut the long center post.

5 Cut the lintels to length, then level and rest them on temporary blocks. Mark the height of the center 2x4s, then cut them off with your circular saw.

LONG 2x4

SHORT 2x4s

CUT MARK

2x8 LINTEL

TEMPORARY BLOCK

We designed the trellis grid work with close spacing to support climbing plants. You can make your grid work with larger spaces, or tighter if the trellis alone will be the screen, without vines. We fastened the grid work high enough above the patio to allow space for a planter box below. If you're building the grid work to look like ours, get five cedar 2x4 "rungs" (horizontal members; Figure A) long enough to span between posts. Also pick up three 8-ft.-long 2x2 pickets (verticals) for each foot of width, or rip them from 2x4s.

Build a template and dig the postholes

A 2x4 template makes quick work of marking accurate post positions and of setting the posts (Photo 1). Decide on the best footprint for the arbors and make the template dimensions to match the corners of the posts. Be sure to square up your template by matching diagonal measurements (distances between opposite corners should be the same) and then add a brace to keep it square. Use screws for fasteners so you can take the template apart easily after you're through setting the posts.

Drive stakes into the ground at the corners to mark the holes and then set aside the template. Dig 8-in.-wide holes about 3 ft. deep and pack the bottom of

each hole with a shovel handle so the posts won't settle later. After the holes are dug, return the template to the same spot for setting the posts.

The template helps keep the posts plumb and aligned. Push the preassembled posts against the template and plumb each post in both directions. Toe-screw each one to the template to hold it plumb while you fill in the hole with soil (Photo 3). If the template moves around too much, just anchor it to the ground with a few temporary stakes.

Use a single 2x4 for a template when you're setting the two posts for the trellis. Make sure the posts lie flat against the 2x4 to ensure that the post sides remain aligned. After plumbing each post

Materials list

Treated wood: For each post, you'll need a treated 12-ft.-long 2x4 for the center and an 8-ft.-long treated 2x4 cut in half for the shorter post sides (Photo 2).

Cedar: For wrapping each post, buy two 8-ft. cedar 2x4s and two 8-ft. 2x6s. Also buy two 2x8 cedar lintel boards at least 3 ft. longer than the distance between the posts (outside-to-outside dimension).

Hardware: Buy a 1-lb. box of 3-in. deck screws for joining all of the components except the pickets. Buy a 1-lb. box of 10d galvanized finish nails for that job. And get one 60-lb. bag of premixed concrete for each pair of posts.

with a level, add fill, packing it as you go. Fill the top 8 in. with concrete. If you're going to quit for the day, mix the concrete now and collar each post with a half bag (60-lb. bags). Otherwise, go on to the next step, adding the cedar trim, and add the concrete later.

Assemble the cedar parts

Start by cutting off the short treated 2x4s a couple of inches above the final grade (Photo 4). Be sure to account for the finished height, including sod, pavers or mulch. The idea is to keep the cedar above the ground to prevent rot.

Cut the 2x8 lintels to length and cut the decorative angles on the ends (Figure A). Support one of the leveled 2x8 lintels on temporary blocks at the desired height to mark the top of the center 2x4 for trimming (Photo 5). Before you take the 2x8 down, use a level and a long straightedge to transfer the post height to the posts on the opposite arbor. That way the arbor tops will match.

Installing the cedar cladding is simple; it's just a matter of measuring, cutting and screwing the parts together. Photos 6 and 7 show you how.

If you're building a trellis next to a wall as we did, you may not be able to fit a screw gun between the wall and the trellis to drive the screws. If so, just toe-screw those parts from the front.

Tip

You'll save tons of time by painting or sealing the cedar parts before assembly. You'll still have freshly cut ends to touch up, but that only takes moments.

1' SUPPORT BOARDS

RUNGS

2x2 PICKET SPACING

6 Cut the cedar 2x4 post trim boards to length and screw them to the center treated post. Then screw the lintels in place flush with the post top.

2x4 TRIM

7 Cut the 2x6 post trim to fit directly under the lintel and screw it to the cedar 2x4s, keeping an even overhang on both sides.

2x6 TRIM

8 Set the trellis posts, then cut the 2x4 rungs to fit between them. Cluster the rungs and lay out the picket positions.

VERTICAL-SUPPORT

GUIDE BOARD

2x6 TRIM

9 Stack the rungs over the vertical supports, screwing each one to the tops below it as you work. You'll cover the joints with 2x6s later.

10 Tack a level guide board across the posts. Push the pickets against the guide and nail them to each rung with 10d finish nails. Add the last 2x6 trim boards.

Install the trellis grid work

Assemble the trellis exactly the same as the arbor, except leave off the 2x4 post trim on the inside of the posts as well as the outside 2x6 (Photo 9). Cut the horizontal rungs to fit between the posts and work out your picket spacing on one of them. This takes a bit of figuring; allow for the thickness of the inside 2x4 trim and try for even spacing. Or simply position a picket in the center and work out in both directions. Once you have the right pattern, transfer the layout to all of the horizontal rungs (Photo 8).

Photo 9 and Figure A show you the correct assembly order and the spacing we used for the rungs and pickets. Start with the bottom 2x4 blocks, screw a rung to the tops, then another block, another rung and so on. Cut 45-degree angles on the picket ends for a more decorative look if you choose. Tack up a temporary guide board parallel to the lintel to help align the pickets as you nail them up. That'll keep them straight.

Build a compost bin 255
Cedar potting bench 258
Deluxe drum composter 264

17 GARDEN TOOLS & EQUIPMENT

WHAT IT TAKES

TIME: 1 day
SKILL LEVEL: Intermediate

This "log cabin" bin will keep your compost pile from becoming an eyesore

Why not turn your yard waste into yard gold by building this compost bin? Build it now, then start your compost pile with leaves, garden plants and some grass clippings. (Leave most of the clippings on the lawn to return nitrogen to the grass as they decompose.)

You probably already own all the tools you'll need. Round up a circular saw, a coping saw, a tape measure, a drill/driver, 1/16-in.-dia. and 3/8-in.-dia. drill bits, a carpenter's square, two pipe clamps and a wood chisel.

The bin is constructed from "five-quarter" (5/4) rounded-edge decking

boards. (Although the name implies that these are 1-1/4 in. boards, they're actually only about 1 in. thick.) The boards are pressure-treated, which makes the bin resistant to rot and insects. There's very little hardware because the pieces fit together like classic Lincoln Logs.

Cutting the pieces

All of the 5/4 decking needs to be cut to 42-in. lengths—you'll get four 42-in. boards from each 14-ft. board. (Hauling 14-ft. boards can be a hassle, so have the lumberyard cut each one into two 7-footers.) The 42-in. boards, when assembled, give you a compost bin that's

approximately a 3-ft. cube.

Two of the 42-in. boards will need to be ripped in half (cut down their length). Two of the ripped pieces (parts D) need to be cut to 2-3/8 in. wide and then notched (see Figure A). One of the pieces should be cut to 1-1/2 in. wide (part C). The remaining piece is scrap, which you'll use later.

Cutting treated lumber requires special precautions. Here's what to do:

- Wear a dust mask to avoid inhaling the sawdust.
- Do the cutting outdoors.
- Clean up scraps and throw them in the trash. DO NOT burn treated lumber. It gives off toxic fumes!
- Wash exposed skin after cutting the lumber.

Notching the boards

Interlocking, 1-3/16 in. deep notches hold the bin together. Notches cut to this depth leave about a 3/4-in. space between each pair of boards when interlocked. The exact width of the notches depends on the thickness of the lumber, but remember, 5/4 lumber is actually only about 1 in. thick.

Here's how to cut the notches:

- Clamp the like components together with pipe clamps. Then stand them on edge on a solid work surface (Photo 1). Not all the pieces require the same number of notches; check Figure A for the number required for each component.
- Measure in from the edge of the boards 1-3/4 in. and draw a line at this distance on all of the boards. Now, measure from this line 1 in. (or the thickness of your lumber) toward the center of the boards and draw a second line.

Figure A
Compost bin

PARTS LIST

LID ASSEMBLY

LID

A (QTY. 7)

42"

1-1/2" B (QTY. 1)

35"

C (QTY. 2)

36"

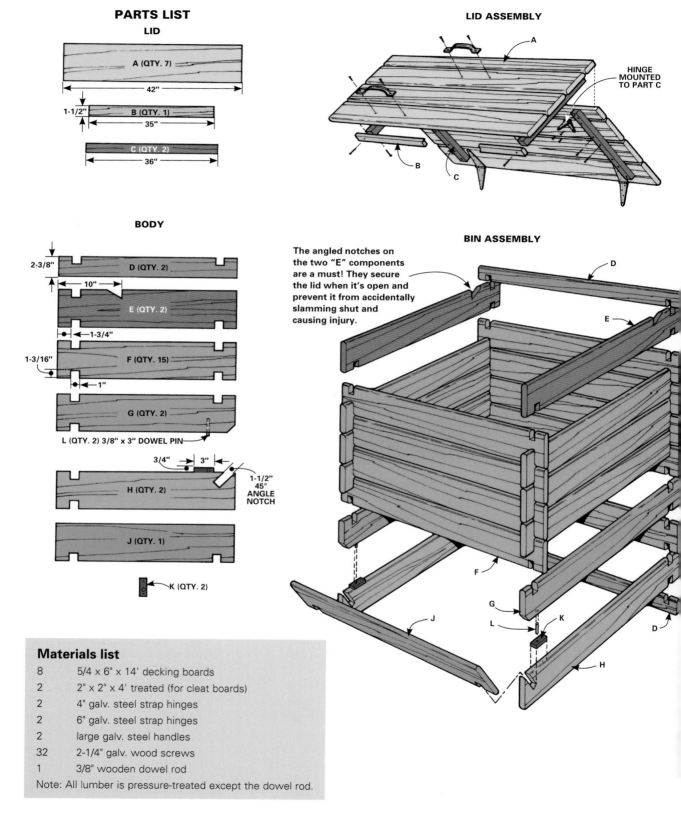

A

HINGE MOUNTED TO PART C

B

C

BODY

BIN ASSEMBLY

2-3/8" D (QTY. 2)

10"

E (QTY. 2)

1-3/4"

1-3/16" F (QTY. 15)

1"

G (QTY. 2)

L (QTY. 2) 3/8" x 3" DOWEL PIN

3/4" 3"

H (QTY. 2)

1-1/2" 45° ANGLE NOTCH

J (QTY. 1)

K (QTY. 2)

The angled notches on the two "E" components are a must! They secure the lid when it's open and prevent it from accidentally slamming shut and causing injury.

D

E

F

G

J

L

K

D

H

Materials list

8	5/4 x 6" x 14' decking boards
2	2" x 2" x 4' treated (for cleat boards)
2	4" galv. steel strap hinges
2	6" galv. steel strap hinges
2	large galv. steel handles
32	2-1/4" galv. wood screws
1	3/8" wooden dowel rod

Note: All lumber is pressure-treated except the dowel rod.

1 Clamp the like components together with pipe clamps on both ends. Use a circular saw to cut 1/4-in.-wide slices to make the 1-in.-wide, 1-3/16-in.-deep notches.

2 Remove the slices with a wood chisel. Use a coping saw to square the corners of the notches to make a tight-fitting joint.

- Set your circular saw to cut at a depth of 1-3/16 in. and cut along the entire length of both lines. Now make a series of 1/4-in.-wide cuts or slices (Photo 1).
- Remove the slices with a wood chisel (Photo 2). Square the bottom corners of each notch with a chisel for tight-fitting corners.

After you finish the interlocking notches, cut the 45-degree diagonal notches in the two bottom side boards (parts H). The cuts can be started with the circular saw, but finish them with a coping saw.

Next, cut two 3/4-in.-thick, 3-in.-long spacer blocks (parts K) from the scrap lumber. Drill a 1/16-in.-dia. hole through

each end of each spacer and a 3/8-in.-dia. hole in the center of the spacer. Then nail the spacers to the bottom side boards (parts H).

Measure from the front edge of parts H to the center of the 3/8-in. hole in the spacer. Mark this measurement on the bottom front of the part G boards and drill a 1-1/4 in.-deep, 3/8-in.-dia. hole for the dowel (L).

Cut two, 3-in. lengths of 3/8-in.-dia. dowel and tap them into the holes through the spacers.

Now you're ready to assemble the other components Lincoln Log style. First, move all of the components to the bin site before you start. The bin's not easy to move once it's fully assembled.

Constructing the top

Building the lid is quick and easy. Here's how:
- Lay out the seven remaining 42-in. boards, making sure they're tight together, edge to edge.
- Measure in 3-1/2 in. from both ends and mark. This is where you'll attach the 2 x 2-in. cleats (C). Use 2-1/4-in. galvanized wood screws.

Don't put screws into the cleat board that's directly over the center of the top's middle board. Now rip the center board in half to form the two lid sections. Cut completely through the cleat board when you rip the center board.
- Connect the two lid sections with 4-in. strap hinges using the screws that come with the hinges.
- Mount one leaf of the 6-in. strap hinges (they secure the lid to the bin) just inside the cleat boards. Mount the other leaf on the outside of the back of the bin.
- Finally, attach the handles as shown in the illustration on p. 112.

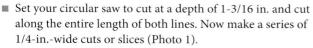

What to compost
- Green plant material (the nitrogen supply) with brown materials such as fall leaves (the carbon supply).
- Any plant materials (except weeds with seeds and poisonous plants such as poison ivy), straw, coffee grounds, eggshells (not the whole egg), and raw fruit and vegetable scraps. Do NOT compost meat, dairy products or pet feces.

Starting the pile

The pile needs to be built in layers. The bottom layer should be 8 to 10 in. of an even mix of grass and leaves or other plant trimmings.

Water this layer so that it's moist, but not soggy. You can add a 1-in. layer of soil over the nitrogen-rich plant matter to increase the number of decomposing microorganisms.

Repeat these layers until the pile fills the bin.

Cedar potting bench

Build this handy potting bench in a weekend

SOLID NOTCHED JOINTS

BUILT-IN POTTING SOIL CONTAINER

GRATE-COVERED DIRT CATCHER

REMOVABLE CONTAINER COVER

WHAT IT TAKES

TIME: 1 weekend
SKILL LEVEL: Intermediate

Whether you're a spare-time gardener or a hard-core enthusiast, this bench is for you. It has plenty of storage to keep all your plant supplies in one convenient location, and it features a built-in potting soil container and a grate-covered dirt catcher to make messy potting and cleanup a snap.

Here you'll learn how to build this cedar potting bench in a weekend.

This bench was designed to be strong without complex joints. An experienced woodworker can complete this potting bench in a day. If you're a beginner, allow two or three days.

You'll need basic carpentry tools like a tape measure, large and small squares, and a chisel. You could make most of the cuts for this potting bench with a circular saw. However, a power miter saw will ensure perfectly square end cuts, and a table saw is almost essential for cutting the grate slats. If you don't have a table saw, ask a friend, neighbor or the staff at the lumberyard to cut the pieces for you. You'll also need a drill with the bits mentioned here, and a jigsaw.

Choose straight, nice-looking lumber

Use the Materials List below to buy your materials. Shown is cedar, but pine is cheaper. Consider using pressure-treated pine if you'll be leaving the bench outside. All of these are available at home centers and lumberyards.

Make tight-fitting joints for a strong bench

Photos 1 and 2 show how to notch the legs for the horizontal cross members. Notching looks tricky, but it's simple if you follow these key steps: First clamp each pair of legs together, and using dimensions from Figure A, mark the

lower edge of each notch. Use a square to draw lines across the boards at these marks. Then align the corresponding horizontal board with this line and mark along the opposite edge to get an exact width. Using the boards in this manner to mark the width of the notch is more accurate than measuring. When you saw the notch, cut to the waste side of the pencil line, leaving the line on the board. You can always enlarge the notch or plane the board to fit a notch that's too tight, but you can't shrink a notch that's too wide. Tight-fitting joints strengthen the bench and look better too.

Assembly is quick once the parts are cut

Photos 3 and 4 show how to assemble the leg sections and connect them to form the bench frame. Before you screw the horizontal pieces to the legs, pick the best-looking side of the boards and make

Materials list

ITEM	QTY.
2x6 x 8' cedar (rip to 2-1/2" for legs)	1
2x4 x 6' cedar (rip to 2-1/2" for lower cross members)	1
2x4 x 4' cedar	1
1x2 x 4' cedar	3
1x3 x 8' cedar	1
1x4 x 8' cedar	2
1x8 x 4' cedar	3
5/4 x 6 x 4' bullnose cedar	9
2' x 2' 3/4" plywood	1

Hardware

1-1/4" stainless steel screws	80
2" stainless steel screws	50
3" stainless steel screws	10
1-1/4" finish nails	1 lb.
3/8" wood screw plugs*	30
3/8" wood buttons*	10
10-oz. tube of construction adhesive	1
Water-resistant wood glue	1
6" x 8" decorative shelf brackets	4
10" x 14" x 18"-deep wastebasket	1
14" x 20" x 4"-deep litter pan	1
100-grit sandpaper sheets	2

* Wood plugs and buttons are available from home centers and woodworking stores.

1 Mark the notch locations on the legs (A and B) using the dimensions in Figure A. Make a series of 3/4-in.-deep saw kerfs about 1/4 in. apart to create the notches.

SQUARE
BACK LEGS (A)
3/4"-DEEP KERFS

Choosing lumber

Make sure to pick straight boards with at least one nice-looking side. You can hide a few minor defects on the back or underside of the bench. Also, avoid boards with large knots, which will weaken key parts and make it harder to cut the notches.

When you get your materials home, cut the pieces to size using the Cutting list p. 116. Many of the parts, like the 1 x 1-in. slats for the grate and the 2-1/2-in.-wide legs, have to be cut the length of the board. This operation, called ripping, is possible with a circular saw, but it's much quicker, easier and more accurate with a table saw.

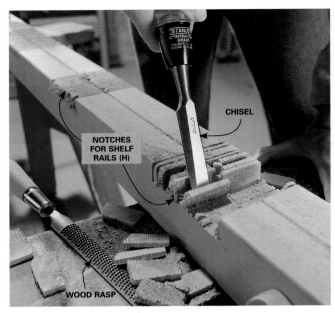

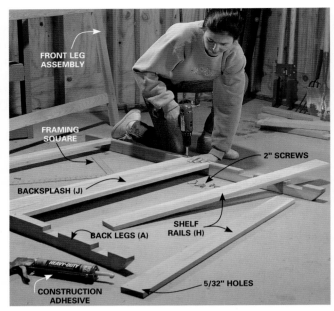

2 Chisel out the waste wood from the notches and smooth the bottom with a wood rasp.

3 Spread a small bead of construction adhesive in each notch and lay the horizontal pieces in place. Use a framing square to make sure the cross members are at right angles to the legs, then drive a pair of 2-in. screws at each joint.

sure it's facing the front of the bench. (The best sides are facing down in Photo 3.) Drill 5/32-in. clearance holes through the cross members to avoid splitting them and to allow the screws to draw the boards tight to the legs.

Use only one 1-1/4-in. screw to attach parts F and G to the front legs. Center the screw so it doesn't interfere with the 3-in. screws you'll be installing to secure the leg assembly (Photo 4). Use a 3/4-in. spacer block (Photo 4) to align the cross members (E) before you drive in the 3-in. screws.

If you'll be leaving your bench outdoors, use stainless steel screws or corrosion-resistant deck screws. For extra strength and durability, put a small dab of construction adhesive on each joint before you screw the pieces together. To hide the 3-in. screws that secure the front legs, use a 3/8-in. brad point drill bit to drill 1/4-in.-deep recesses before you drill the 5/32-in. clearance holes. Then glue 3/8-in. wood buttons into the recesses after you screw the parts together.

Keep a framing square handy as you assemble the leg sections and bench frame and use it to make sure the assemblies are square before you tighten the screws.

Photo 5 shows how to mark and cut the plywood that supports the potting soil container. Shown is a plastic wastebasket, but any container with a lip will work. Trace the shape on a piece of plywood and then cut the hole a little smaller so the plywood supports the lip.

The bench top is made of 1-in.-thick bullnose cedar decking. Join two pieces with cleats to make a removable cover for the dirt catcher (Photo 7). Glue 1 x 1-in. slats together with water-resistant wood glue to form the grate (Photo 6). Scrape off excess glue before it dries. Then allow the glue to dry overnight before you sand the grate and trim the ends flush.

Cutting list

KEY	QTY.	SIZE & DESCRIPTION
A	2	1-1/2" x 2-1/2" x 62" (back legs)
B	2	1-1/2" x 2-1/2" x 33" (front legs)
C	2	1-1/2" x 2-1/2" x 21" (lower cross members)
D	1	1-1/2" x 2-1/2" x 21" (middle cross member)
E	2	1-1/2" x 3-1/2" x 21" (upper cross members)
F	2	3/4" x 2-1/2" x 47" (lower rails)
G	1	3/4" x 3-1/2" x 47" (upper rail)
H	2	3/4" x 3-1/2" x 47" (shelf rails)
J	1	3/4" x 7-1/4" x 47" (backsplash)
K	2	3/4" x 7-1/4" x 47" (shelves)
L	1	3/4" x 3-1/2" x 42-1/2" (bench-top support)
M	2	3/4" x 1-1/2" x 10-1/2" (cover cleats)
N	2	3/4" x 1-1/2" x 12-1/2" (grate cleats)
P	2	1" x 5-1/2" x 23" (bench-top ends; cut to fit)
Q	5	1" x 5-1/2" x 23" (bench top)
R	7	1" x 1" x 23-1/2" (slats)
S	12	1" x 1" x 4" (spacers)
T	2	3/4" x 1-1/2" x 25-1/2" (container cleats)
U	2	3/4" x 1-1/2" x 16-3/4" (bench-top cleats)
V	4	1" x 5-1/2" x 47" (lower shelf)
W	1	12-3/4" x 20-1/4" x 3/4" plywood (container support)

Screw cleats to the bottom of the grate to keep it positioned and allow easy removal.

The width of the end pieces (P) varies, depending on the dimensions of your decking. To determine the width, first

Figure A
Potting bench

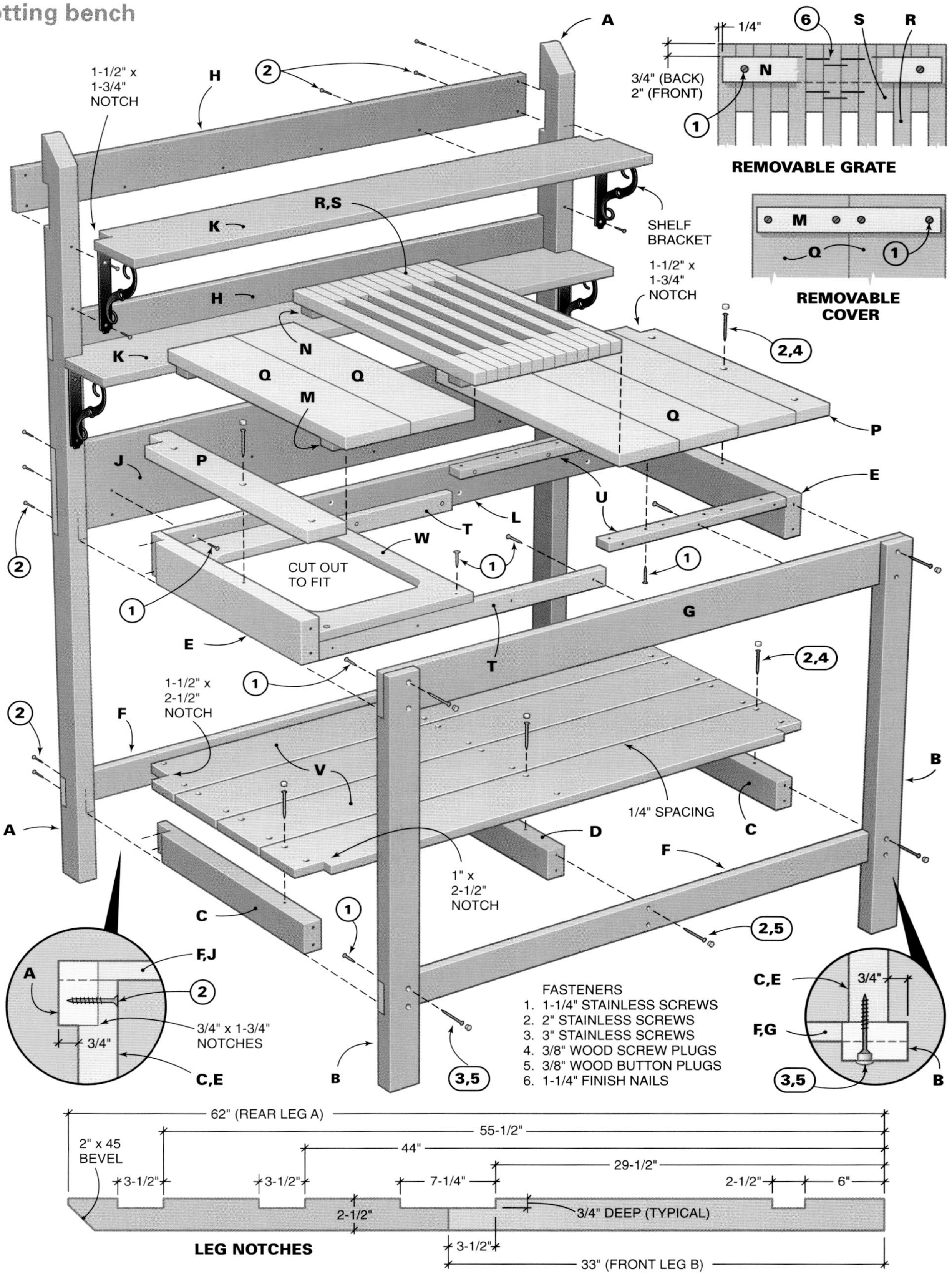

1-1/2" x 1-3/4" NOTCH

H

2

A

1/4"

6

S

R

3/4" (BACK)
2" (FRONT)

N

1

REMOVABLE GRATE

K

R,S

SHELF BRACKET

1-1/2" x 1-3/4" NOTCH

M

REMOVABLE COVER

Q

H

2,4

K

N

Q

Q

M

P

J

P

E

T

L

U

G

1

W

CUT OUT TO FIT

T

1

1

2,4

E

T

Q

P

1-1/2" x 2-1/2" NOTCH

1

V

B

F

1/4" SPACING

C

A

D

C

F

1" x 2-1/2" NOTCH

C

1

2,5

F,J

A

2

3/4" x 1-3/4" NOTCHES

C,E

B

C,E

3/4"

F,G

3,5

B

3,5

FASTENERS
1. 1-1/4" STAINLESS SCREWS
2. 2" STAINLESS SCREWS
3. 3" STAINLESS SCREWS
4. 3/8" WOOD SCREW PLUGS
5. 3/8" WOOD BUTTON PLUGS
6. 1-1/4" FINISH NAILS

62" (REAR LEG A)
55-1/2"
44"
29-1/2"

2" x 45 BEVEL

3-1/2"
3-1/2"
7-1/4"
2-1/2"
6"

2-1/2"
3/4" DEEP (TYPICAL)

3-1/2"

LEG NOTCHES

33" (FRONT LEG B)

LOWER RAIL (F)

FRONT LEGS (B)

3" SCREWS

3/4" SPACER BLOCK

LOWER CROSS MEMBERS (C)

UPPER CROSS MEMBERS (E)

LOWER RAIL (F)

2" SCREWS

4 Screw the horizontal cross members (C and E) to the back leg assembly. Drill and countersink the front leg assembly and attach it to members C and E with 3-in. screws. Cover the screws with decorative wood buttons.

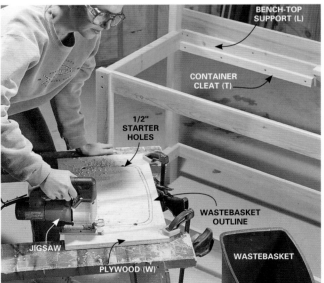

BENCH-TOP SUPPORT (L)

CONTAINER CLEAT (T)

1/2" STARTER HOLES

WASTEBASKET OUTLINE

JIGSAW

WASTEBASKET

PLYWOOD (W)

5 Trace the wastebasket onto the 3/4-in. plywood (W). Draw a second line about 1/2 in. inside the traced outline. Drill a 1/2-in. starter hole and cut along the inside line with a jigsaw. Screw the bench-top support (L) and container cleats (T) to the bench and screw the plywood (W) into place.

center the grate, removable cover and three more boards on the bench top, leaving an equal space on each end. Then measure the distance from the last board to the outside edge of the back leg and cut and notch the end pieces to fit.

Glue 3/8-in. wood plugs into 3/8-in. by 1/4-in.-deep recesses to hide the screws that hold the two end pieces (P) and lower shelf boards in place. Sand them flush after the glue dries.

Complete the potting bench by notching the 1x8 shelves (Photo 9) and securing them with 2-in. screws through the horizontal 1x4 shelf rails (H).

Protect your bench with a good finish

Unfinished cedar has some resistance to decay, but the best strategy is to apply a top-quality exterior finish to keep the wood from cracking, splitting and rotting. Penetrating oil–type finishes with a small amount of pigment provide a natural look and reduce fading. Finishes that leave a film provide the best protection. Spar varnish or Sikkens are two examples. Take extra precautions to seal the bottom of the legs to keep them from absorbing moisture from the damp ground.

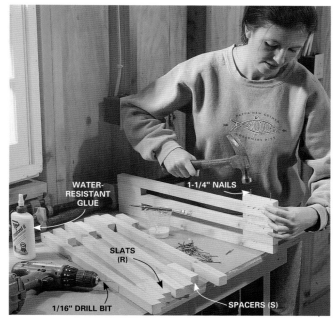

6 Glue and nail the slats and spacers together to make the grate. Drill 1/16-in. pilot holes for the nails to prevent splitting the wood. Spread water-resistant glue on both surfaces and nail the slats and spacers together with 4d galvanized finish nails. Clamp the completed assembly with bar clamps and allow it to dry overnight. Trim the 23-1/2-in. grate to 23 in. with your circular saw or table saw and sand the edge smooth.

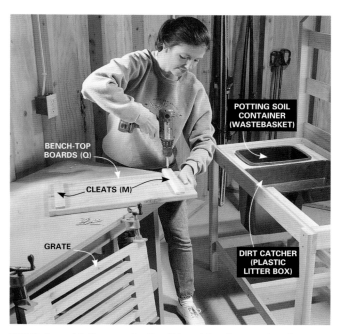

7 Assemble the cover for the dirt container by screwing cleats (M) to the bottom of the 5/4 x 6-in. decking (Q). Screw cleats (N) to the bottom of the completed grate.

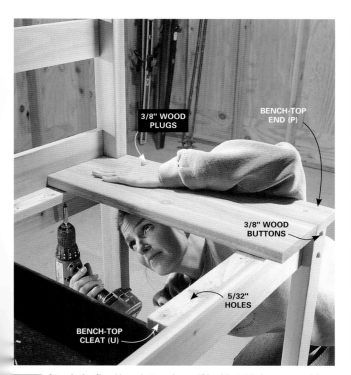

8 Attach the fixed bench-top pieces (Q) with 1-1/4-in. screws driven up through the bench-top cleats (U). Secure the bench-top ends (P) and bottom shelf boards (V) by driving 1-1/4-in. screws through predrilled and countersunk holes. Conceal these screws with wood plugs glued into the recesses. Sand the plugs flush when the glue dries.

9 Notch the shelves (K) and slide them into place. Screw through the shelf rails (H) into the shelves. Support the front of the shelves with metal brackets.

Deluxe drum composter

It's large and loaded with features—but you can build it for the cost of a bargain model

Drum composters convert yard waste to finished compost much faster than stationary compost bins do because they allow you to churn and instantly aerate the waste. Plus, drum composters are easier on your back. You can buy them online or at any garden center in a wide range of sizes and prices. But they all follow the same basic design—a drum on a stand. Our version is an adaptation of that, using a plastic 55-gallon drum. The drum and stand together cost about the same as the low-price models, but our composter is built stronger and has more features. It takes a full day to customize the drum and build the stand. We used rivets to speed up the assembly, but screws, nuts and lock washers work too.

Finding and customizing the drum

Ask for free used 55-gallon polyethylene drums at car washes and food processing and industrial manufacturers. Since beggars can't be choosers, you'll probably wind up with a white, green or blue drum. If that doesn't fit your backyard color scheme (paint doesn't stick well to polyethylene), contact a container firm and order the color you want. We ordered a black "tight-head" drum (top permanently sealed to the drum) from a local supplier.

Next, use a jigsaw to cut a door panel slightly smaller than the width of your wheelbarrow. The next step takes the most time and isn't mandatory, but it adds strength and stability to the entire door assembly: Bend 1/8-in. x 1-in. flat aluminum stock around the drum to form side reinforcements for the door opening. Cut the bent aluminum slightly longer than the door opening and mount it to the drum (Photo 1, p. 123).

Then cut flat aluminum pieces for the top and bottom of the door opening and the hinge side of the door. Mount the top and bottom door opening reinforcements in the same manner. Mount the hinges at the bottom of the door opening so the door hangs down when you empty the drum. Finish the door by adding the latches (Figure A).

To make stirring paddles, cut an 8-ft. piece of 4-in. PVC pipe in half lengthwise using a jigsaw. Cut the halves to length so they're slightly shorter than the inside height of the drum. Arrange two halves back-to-back. Then drill and screw the pieces together to form one paddle unit. The back-to-back design is stronger than a single "scoop" and allows you to rotate the drum in either direction. Repeat for the second paddle unit.

Since the drum has a taper at the top and bottom, you'll have to sand the ends of the paddles to match (Photo 2). Mount the paddle units 180 degrees apart and secure them to the drum with screws, nuts and washers. Finally, mount grab handles around the drum to help you rotate it.

A tight-head drum comes with two threaded "bungholes." Remove the threaded caps to provide ventilation. You may need to drill additional ventilation holes if the mixture stays too wet.

Build the stand and mount the rollers

Cut the legs and deck boards to length according to the Cutting List. Then assemble the stand using a drill and exterior screws (Photo 3). Add diagonal struts to prevent front-to-back and side-to-side movement when spinning the drum.

Flip the stand upright and mount two casters so they ride in the recess around the drumhead. Then level the drum and mount the remaining two casters (Photo 4).

Load, spin and dump

Load the drum with yard waste and add a compost starter to get the batch cooking (sold at any home or garden center). Rotate at least once every day to mix and aerate the batch. When the compost is ready, just dump it out.

How it works

Waste becomes compost thanks to millions of hungry microbes, which break it down and convert it to nutrient-rich fertilizer. Those microbes need oxygen to thrive, and turning the drum daily creates fresh air pockets in the mix. You can accomplish the same thing by churning a pile of compost with a shovel, but a drum composter makes it easier. And the more thorough mixing speeds decomposition.

Rotate daily. Screw the bung caps into the holes to prevent compost from leaking out. Then grab the handles and rotate the drum several times in either direction to stir the mixture.

Drop, roll and dump. Park your wheelbarrow under the drum and open the door. As you roll the drum downward, the compost will dump right into the wheelbarrow.

Overall dimensions: 39" W x 30" D x 58" H

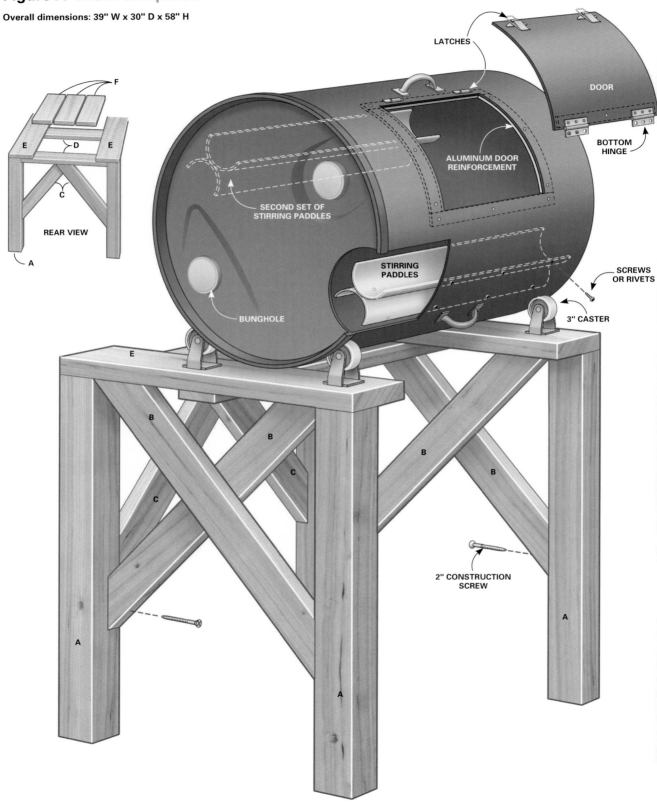

F

E — D — E

C

REAR VIEW

A

LATCHES

DOOR

ALUMINUM DOOR REINFORCEMENT

BOTTOM HINGE

SECOND SET OF STIRRING PADDLES

STIRRING PADDLES

SCREWS OR RIVETS

3" CASTER

BUNGHOLE

E

B

B

B

B

C

C

2" CONSTRUCTION SCREW

A

A

A

1 Reinforce the door opening. Clamp aluminum strips in place so 1/2 in. extends into the door opening. Fasten the strips with rivets or nuts and screws.

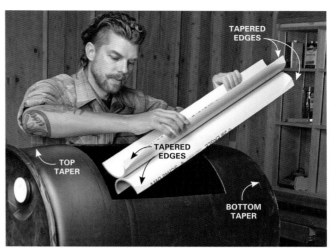

2 Install the paddle. Taper the ends of the paddle to match the tapered ends of the drum. Sand the paddle with a belt sander until it fits. Then install the paddle with screws.

3 Assemble the stand. Screw the legs to the rails. Then install the cross braces. Strengthen with diagonal struts.

4 Mount the casters. Then set a level on top of the drum and pry the drum up with a board. When the drum is level, position the last caster, mark its location and screw it into place.

Cutting list

KEY.	QTY.	SIZE & DESCRIPTION
A	4	4x4 x 32-1/2" (legs)
B	4	2x4 x 32-3/8" (side braces; cut at 45-degree angle, long point to long point)
C	2	2x4 x 30" (back braces; cut at 45-degree angle, long point to long point)
D	2	2x4 x 32" (cross braces)
E	2	2x8 x 30" (drum deck)
F	3	2x8 x 13-1/2" (deck, evenly spaced; optional)

Materials list

ITEM	QTY.
12' 4x4 treated lumber	1
8' 2x4 treated lumber	3
10' 2x8 treated lumber	1
6' of 4" PVC pipe	

Rivets (aluminum), nuts and bolts (stainless steel), hinges, handles, 1" flat aluminum stock, latches, exterior screws, 3" casters.

Faux stone patio table 269

Fold-up grill table 272

Stone-top table 276

A-frame picnic table....................................... 278

18 OUTDOOR TABLES

Faux stone patio table

WHAT IT TAKES

TIME: 1 day, plus a week for drying time

SKILL LEVEL: Intermediate

A different kind of grout

Construction grout is used mostly for heavy construction projects like anchoring steel columns. But it's also perfect for casting projects because it has a creamy consistency that takes on the shape and texture of the form almost perfectly. Use a smooth form and you're guaranteed a smooth, uniform tabletop. Most home centers carry construction grout in 50-lb. bags. (Quikrete Precision Grout and Sakrete Construction Grout are two brands.) Go to quikrete.com or sakrete.com to find a dealer if your store doesn't carry it. Darken the grout by adding cement colorant to the water (Photo 2).

The top is made from construction grout tinted with colorant. Tile grout creates the dark veins.

Build the form

Plastic-coated particleboard (called melamine) is perfect for form work because it's inexpensive and smooth. Cut the form base to 31-1/2 x 31-1/2 in. and then cut 2 x 32-in. strips for the form

Forming a crinkled edge

Smooth edges on the tabletop are fine, but a crinkled edge will give it a more natural look. To start, cut four strips of aluminum foil tape about an inch longer than the form sides. Then...

Scrunch it up.   Straighten it out.   Stick it on the form sides.

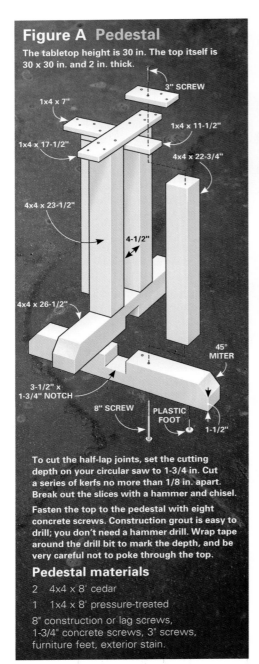

Figure A Pedestal

The tabletop height is 30 in. The top itself is 30 x 30 in. and 2 in. thick.

- 3" SCREW
- 1x4 x 7"
- 1x4 x 11-1/2"
- 1x4 x 17-1/2"
- 4x4 x 22-3/4"
- 4x4 x 23-1/2"
- 4-1/2"
- 4x4 x 26-1/2"
- 45° MITER
- 3-1/2" x 1-3/4" NOTCH
- 8" SCREW
- PLASTIC FOOT
- 1-1/2"

To cut the half-lap joints, set the cutting depth on your circular saw to 1-3/4 in. Cut a series of kerfs no more than 1/8 in. apart. Break out the slices with a hammer and chisel.

Fasten the top to the pedestal with eight concrete screws. Construction grout is easy to drill; you don't need a hammer drill. Wrap tape around the drill bit to mark the depth, and be very careful not to poke through the top.

Pedestal materials

2 4x4 x 8' cedar
1 1x4 x 8' pressure-treated
8" construction or lag screws, 1-3/4" concrete screws, 3" screws, furniture feet, exterior stain.

Tabletop materials

150 lbs. of construction grout
3/4-in. melamine (sold in 4 x 8-ft. sheets)
Quikrete Cement Color (10 oz.)
Spray lubricant
Plastic cement tub
2-1/2-in.-wide foil tape
2-in. nails or screws
Unsanded tile grout (black or charcoal)
Tile or stone sealer
Welded wire mesh

1 **Build an upside-down form.** Assemble the form, spray on lubricant and wipe off the excess. Cast upside down, the tabletop's surface face will turn out as smooth and flat as the melamine form.

2 **Mix one bag at a time.** Add grout to water mixed with colorant. Turn a bucket into a giant measuring cup so you can easily use the correct amount of colored water with each bag.

HOMEMADE MEASURING BUCKET
BATCH 1
BATCH 2
BATCH 3

3 **Pour a pattern.** Sketch a pattern on the form and fill the outlined areas with mounds of construction grout. This pattern will show up on the top of the table.

sides. Attach the sides to the base as shown in Photo 1. The overhanging sides make dismantling the form easier; you can just whack them loose with a hammer. Coat the form with spray lubricant (Photo 1). Important: Use a lubricant that dries instead of leaving an oily coating. The label will say something like "leaves a dry film."

Next, grab a pencil and sketch a random pattern on the form outlining the areas you'll cover with grout first (Photo 3). The pencil lines will determine where the dark veins appear in the finished top. Set the form on a sturdy work surface

and level the form with shims. Construction grout is slushy and will overflow if the form tilts. Spilled grout will leave stains, so cover the floor with plastic drop cloths.

Get ready to mix

Mixing and pouring the construction grout is a three-phase process: You'll use most or all of the first bag to pour a pattern (Photo 3), the second to fill in the pattern (Photo 6) and the third to completely fill the form.

Turning a bucket into a giant measuring cup (Photo 2) will let you add equal amounts of water and

4 **Create the veins.** Sprinkle dry tile grout along the edges of the mounds. The colored powder will form dark lines in the finished top.

5 **Blow the grout.** Turn down the pressure on your compressor and blow the tile grout against the edges of the mounds.

6 **Fill in the blank spots.** Cover the bare areas of the form. Pour between the areas you covered first, not on top of them. Jiggle the form to spread and level the mix.

7 **Add the mesh.** With the form about half full, lay in the welded wire mesh for reinforcement. Then completely fill the form.

8 **Screed it off.** Scrape off the excess using a straight board and a sawing motion. Cover the wet grout with plastic. The longer it stays wet, the stronger it will cure.

9 **Seal the tabletop.** Bring out the color with sealer. Before you apply the sealer, ease the tabletop's sharp edges with 80-grit sandpaper.

cement colorant to each of the three bags without measuring each time. First, measure the correct amount of water into the bucket (about 4.5 liters per bag) and mark the water level on the bucket. Measure in more water to locate the other two marks (at 9 and 13.5 liters).

Next, empty the bucket and dump in the cement colorant. Much of it will remain in the bottle. To wash it out, pour in a little water, shake hard and pour again. Repeat until all the colorant is washed out. Refill the bucket with water and you'll have tinted water, premeasured into three equal amounts. The colorant tends to settle to the bottom, so stir the colored water before each use.

Construction grout hardens fast. In warm weather, it will become stiff and difficult to work with in just 15 minutes. Minutes wasted cutting the wire mesh or searching for a tool can ruin the project. So have absolutely everything ready to

go before you start mixing. It's best to have a helper, too. To slow down the hardening, use cold water only.

Mix the construction grout in a plastic cement tub. Don't pour the water directly from the bucket into the mixing tub; it's too hard to control the flow. Instead, ladle the water into the tub with a smaller container. Dump in about half the bag and mix it thoroughly. Gradually add the rest of the bag as you mix. If the mixed grout stiffens before you can use it, stir it to restore the slushy consistency. If it becomes too stiff to stir, toss it. The tabletop only requires about 2-1/2 bags, so you can afford to waste some.

Pour, wait patiently and seal

Photos 3 – 9 show how to complete the top. Don't forget to turn down your compressor's pressure to about 5 psi before you blow the tile grout (Photo 5). Cut the 2 x 2-ft. section of mesh (Photo

7) using bolt cutters. Wire cutters won't do the job.

Resist the temptation to tear off the form as soon as the grout is hard. The longer the grout stays wet, the stronger it will get. Give it at least three days. A week is even better. To remove the form, get a helper and flip the form upside down. (Don't let the top tip out of the form!) Then knock the form sides loose with a hammer and lift the form off the top. Don't despair when you unveil the bland, gray top. The sealer will deepen the color and accentuate the black veins (Photo 9). Most sealers can't be applied until the grout has cured for at least 28 days. Before you apply sealer to the top, try it on the underside to make sure you like the look. We used a glossy "stone and tile" sealer to bring out the most color. A sealer with a matte finish will have a subtler look.

Fold-up grill table

WHAT IT TAKES

TIME: 4 hours
SKILL LEVEL: Intermediate

A handy companion for your barbecue that collapses for easy storage

After building this collapsible cedar table, your family will wonder how they ever grilled without it. The legs nest under the top for quick storage or carrying to all kinds of other jobs, indoors or out. All you need to build it is a drill, a saw, basic hand tools, a short stack of cedar boards and half an afternoon.

The table is made entirely from 1x4 cedar boards. Wood quality varies, so pick over the lumber for flat, straight boards that are free of large or loose knots. You can make the table from eight 6-ft. boards, but buy 10 to allow for possible miscuts and to give you more choice for the top slats.

Figure A
Fold-up grill table

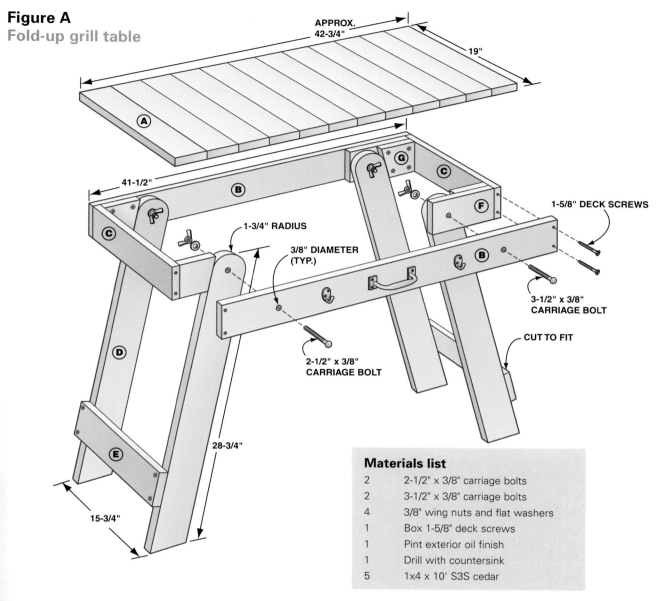

APPROX. 42-3/4"

19"

41-1/2"

28-3/4"

15-3/4"

1-3/4" RADIUS

3/8" DIAMETER (TYP.)

2-1/2" x 3/8" CARRIAGE BOLT

1-5/8" DECK SCREWS

3-1/2" x 3/8" CARRIAGE BOLT

CUT TO FIT

Materials list

2	2-1/2" x 3/8" carriage bolts
2	3-1/2" x 3/8" carriage bolts
4	3/8" wing nuts and flat washers
1	Box 1-5/8" deck screws
1	Pint exterior oil finish
1	Drill with countersink
5	1x4 x 10' S3S cedar

Cutting list

Overall Dimensions: 28-1/2"H x 42-3/4"W x 19"D

KEY	NAME	QTY.	DIMENSIONS IN INCHES
A	Top slat	12	1x4 x 19"
B	Long side pc.	2	1x4 x 41-1/2"
C	Short side pc.	2	1x4 x 15-3/4"
D	Leg	4	1x4 x 28-3/4" (15 degree angled end cut)
E	Leg stretchers	2	1x4 x 15-3/4" (Cut to fit)
F	Leg spacers	2	1x4 x 6-3/4"
G	Leg stop blocks	4	1x4 x 4-3/8" (15 degree angled end cut)

Note: All parts cut from "1x4 S3S" cedar, so each board is a "fat" 3/4" thick and 3-1/2" wide, with two smooth edges, one smooth side and one rough side.

Cut the parts

You can use a handsaw to cut the parts, but a miter saw and jigsaw speed up the job significantly. Use a square to help make straight cuts (Photo 1). To ensure matching legs and frame parts, clamp two boards together and mark and cut them at the same time (Photo 2). Cut slats one or two at a time. You'll cut the stretchers after bolting on the legs.

To assemble the frame, drill two holes in the ends of the longer frame boards and add a countersink hole for the screwheads to nestle into. Cut the slats and place them top-side up on a flat surface (Photo 3). Center the frame on the slats to create a 3/4-in. overhang on all four sides. Then lightly trace the frame shape on the slats with a pencil.

Lift off the frame and drill and countersink screw holes in the slats using the traced lines as a guide. Then screw the slats to the frame (Photo 4). Lightly tap a couple nails between the slats while

1 Cut the boards for the top and the frame that supports it using a jigsaw or handsaw and a square. (See the exploded view diagram on p. 129.)

2 Clamp the leg boards together (rough side in) and cut both of them at once to create identical leg pairs. Drill the 3/8-in. bolt hole in the upper end before unclamping.

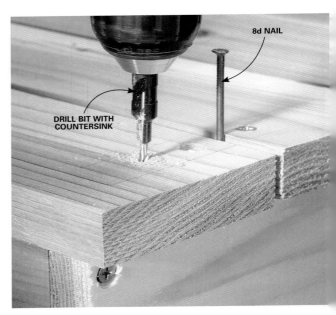

FRAME

3/4" OVERHANG

TOP BOARDS

8d NAIL

DRILL BIT WITH COUNTERSINK

3 Lay the frame on the top boards and lightly trace the frame shape so it's easy to see where to drill holes. Space the top boards with about 1/16-in. gaps between them.

4 Drill two holes on each top board end with a countersink bit and screw them to the frame. A nail is handy for creating even spacing.

screwing them to the frame in order to create the approximate 1/16-in. spacing between the slats. The end slats will overhang the frame approximately 3/4 in. to match the slat overhang along the frame sides.

Attach the legs

Flip the tabletop upside down and screw the pair of angled leg stop blocks to the corners of one end (Photo 5). Butt the rounded leg ends against the blocks, then drill and bolt on the

outer leg pair with the shorter 2-1/2-in. carriage bolts, washers and wing nuts. Attach the inner leg pair to the other frame, first screwing in the spacer blocks to allow the legs to nest inside the other pair (Photo 6). Add the angled leg stop blocks, then drill and bolt on the second leg pair with the longer 3-1/2-in. carriage bolts.

With the legs flat on the underside of the table, measure for the stretchers, cut, drill and fasten them to the legs (Photo 7). To pull out the legs, lift the more widely spaced pair first so the

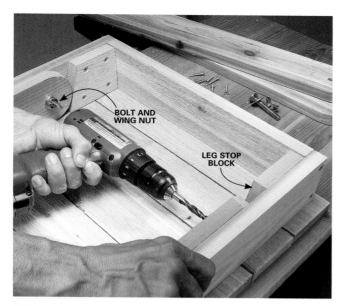

5 Screw a pair of angled leg stop blocks in one end of the frame, then butt the rounded ends of the legs against the blocks. Drill through the frame and bolt on the legs.

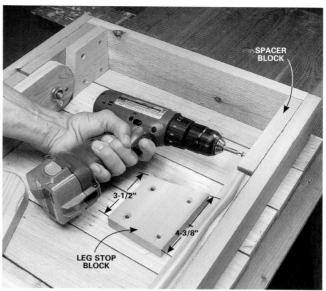

SPACER BLOCK

3-1/2"

4-3/8"

LEG STOP BLOCK

6 Screw spacer blocks in the other frame end. These allow the other pair of legs to nest inside the first pair. Then drill and bolt on the second pair of legs and leg stop blocks.

STRETCHER

7 Screw stretchers across each pair of legs. For best fit and overall results, mark and cut the stretchers based on the actual spacing between the legs.

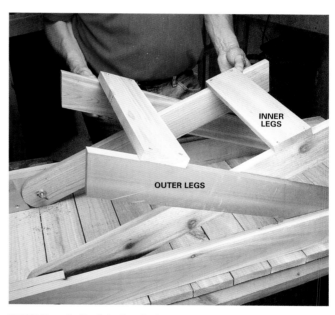

INNER LEGS

OUTER LEGS

8 Test the fit of the legs in the frame by pulling the legs up from the frame. If they bind and scrape, sand the sides for a smoother fit.

second pair can be raised without catching on the first pair's stretcher (Photo 8).

Sand, finish, then grill

Sand the table with 100-grit paper and, with a sanding block or rasp, slightly round the top edges of the slats. Put on your favorite finish; we used two coats of penetrating oil finish. Pull out the legs, tighten the wing nuts and throw some rib eye steaks on the grill—just in time for dinner!

Stone-top table

The inspiration for this small end table came while browsing through a local tile store, looking at the huge variety of slate, granite, limestone and marble that's available. The table top shown here is 16-in.-square copper slate—a perfect match for the oak base—but many other stone tiles are available.

To make this table, you'll need a power miter saw, drill and hand tools. The stone top doesn't need cutting—just soften the sharp edges with 120-grit sandpaper. The base is made from standard dimension oak, available at home centers. And once you put together the simple cutting and assembly jigs shown in the photos on the next page, the table base almost builds itself.

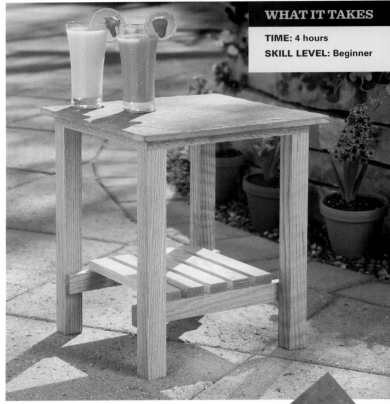

Figure A
Stone-top table

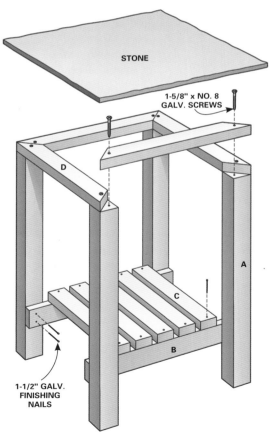

STONE

1-5/8" x NO. 8 GALV. SCREWS

D

A

C

B

1-1/2" GALV. FINISHING NAILS

Materials list

Wood

2 2x2 x 3' oak

14' 1x2 oak

Note: If the table is for outdoor use, use white oak or ash, which are more rot-resistant.

Stone Tile

1 16" x 16" x 1/2"

Hardware

1 lb. 1-1/2" galvanized finishing nails

8 1-5/8" x No. 8 galvanized screws

4 Nylon chair glides

   Exterior wood glue

   Exterior construction adhesive

Cutting list

KEY	NAME	QTY.	DIMENSIONS
A	Leg	4	2x2 x 16-3/4"
B	Shelf supports	2	1x2 x 13-3/4"
C	Shelf slats	5	1x2 x 10-3/4"
D	Mitered top support	4	1x2 x 13-3/4"

BLACK SLATE

CREAM QUARTZ

INDIAN AUTUMN SLATE

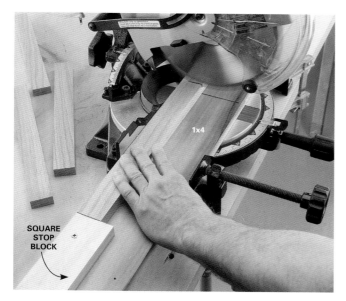

SQUARE STOP BLOCK

1x4

MITERED STOP BLOCK

1 Make a jig with square and mitered stop blocks screwed to a straight 1x4. Slide the 1x4 to the right length for each piece and clamp it down. When you cut the miters, set the saw for 45-1/2 degrees. That way, the outside corners of the top—the only part that shows—will be tight even if the top isn't perfectly square. Sand all the oak pieces before beginning assembly.

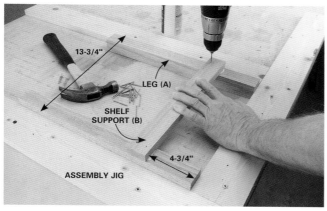

13-3/4"

LEG (A)

SHELF SUPPORT (B)

4-3/4"

ASSEMBLY JIG

2 Set up a square assembly jig with 1x4s attached to your work-bench. Use two shelf supports as spacers to ensure that the jig is the correct width. Set two table legs (A) in the jig and attach a shelf support (B) with glue and nails. Predrill with a 5/64-in. drill bit, or use one of the nails with the head clipped off as the drill bit.

TOP SUPPORT (D)

COMBINATION PILOT/ COUNTERSINK BIT

3 Screw down the mitered top supports (D) with the table still in the jig, using glue and 1-5/8-in. galvanized screws. Predrill and countersink with a combination bit at a slight angle, toward the center of the leg.

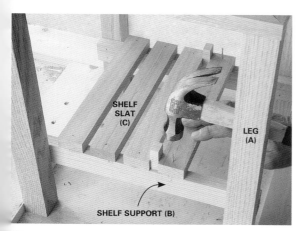

SHELF SLAT (C)

LEG (A)

SHELF SUPPORT (B)

4 Predrill and nail the shelf slats with the legs tight and square against the sides of the assembly jig. Attach the center slat first, centering it on the shelf support. Wipe off excess glue and set the remaining slats, using two 1/2-in. spacers. Set the nails, fill the holes, then sand.

CONSTRUCTION ADHESIVE

5 Glue the stone top to the base. First, center the table and trace the top onto the tile. Lay a bead of construction adhesive within the outline, keeping the glue away from the outer edge to avoid oozing. Press the table into the glue. Place a weight on the table for 24 hours until the glue sets. Leave excess glue until it's dry, and then peel it away. Finish the wood with exterior oil or varnish and add a nylon chair glide on the bottom of each leg.

A-frame picnic table

An outdoor dining table you can build in a weekend

WHAT IT TAKES

TIME: 1 weekend
SKILL LEVEL: Intermediate

H ere's a great-looking, sturdy picnic table that's strong enough to support eight or more bulky NFL linemen, even after a pregame feast. Plus, it's easy to build and inexpensive because it's made from construction-grade Douglas fir lumber.

This isn't a project that'll take weeks to build. You can buy the lumber, build the table, and apply the finish all in one weekend. You can do it all yourself, but an extra pair of hands comes in handy during assembly.

And it does comfortably seat eight people, even 10, if everyone gets along!

What you need to build it

You'll need a circular saw, belt sander, drill, a 1-in. dia. spade bit, a few drill bits, a ratchet with a 9/16-in. socket to tighten the nuts, a hammer, tape measure, screwdriver, four bar clamps and a pair of sawhorses. If you have a Speed square, use it to guide the circular saw as you cut the ends of the top and seat boards.

The A-frame pieces (B, C and D) are joined with carriage bolts. A carriage bolt doesn't look like a regular bolt. It has a round head

with a short, square nub directly under it. You drive it into its hole with a hammer, and the square part locks it into the wood to keep it from turning as you tighten the nut. We used carriage bolts to give the outside ends a more decorative look.

Instead of standard wood screws, use deck screws to prevent rust. The deck screws also have coarse threads for extra grip. To prevent splitting, be sure to drill pilot holes before driving the screws.

Materials list

5	2x10 x 8' construction-grade Douglas fir (or other rot-resistant wood)
2	2x8 x 8' construction-grade Douglas fir
3	2x6 x 8' construction-grade Douglas fir
16	3/8" x 3" galvanized carriage bolts, washers and nylon lock nuts
34	3" deck screws
1 qt.	exterior penetrating clear wood finish and preservative

Figure A
Picnic table details

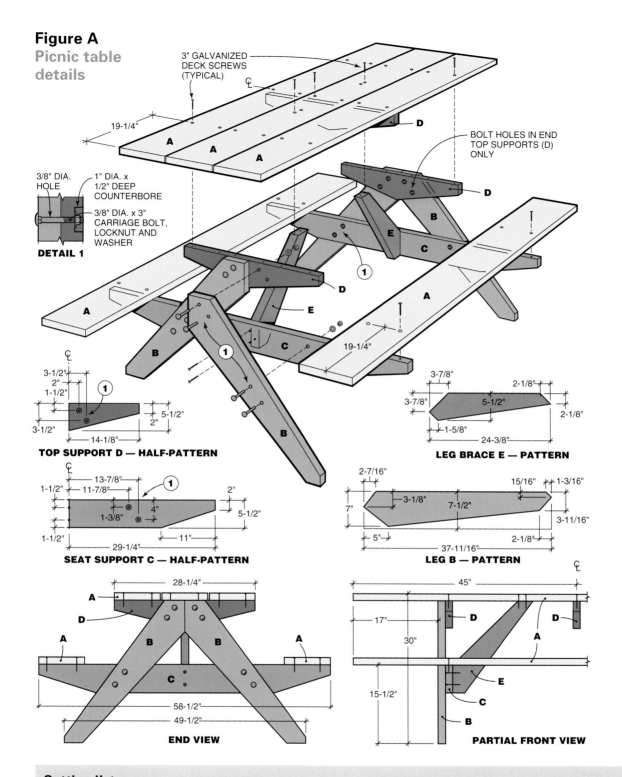

3" GALVANIZED DECK SCREWS (TYPICAL)

19-1/4"

A

A

A

3/8" DIA. HOLE

1" DIA. x 1/2" DEEP COUNTERBORE

3/8" DIA. x 3" CARRIAGE BOLT, LOCKNUT AND WASHER

DETAIL 1

BOLT HOLES IN END TOP SUPPORTS (D) ONLY

D

D

B

E

C

A

1

A

D

E

C

B

1

B

19-1/4"

3-1/2"
2"
1-1/2"
3-1/2"
1
5-1/2"
2"
14-1/8"

TOP SUPPORT D — HALF-PATTERN

3-7/8"
2-1/8"
3-7/8"
5-1/2"
2-1/8"
1-5/8"
24-3/8"

LEG BRACE E — PATTERN

13-7/8"
11-7/8"
1-1/2"
1-3/8"
4"
2"
5-1/2"
1-1/2"
29-1/4"
11"

SEAT SUPPORT C — HALF-PATTERN

2-7/16"
7"
3-1/8"
7-1/2"
15/16"
1-3/16"
3-11/16"
5"
2-1/8"
37-11/16"

LEG B — PATTERN

28-1/4"
A
D
A
B
B
A
C
58-1/2"
49-1/2"

END VIEW

45"
17"
D
D
30"
A
15-1/2"
E
C
B

PARTIAL FRONT VIEW

Cutting list

KEY	QTY.	SIZE & DESCRIPTION
A	5	1-1/2" x 9-1/2" x 90" fir (top and seats)
B	4	1-1/2" x 7-1/2" x 37-11/16" fir (legs)
C	2	1-1/2" x 5-1/2" x 58-1/2" fir (seat supports)

KEY	QTY.	SIZE & DESCRIPTION
D	3	1-1/2" x 5-1/2" x 28-1/4" fir (top supports)*
E	2	1-1/2" x 5-1/2" x 24-3/8" fir (leg braces)

*D length is equal to the total width of the three top pieces (A) plus 1/2 in.

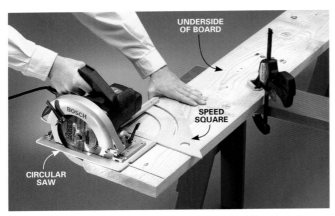

1 Use a circular saw to cut the seat and top boards to length. Try to cut away the checks (cracks) on both ends of the boards. If you have a Speed square, use it to guide the saw as you cut the ends square.

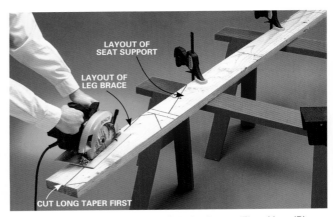

2 Cut the long tapered sides of the leg braces (E) and legs (B) before you cut the pieces to length. This way you can easily clamp the boards to your sawhorses to hold them as you make the cuts.

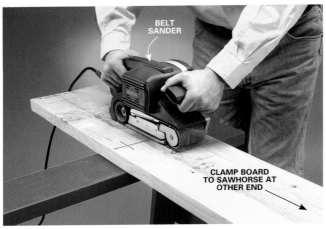

3 Use a belt sander and an 80-grit belt to smooth the boards. To sand board edges, clamp them upright between your sawhorses and sand them with the belt sander or by hand.

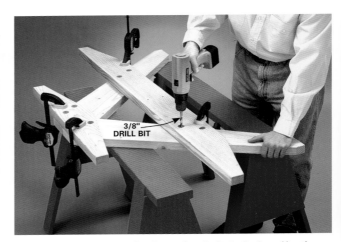

4 Drill the pilot holes for the carriage bolts in the legs. Use the holes drilled in the seat and top supports as drilling guides.

Step-by-step instructions

1. As shown in Photo 1, cut the top and seat pieces (A) to the length given in the Cutting List.
2. Using the dimensions in Figure A, draw the shapes of pieces B through E on your boards. To get the most out of your lumber, place one leg brace (E) and one seat support (C) on one 2x6 board. Put the narrow end of the leg brace at the end of the board. Duplicate this layout on one more 2x6, then draw the three top supports (D) on the remaining 2x6. Also lay out the legs (B) on the 2x8 boards with the narrow ends of the legs at the ends. To make cutting the tapers a bit easier, cut the long sides of the leg braces (E) and legs (B) first, then cut the pieces to length (Photo 2).
3. Drill the holes for the screws and carriage bolts in every part except the legs and leg braces. You'll drill these later during assembly.
4. Use a belt sander with an 80-grit belt to smooth all of the surfaces (Photo 3). Then finish any sharp edges by hand, sanding with 80-grit sandpaper.

5. Now make the A-frame assembly from parts B, C and D. Align the top edge of the seat support (C) 15-1/2 in. up from the bottoms of the legs (B), and center it. Then align the top support (D) parallel to the seat support, and centered as well. Now, drill the carriage bolt holes through the legs using the counterbored holes in the seat support and top support as drilling guides (Photo 4).
6. Keeping each A-frame assembly clamped, flip the end over and hammer in the carriage bolts (Photo 5).
7. Flip the assembly again and put on the washers and nuts. Tighten them with a ratchet and 9/16-in. socket (Photo 6).
8. Align and screw the outside top pieces (A) to the top supports (Photo 7).

Tip

When cutting with a circular saw, cut with the underside of the board facing up. This will help eliminate nasty-looking edges.

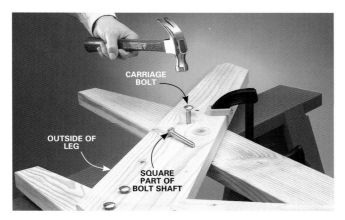

5 Hammer the carriage bolts into their holes. Insert them all the way to "seat" the square part of the bolt shafts securely in the wood.

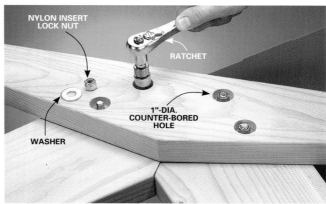

6 Tighten the nuts with a ratchet and socket. Use nylon insert lock nuts to eliminate lock washers.

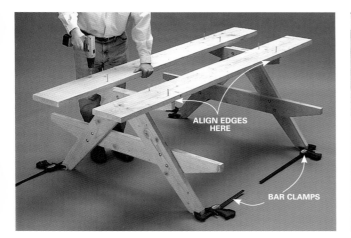

7 Screw the outside top boards to the top supports. Hold the assembled ends upright by placing bar clamps at the bottoms of the legs.

8 Align and mark the spot where the leg braces (E) land on the center top board. If you're working alone, you can do it from underneath.

9. Align and screw the center top board (A) so the gaps between all the boards are equal. Square the top of the table by measuring the diagonal dimensions of the top until they're equal.

10. A helper can make this step easier. Flip the table over and align the leg braces (E) with the top as shown in Figure A. Drill pilot holes, then screw the leg braces to the seat supports and center top board.

11. Align and screw the center top support (D) in place, then attach the seat boards (A).

12. Before applying the finish, unscrew the seat boards and the outside top boards. Removing just these pieces lets you get into tight corners without taking apart the whole table.

13. Apply the finish in a shaded area using the directions given on the can of clear wood preservative finish. Use a 3-in. disposable foam roller to apply the finish on the large surfaces, and a brush for the tight areas.

14. Let the finish dry for two days, then reattach the seat boards and top boards, and you're ready to picnic!

Using construction-grade lumber

Construction-grade lumber is milled for use in home construction. It has lots of knots, cracks and other defects. You can use it to build this table and other outdoor furniture, if you're cautious.

Look for straight, flat boards with no loose knots. Inspect the edges and ends for defects and cracks. Look for bad edges that may turn into nasty splinters later. If you're stuck with bad edges, hide them underneath and on the insides of the seat and top boards.

Finding boards with no end checks is nearly impossible. The table is 90 in. long so you could cut off a total of 6 in. from the checked ends. Don't worry about minor surface roughness; you can sand the wood smooth with a belt sander.

If you plan to buy your wood a few days before you start, store it in a shaded area. When you build the table, pick a shaded area so the sun doesn't dry the wood too fast and cause more cracking.

Mud-busting boot scraper 283

Quick workbench for outdoor projects 284

Compost sifter 285

Build a rain barrel 286

Rock dolly 287

Big-foot shoe cleaner 287

Grow your own 2x4s 288

19 QUICK PROJECTS

WHAT IT TAKES

TIME: All the projects in this chapter can be built in half a day or less.

SKILL LEVEL: Beginner

Mud-busting boot scraper

Ordinary doormats simply can't handle serious muck, but you can clean out packed dirt from even the deepest boot treads with this boot scraper made from 2x4s.

1. Screw the base pieces (A and B) together upside down so that the screw heads are hidden.
2. Fasten the uprights (C) to the sides (D), then screw the side brushes on with 2-in. screws.
3. Screw the bottom brushes to the base with 2-in. screws.
4. Space the side pieces so that the bristles are roughly 4-1/2 in. apart.
5. Add a piece of aluminum angle to the front edge so you can scrape boots before brushing them.

Use stiff-bristle brushes—either "bilevel" brushes or deck scrub brushes. You may need to cut off part of the handle so the brush will lie flat.

Figure A
Boot scraper

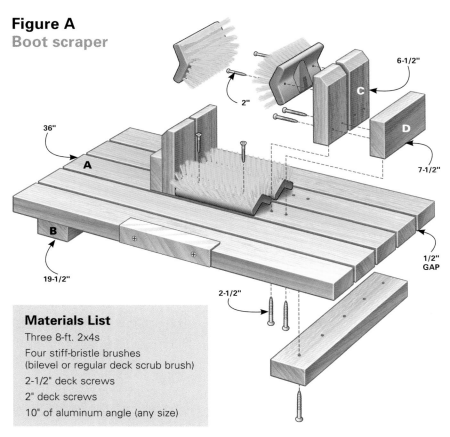

Materials List
Three 8-ft. 2x4s
Four stiff-bristle brushes
(bilevel or regular deck scrub brush)
2-1/2" deck screws
2" deck screws
10" of aluminum angle (any size)

Quick workbench for outdoor projects

FIVE-MINUTE WORKBENCH

CARRYING HANDLE

SHELF

Build a five-minute workbench

You can set up a semipermanent workstation with sawhorses when you're working outside. Screw 2x4s to the tops of the sawhorses and a plywood platform to the 2x4s and you're ready to build. Let the 2x4s project a few inches beyond the plywood to make it easier for someone to help you pick up the whole works and move it around as needed. To keep the clutter out from underfoot, install a temporary plywood shelf across the braces.

Compost sifter

Sifting compost through a coarse screen of 1/4-in. hardware cloth removes sticks and other large chunks, and leaves you with a wheelbarrow full of rich, fluffy compost. Return the large stuff to the compost pile, where it will continue to break down. Size the sifter to fit over your wheelbarrow or just prop one end up and sift right onto the ground.

You'll need about 10 ft. of 1x6 lumber for the sides and another 10 ft. of 1x2 to clamp the screen to the bottom for the bottom screen molding. The lumber species doesn't matter, but cedar will last longer than untreated pine. Buy a 24-in. x 36-in. piece of 1/4-in. hardware cloth and cut it with tin snips to cover the bottom of the completed frame.

OVERHANG PROTECTS AGAINST SHARP SCREEN

1x2

1/4" HARDWARE CLOTH

1/4" HARDWARE CLOTH

1x6

2" GALVANIZED DECK SCREWS

1x2

STAPLER

TIN SNIPS

Cut two 36-in. lengths and two 22-1/2 in. lengths of 1x6 pine. Drill 7/32-in. clearance holes 3/8 in. from the ends of the 36-in. boards and screw the corners together with 2-in. deck screws to form the sifter frame. Cut a piece of 1/4-in. hardware cloth to fit and staple it to the bottom of the box. Cut two 37-in. pieces and two 22-in. pieces of 1x2. Drill clearance holes and screw them to the bottom. Overhang the 1x2s 1/2 in. to cover any sharp edges of screen that may be sticking out.

Build a rain barrel

Install a large valve to quickly fill watering cans and a smaller valve for a garden hose. Secure the valves to the cross brace with J-brackets.

Rain barrels are expensive, but it's pretty easy to build your own from plastic drums or trash cans. Check online for an "open head" plastic 55-gallon drum with a cover. Or find a used barrel by talking to car wash managers (they buy soap and wax by the barrel). If you can't find a container you like, buy a large, heavy-duty garbage can at a home center. All the other materials will be available there too.

Place the drum near a downspout, drill a hole in the side near the bottom and screw in a drain valve. That's an OK installation if you plan to run a soaker hose to your garden. But if you want to use a wand or a spray nozzle, you'll need to elevate the barrel on a stand for more water pressure. Water is heavy (55 gallons weighs 440 lbs.), so use 4x4 treated lumber for the legs and secure everything with construction screws or stainless steel lags. But don't place the stand on soft ground. You could kill somebody if the rig toppled over. If

Figure A Trash can rain barrels

You can make cheap, functional rain barrels with trash cans and simple PVC plumbing and electrical conduit fittings. Line up as many as you need to meet your watering needs.

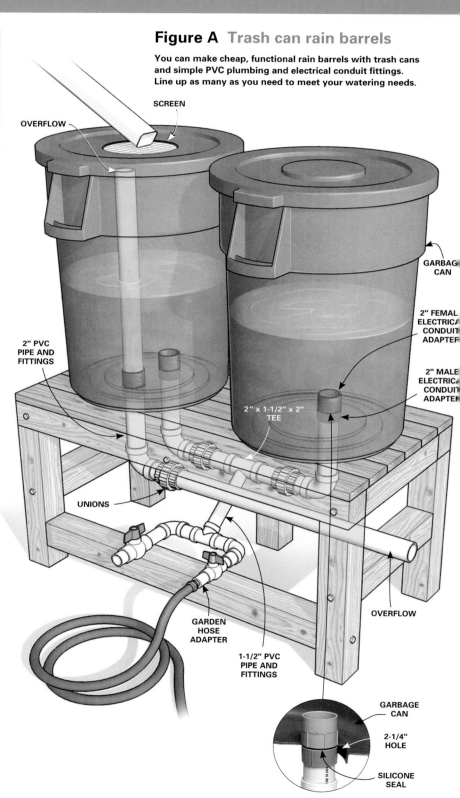

you have large gardens and want to store more water, double-size the stand and add a second barrel.

Cut holes in the bottoms of the barrels with a 2-1/4-in. hole saw. Then screw in a 2-in. male threaded electrical (gray PVC) conduit adapter (electrical adapters aren't tapered like plumbing adapters, so you can tighten them down all the way). Squirt a thin bead of silicone caulk around the opening and screw on a threaded electrical PVC coupler to cinch the barrel between the two fittings (Figure A). Next, glue together sections of 2-in. PVC pipe, unions (to make winter disassembly easier), reducers and valves. As long as you're at it, install an overflow pipe so you can direct the excess where you want it.

Finally, cut a hole in one of the covers and mount a screen to filter out leaves and debris. Then just wait for the next big rain.

Rock dolly

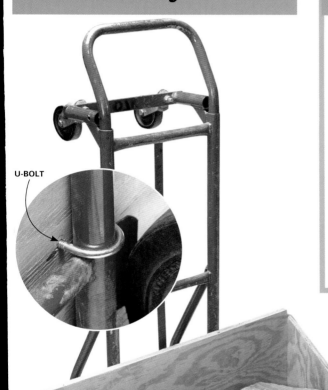

U-BOLT

Big-foot shoe cleaner

Don't give grass clippings and sawdust a free pass indoors. Screw a stiff brush to a hunk of plywood and give grass and gunk the brush-off before they enter your home.

STIFF BRUSH

BIG PLYWOOD FOOT

Need to move stones, potted trees or bags of soil? Make your own sturdy garden dolly from a two-wheel hand truck and plywood. You can make the box any size you want (a box 31 in. wide will still fit through a doorway) and then attach it to your hand truck with U-bolts. It can handle a lot of weight and is easily removed. It's also low to the ground, so you can just roll stones and other heavy items right into it without lifting.

Grow your own 2x4s

Caution: A few days before you dig, call 811 to have your underground utilities marked.

Don't add soil amendments

For years, experts recommended adding compost, peat moss or fertilizer to the planting hole. However, most now agree that you shouldn't backfill with anything other than the original soil from the planting hole. Soil amendments in the planting hole can discourage the tree roots from spreading into the surrounding soil and can cause poor water drainage. Also, in some instances, fertilizers can kill young roots.

Plant in fall or early spring

The ideal time to plant a tree is in early spring before "bud break" or in the fall before the tree goes dormant. Cool weather allows the tree to establish roots in its new location before new top growth puts too much demand on it. Some trees establish better if planted in early spring. These include oaks, pines, dogwoods, American holly, willows and black gum. Avoid planting trees during the summer when they're in full leaf and susceptible to heat stress.

Dig a shallow, broad hole

Dig a saucer-shape hole three to five times the diameter of the root-ball (or the spread of the roots for a bare-root tree). This allows the roots to easily penetrate the softened backfill and properly anchor the tree.

If you're planting in clay or wet soil, use a garden fork or your spade to roughen the bottom and sides of the planting hole to avoid "glazing." Glazing happens when the sides and bottom of a hole become so smooth and compacted that water can't pass easily through the soil. In extreme situations, it could block roots from penetrating the sides of the planting hole.

Don't plant too deep

If you plant the root-ball of a tree too deep, new roots can girdle the trunk and may also suffer from a lack of oxygen. Plant a tree so the root collar—where the uppermost roots attach to the trunk—is about an inch above the soil level.

In many cases, containerized trees from nurseries are planted too deep. Don't go by the soil level in the container. Dig down into the planting medium to find the root collar so you know how deep to plant the tree.

If you're planting a bare-root tree, leave a cone of soil at the bottom of the planting hole and set the root system on top. Place the handle of your shovel flat across the hole from one side to the other to make sure the crown is level with the surrounding soil. You should be able to partially see the root collar, or trunk flare, after the tree is planted.